*f*P

BEYOND THE CRASH

*Overcoming the First Crisis
of Globalization*

GORDON BROWN

FREE PRESS

New York   London   Toronto   Sydney

FREE PRESS
A Division of Simon & Schuster, Inc.
1230 Avenue of the Americas
New York, NY 10020

First Free Press hardcover edition December 2010

FREE PRESS and colophon are trademarks of Simon & Schuster, Inc.

For information about special discounts for bulk purchases,
please contact Simon & Schuster Special Sales at 1-866-506-1949
or business@simonandschuster.com

The Simon & Schuster Speakers Bureau can bring authors to your live event.
For more information or to book an event contact the Simon & Schuster Speakers Bureau
at 1-866-248-3049 or visit our website at www.simonspeakers.com.

DESIGNED BY ERICH HOBBING

Manufactured in the United States of America

1 3 5 7 9 10 8 6 4 2

Library of Congress Cataloging-in-Publication Data

Brown, Gordon, 1951–
Beyond the crash : overcoming the first crisis of globalization /
Gordon Brown. — 1st Free Press hbk. ed.
p. cm.
Includes bibliographical references and index.
1. Global Financial Crisis, 2008–2009. 2. Financial crises. 3. International trade.
4. International finance. 5. International economic relations. 6. Economic policy—
International cooperation. 7. Economic development—International cooperation. I. Title.
HB37172008.B76 2010
330.9'0511—dc22   2010043118

ISBN 978-1-4516-2405-2
ISBN 978-1-4516-2407-6 (ebook)

CONTENTS

CONTENTS

ACKNOWLEDGMENTS

Why write a book on the financial crisis? Or perhaps more pertinently, why write another book on the financial crisis when so many accounts of the events of 2007–2010 have already appeared that there may be little appetite for more?

My case for writing this account is that I was there. If we do not understand fully the biggest economic shock of our generation, then we are destined to repeat its mistakes. I believe a firsthand account can best illuminate how choices (and mistakes) were made.

My case for writing this *now* is that the crisis is not yet over. If it is to end with a full recovery, we need to learn quickly the lessons of what went so wrong that the global financial system froze, and we need to come to a firm and shared view regarding what we can do to make things right. So, while some will say this is a book written in (extreme) haste that I will repent of at leisure, it is for me a necessary means of provoking a much-needed debate about what I believe is the only way to overcome the disastrous economic collapse: coordinated global action.

This book is not, therefore, a comprehensive account of the crisis. But it does cover the misjudgments that brought the crisis about and proposes how best they can be overcome. This is my first attempt at a set of recommendations for the next stage of our economic recovery. As I discuss this book's content with people across the world I will be ready to learn from their knowledge, to review and amend my recommendations, and to update and reconsider my conclusions.

I am neither a finance expert not a trained economist, but fear of making technical mistakes (of which, I'm sure, this book is full) should not silence us altogether when the task before us is so urgent.

We are of course summoned to address many great challenges that arise from the global changes that are shaping our twenty-first century lives—combating global terrorism and nuclear proliferation, and in the wider economy itself, curbing the volatility in oil, food, and commodity prices and fighting climate change with the opportunity that I would like to write about later for a transformation in the way our economies consume energy. But in this book, the priority is to address head-on the new and gnawing insecurity that millions now experience in their daily lives. And so my priorities are jobs and justice. This book is a call for the world to achieve together what we now know is possible in the immediate future: to create and save 50 million jobs worldwide and to lift nearly 100 million people out of poverty. We are on an uneven and hazardous journey whose route and destination should not be left to chance, but must be shaped by our common endeavors and by the values we share in common. And for me at least, the oft-quoted phrase I hear spoken and sometimes use myself of "restoring the global economy to full health" cannot be an accurate description of the outcome we seek without its including millions more hard-working families in decent jobs.

This is my first draft, a work in progress. But of this I am certain: the basic thesis—that global problems need global solutions and that there must be an alternative to a decade of low growth and lost jobs—will withstand the arguments about culpability for the crisis and the questions about specific recommendations.

* * *

I, of course, take full responsibility for the contents of this book. Only I am to blame for any mistakes that I have made and that are inevitable in a project of this speed and scope. I did not start to write until the end of May 2010 and completed the work in the fourteen weeks that followed, alongside my work as a Member of Parliament. It would not have been possible to deliver it on deadline without the prior support I had from all those who served with me in government, and I could not even have contemplated it without the amazing and unsurpassable commitment and loyalty of those who are still assisting me today.

My debt to Alistair Darling as my friend and Chancellor and recent Chief Secretaries—Yvette Cooper, Stephen Timms, Andy Burnham, and Liam Byrne—Paul Myners and other Treasury ministers, and the civil servants responsible for economic policy is unpayable and readily acknowledged. This is not the right place to thank all the individual members of the No. 10 team; each and all can be proud to have served their country during a major crisis.

But it is right to acknowledge in particular the economic and policymaking team, for this is their story as much as it is mine. I was beyond lucky to work with Jeremy Heywood, who has not only a superb mind and a real flair for management, but true expertise on economic matters through his City and Treasury experience. I was also fortunate that James Bowler, who was my Principal Private Secretary in the Treasury, stayed with me as Principal Private Secretary in No. 10. He is a man of great integrity and prodigious effort and led a formidable private office team that included Matthew Style, Christina Scott, and Gila Sacks, who will be future leaders in our civil service. Leeanne Johnston was indispensable in both the Treasury and Downing Street, and remains so now in her new incarnation at the IMF, and I am grateful too to Carol Bird. I would also like to relay, through Nick Macpherson and Gus O'Donnell, my thanks to the Treasury and to the wider civil service.

Tom Scholar is the civil servant who helped me as we made the Bank of England independent, and he was a brilliant representative of Britain at the IMF and World Bank. He has always been there ready to take on the most difficult of tasks, including, most recently, succeeding another civil servant with a great mind, John Kingman, as the official in charge of financial reconstruction. He and Ollie Robbins, who was my first private secretary in No. 10, exemplify the British civil service at its best. Sir Jon Cunliffe, who also worked with me for several years at the Treasury as we dealt with European negotiations, kindly came to work with me at No. 10 as European and global economic policy adviser. As we will see in the chapters that follow, he consistently delivered for me and for Britain. His work and that of his team in shaping the G20 will go down in history. Jonathan Portes's phenomenal abilities and his grasp of global economic issues have been invaluable.

For more than ten years Shriti Vadera, more than anyone else, challenged and helped develop my understanding of globalization, and her contribution to everything I did right is evident in these pages. She is a brilliant lateral thinker who characteristically stepped up to the challenge of formulating policy out of the box and led with conviction during the crisis. Her business acumen, her intellectually rigorous insights, and her prodigious energy make her one of the best economic and financial thinkers I have come across. David Henderson, Theo Bertram, Steve van Riel, and all those who worked with me on economic research in both No. 10 and the Labour Party are owed a huge debt of thanks for the level of detail in what follows.

Mike Ellam is not only an expert on global economic matters but was also a brilliant head of communications at No. 10. He and my other media advisers (including Iain Bundred, Nicola Burdett, Michael Dugher, Simon Lewis, John Woodcock, Katie

Martin, and the teams in No. 10 and the Labour Party) have my thanks for their unstinting efforts in helping me communicate to the wider world the decisions that are discussed in this book.

I am grateful to all members of the policy unit who served with me in No. 10 and on the Council of Economic Advisers (including Ed Miliband, Maeve Sherlock, Kirsty O'Brien, Michael Jacobs, Matt Cavanagh, Greg Beales, Will Paxton, Patrick Diamond, Jennifer Moses, and Oona King), and in particular Dan Corry, an amazingly conscientious chief adviser on economic matters; Nick Pearce, a wonderfully innovative and deep-thinking head of the policy unit; and Gavin Kelly, an incredibly warm individual and a rock through thick and thin as Deputy Chief of Staff.

To both Tom Fletcher, who combined a mastery of detail with a mastery of diplomacy, and Stewart Wood, whose knowledge of Europe, America, and so much else was a constant pleasure, I owe a huge debt I can never repay.

Justin Forsyth, who is now head of Save the Children UK, served as my Director of Strategic Communications. He is not just a committed internationalist but an excellent leader of people, and I know that he will mobilize people in the cause of economic justice for the rest of his life. No one I know has the creativity and total commitment to delivery that David Muir brought when he came to work in government, and nobody could have done his difficult job with greater skill, loyalty, or strategic flair. Sue Nye has been, as always, a constant source of support.

Ed Balls and I have worked together on economic policy for most of the past twenty years. His speeches and insights have proved invaluable in the conduct of economic policy, where I freely acknowledge my long-standing debt to his advice.

Stuart Hudson's acute observations and attention to detail have improved so much that I have done over the years, but in particular this manuscript. I am grateful for his time and talents.

I am grateful also to Andrew Small, who has brought to me not only an encyclopedic knowledge of the Asian economies but also a rigorous analysis. I am also pleased to acknowledge the contribution of his colleagues at the German Marshall Fund.

I am grateful to Jim O'Neill and Anna Stupnytska and their team at Goldman Sachs for allowing me to test my arguments against their very brilliant modeling of the world economy, and to Dominique Strauss-Kahn and the staff of the IMF for their swift and stunning research capabilities and generosity in sharing their thoughts.

Let me also thank for their insights over many years Mervyn King and the staff of the Bank of England, and Adair Turner and his predecessor Callum McCarthy and their teams at the FSA.

Wilf Stevenson has done exhaustive checks on the meetings and telephone calls I reference here and has been on constant call for checking, polishing, and support.

For his help in drafting and editing I am also grateful once again to someone whose writing skills are far superior to mine, Colin Currie.

I am grateful to Jayne Baxter, a fellow Fifer, who, out of work hours, has managed to combine her successful voluntary work as an elected member of Fife Health Board with help for me. Her acute eye for detail has made this project possible.

While I have worked all summer on this book, this project could not have been delivered and indeed could not have happened without Dominick Anfuso and all the team at Free Press and without the advice and wisdom of Flip Brophy at Sterling Lord.

There are so many people whose research or conversation has particularly influenced my thinking; I will not name those in governments around the world, other than to thank all those finance ministers and leaders who have worked with me over the years. I owe a particular debt, however, to Amartya Sen and Emma Rothschild, to Joe and Anya Stiglitz, to Larry Summers and his wife Elisa, to Jim Wolfensohn and to Alan Greenspan and Andrea Mitchell. I am grateful too for the debates with and advice from Michael Klein, Bob Rubin, Hyun Song Shin, Paul

Krugman, and Gavyn Davies. I have also enjoyed conversations about the fortunes of the continents of the world with Lashi Mittal, Lord Swaraj Paul, Nigel Doughty, and Sir Gulam Noon. And I am grateful for the detailed conversations I enjoyed with Mervyn Davies, David Sainsbury, Paul Myners, Paul Drayson, Sir Ronald Cohen, Geoffrey Robinson MP, Lord Robert Skidelsky, and Lucy Parker, who has published brilliant studies of the new future that globalization offers and has been an inspiration in the advice she has given.

My friendship with Bob Shrum and Marylouise Oates has lasted from the moment I met them in Washington nearly twenty years ago. Bob and Marylouise are not only friends of our entire family but also brilliant observers of global trends with strong, deep-rooted convictions about justice. I am grateful to Bob and to my good friend John Sexton, the President of NYU, for their insights about the global changes under way that have enriched the argument I am making.

Gil McNeil has been both a formidable project manager for this book and an inspiration in assisting in the writing and editing. This and so much else would have been impossible without her nonstop encouragement and unflinching support for both Sarah and me.

For help beyond the call of duty I want to thank Helen Etheridge, Beth Dupuy, Ray Collins, and all the staff of the Labour Party, including Joe Irvin, Jonathan Ashworth, and the team in the Political Office. I am also indebted to those who have served as Parliamentary Private Secretary to me over the years: Ann Keen, Anne Snelgrove, Jon Trickett, Angela Smith, and Alison McGovern.

While I wrote this book I also had an intensive set of constituency engagements; being able to do both has been possible only because of the organizing skill of Alex Rowley, who is leader of the Fife Labour group, my constituency agent, and the person most knowledgeable on local issues in my constituency.

Nor could I have managed both obligations without the support of Marilyn Livingstone and Helen Eadie MSPs. I want also to thank Jim Metcalfe, Margaret O'Sullivan, John Rowan, Bill Taylor, and Rhona White, and most of all the people of Kirkcaldy and Cowdenbeath constituency for their loyalty and support.

For making it possible for me to write, to perform my constituency duties, and to manage visits to London and Africa I am grateful for the support of my security staff and the Fife police.

My recent trip to Uganda, like much else I have done in the field of international development, was possible because of the strategic support of Brendan Cox, a tireless campaigner for the best of causes and, along with his wife, Jo, a good friend. They both have a great future as they work to change the world ahead.

I owe an enormous debt to the ministerial colleagues I was privileged to serve with through Labour's thirteen years in office and all the civil servants and political staff who have served both me and their country with distinction.

And for help with the book itself, there are three people who deserve special thanks.

Cormac Hollingsworth has given me priceless assistance as an adviser on the political economy, an expert with detailed knowledge of the financial system, and a razor-sharp finder of wood among trees. The next Labour government will surely succeed if it is able to draw on his unfailing generosity of spirit, his total commitment to the public interest, and of course the unique insight he brings to economic policymaking. He has been indispensable to me; Hope Not Hate is lucky indeed to have him on board.

For most of the summer my editor has been Kirsty McNeill, who is not only a brilliant writer but one of the most insightful observers and analysts of global politics and its progressive potential. She has given up endless weeks to make possible a project that started as an idea, was quickly and perhaps too rashly turned into a promise, and was then converted—again perhaps too quickly—into a publishing schedule. It all had, in the end, to be delivered by someone who was prepared to see the project through, and she made the impossible possible as usual. She has a unique combination of strategic, intellectual, and political skills and is prepared to constantly challenge my arguments—and test to destruction their logical coherence. She has been more than an editor: she is in a very real sense the coauthor of what now appears.

Sarah, John, and Fraser have had to endure a summer in which I have been reading, writing, and typing. It has perhaps been my good fortune that Sarah was also working on her book this summer. I cannot say that my sons find what I am writing of interest, but my comfort is that, with books everywhere in our house, John is reading more and more and Fraser is spurred into learning to read more quickly. To Sarah I owe the greatest debt of all. Ours is a love affair that will never end.

PROLOGUE

It was while I was flying across the Atlantic that I resolved what we as a government had to do.

The date was Friday, September 26, 2008, and we were returning overnight from the United States. I had just left the White House and a meeting with George Bush and just finished a phone call with Alistair Darling, Chancellor of the Exchequer, who told me we would be nationalizing the Bradford and Bingley bank that weekend. Not for the first time, I was grateful to have the calm good sense and judgment of my longtime friend holding the reins in the Treasury at a time like this.

As the plane was taxiing down the runway I read a fax that Jeremy Heywood, the peerless and all-seeing Permanent Secretary at Downing Street, had sent just before takeoff.

It set out for the first time the numbers I had asked for from the Treasury, the Financial Services Authority, and the Bank of England on the losses and capital that would be needed to stabilize our banks. I thought I was, at that stage, beyond being shocked, but even I was taken aback by the figures.

Reading the latest grim data about the state of British banks, I knew that doing nothing was not an option. We were days away from a complete banking collapse: companies not being able to pay their creditors, workers not being able to draw their wages, and families finding that the ATM had no cash to give them. As has been my habit for decades, I was writing notes— action points and reflections—as I talked with Shriti Vadera, our brilliant business minister and former banker. As we debated, only one possible course of action remained.

I wrote it on a piece of paper, in one of the thick black felt-tip pens I've used since a childhood sporting accident affected my eyesight. For good measure, I underlined it twice. It said simply:

<u>RECAPITALIZE NOW.</u>

Private capital had already been deployed,[1] and those investors had been severely burned; they and other investors were unlikely to return.

So in that one moment we set upon a course of our own; these banks had to be recapitalized and, if necessary, bought into by the government immediately. We worked through the night. The banks were sure to resist, and some might even oppose us; after all, we were asking some of Britain's proudest businesses to surrender without a fight to semi-nationalization, and we were asking others who had said they did not need capital to go out and get it, a move that could dilute the equity of their shareholders, perhaps at the cost of management's own jobs.

We needed to have a comprehensive, once-and-for-all capital, funding, and liquidity plan for the whole banking system that would restore stability. By the time we landed, I had decided, despite an inconclusive meeting in which it had become clear that the United States was already committed to its course of action, that the solution to the crisis was capital. And for three or possibly four of the banks, this would mean huge amounts of *government* capital. I knew there would be many hurdles to work through—not least the banks' resistance to the whole idea. So we would probably have to force them to recapitalize. They still needed liquidity and medium-term funding in order to lend. I wrote another note to myself with my felt-tip pen: NO LIQUIDITY WITHOUT RECAPITALIZATION.

It didn't have the elegance of "No taxation without representation," but it would do. And there could be no liquidity without the banks dealing with the big problem that businesses and families faced: lack of credit. And as we proceeded, we became resolved that the banks also had to deal with their excessive remuneration, which had been at the cost of the capital on which they depended.

For several months I had been deeply concerned about the banks' failure to lend. At first I believed that confidence could be restored if we got banks to declare their losses, and there had indeed been a wave of private sector rights issues, with companies selling new shares as a way of getting capital. But the work I had commissioned over the summer and the subsequent events of September 2008 convinced me that most banks hadn't been honest; they were just sitting it out, hoping that something would turn up. The process of declaring the extent of losses and the full scale of the toxic assets—of executives telling their seniors, management telling the board, the board telling the market and their shareholders— was proving so painful that too many people in the banks were deluding themselves that the problems would disappear.

The pressure was increasing by the day. It was clear that if there was no resumption of lending in the economy there would be a crash. Worse, if we had a run on the Royal Bank of Scotland, there would be people and shops and schools and hospitals trying to function with no money. The urgency for comprehensive action was further increased by the dramatic volatility in commodity prices, which threatened people's standard of living.[2]

With the major industrial economies hurtling toward a depression, we were facing a perfect storm. Economic orthodoxy was proving irrelevant; the market seemed intent not on self-correction, but on self-destruction.

We were looking at deep structural flaws at the heart of our banks (excessive leverage had left banks undercapitalized for the risks they had irresponsibly assumed), and it was clear from the work my team and the Treasury had done over the summer that the crisis could no longer be characterized, as it had been earlier that year, as just a series of liquidity problems. At the time, no other government was proposing the actions that we determined on as our plane powered through the darkness.

I asked Shriti how she thought that not just the markets and the banks, but also the U.K. overall, would react to such a radical proposal, one different from the American TARP (Troubled Asset Relief Program), which focused on buying assets and equity rather than injecting capital and which we had been investigating while we were in New York and Washington. Shriti said everything was too fragile and unpredictable to call, but that this was the best thing to do. Not exactly the reassurance I had wanted to hear, but I could always rely on her to be laser-like in her focus and direct in her answers. It felt like we were on our own. I resolved to speak immediately to President Nicolas Sarkozy, the current President of the European Union, and other European leaders.

So, as our plane crossed the night sky, we were considering taking action that was unprecedented, potentially isolating, and certainly risky. But I was convinced that, if we did not do so, we would be facing a banking collapse that would make the queues of depositors outside Northern Rock Bank look like a Sunday outing.

I did not have any doubt—and I certainly could not afford to show any—about the decision I was making, even as my mind churned with trepidation about the number of different angles we had to cover. By the time we touched down in London and after I talked to Alistair Darling and we had agreed on the way forward, we had made a government decision that turned the orthodoxy of the past thirty years on its head.

The First Crisis of Globalization

On the evening of Tuesday, October 7, 2008, eleven days after that sleepless night flight from Washington, after we had prepared the banks for the recapitalization announcement the following day, the head of one of Britain's biggest banks told me that his only problem was cash flow, and that all he needed was "overnight finance." His comment undermined any remaining confidence I had in the collective wisdom of our bankers. The next day two of our banks, then among the biggest in the world, became our biggest banking casualties ever. A few months later, in January 2009, they announced losses that were the highest in British history.

His bank's problems were not short term, or simply about liquidity, and help with cash flow could not have helped for more than a few days. The problems were far, far worse than he knew or perhaps would admit. They were structural and fundamental. His bank owned assets of unimaginable toxicity and had been left with too little capital to cover its losses and remain solvent. The market clearly believed that as well.

But as Wall Street tried to work out if and how the Troubled Assets Relief Program would work, bankers, regulators, and governments across the world were still in shock and had not formed a consensus about what needed to be done. Some called for more liquidity to be pumped into the system. Others wanted to cordon off toxic assets. In Europe there was still a view that this was a problem of, and exclusive to, the so-called Anglo-Saxon economies.

It had taken us more than a year to get to this point, but during the summer holiday I had already come to a different and very troubling conclusion: that the banking problems ran so deep, and were so systemic, that Britain could not afford to wait for others to join us before taking root-and-branch action to save our banks. By September I knew we were days away from a complete meltdown. I had set a course, and was prepared to go it alone if necessary.

At five the next morning I told Sarah that she would have to be ready to pack our things for a sudden move out of Downing Street. I was about to announce that we were offering to invest billions and take control of Britain's two biggest banks—something no government in British history had ever done. If what I was about to do failed, I would have no choice but to resign. As I walked into the office that morning I didn't know if I'd still be *in* office when the sun set that evening.

Then I got down to business. On October 8, 2008, Alistair Darling and I announced the biggest recapitalization in Britain's banking history: a government-led recapitalization package in which we offered to buy up to £50 billion of bank capital and equity, with a unique £250 billion credit guarantee scheme for banks to issue debt and £200 billion of extra liquidity. In return, we would hold firm to the tough conditions we had set on the plane back from America: no funding without recapitalization.

This book is my account of how we got there: an insider's story of the financial crisis that burst upon the world in 2008. If the right decisions had not been taken by leaders across the world, we could have faced a worldwide depression, bringing with it a return to the protectionism, mass unemployment, extremism, and political instability of the 1930s.[1] This is a book about what happened then, and what should happen now.

The world has never been faced with such a complex global economic challenge—such fast financial reversals, such great banking threats, and such pronounced economic instabilities—as it faced in 2008.

I want to tell the story of a banking crisis that morphed into an industrial and business and employment crisis, and is now seen by some as a government debt crisis but which is in fact a far bigger crisis, a crisis of globalization itself.

This is my personal recollection of the key political events but also my analysis of what we can learn from them. Part 1 in particular is an account of events as I saw them, events that, even now, are difficult to put in context. As I said in my speech to the Joint Houses of Congress on March 4, 2009, "We tend to think of the sweep of destiny as stretching across many months and years—as if each minute leads inevitably to the next, before culminating in one of the decisive moments we call history. But sometimes the defining moments of history appear suddenly and without warning."

I have long felt that the rhythm of the political day is too often drawn to symptoms, not causes; to reaction, not reflection; to the low-hanging fruit and not the high-placed prize. There are times when high-pressure decisions matter, and that even when we know what is right, policymakers too often fail to act. But in this case, we did act quickly and got to the heart of the problem, but as politicians we must take our share of the blame and responsibility for this crisis, and in the coming chapters I will outline the areas where I put my own hand up and accept that the fault was mine.

But I would also, with some trepidation and considerable humility, like to posit that there is something I brought to the challenge that came from my particular strengths and even my particular weaknesses. One of my oft-remarked-upon failings as a communicator is that I like to talk in numbers, what the British press branded my "tractor statistics tendency." This criticism has some justification. It is also, I believe, relevant to the story that will unfold in the chapters that follow.

I follow data and statistics because the patterns I see within them help me make sense of complicated human reality. While others may see a dry report on employment statistics and consider it boring, I see a set of stories behind each column of numbers, stories about the hopes and fears, the triumphs and disasters of individual lives.

It was that relationship with numbers which first drew me into the Jubilee 2000 campaign for debt cancellation. I had never been to Africa, never visited or met with the communities who could benefit from the writing-off of unjust debts. But given the projections I had been seeing since I first looked at the problem in 1989, it made no sense to me to insist on the repayment of these debts: they were weighted with the human lives that could be saved or changed if we released their countries from the debit to the credit column. When, many years later, I did meet the children in school and the patients on anti-AIDS drugs who were benefiting from the debt cancellation dividend, I put faces to the lives I had sensed were inscribed on those pages of numbers.

This is, for better or worse, a part of how I think, how I make decisions, and how I see the world. So in the pages that follow there will be many statistics. But underlying the data is messy, unpredictable, fragile human life. The decisions I describe here were made by people. Whether those decisions were wise or foolish, moral or immoral, did not have abstract consequences of interest only to academic economists and market traders. As a direct result of globalization, they mattered to all people everywhere. Precisely because the impact of the crisis was so painful and so widespread, people everywhere are asking how it happened and how can we avoid its repetition. I hope this book will be a useful contribution to that debate, and I want to begin it with a basic explanation of why we are where we are.

This crisis was global in scope and scale in a manner that is unprecedented. For the first time everybody, from the richest person in the richest city to the poorest person in the poorest slum, was affected by the same crisis[2] and although its roots are global, its impact is local, directly felt on nearly every main street, on nearly every shop floor, around nearly every kitchen table.

The opening up of trade and the creation of competitive markets have brought the great successes of globalization, including a global growth that has lifted one billion people out of extreme poverty. I remain resolutely in favor of globalization, of free trade, and of liberalized markets.[3] But while the benefits of globalization must never be understated, they cannot be secured without a willingness to address, at a global level, the underlying economic, democratic, social, and political weaknesses of globalization—and its regulation—that have been revealed in the past few years, which make this more than an ordinary crisis or even a crisis similar to that faced between 1929 and 1931: this is the first crisis of globalization. The shift in the world economy is not transient or temporary but permanent and profound. For two hundred years—the entire history of industrialization—Europe and America have produced most of the world's goods, have been the main exporter of goods and services, have accounted for the majority of manufactured products sold, and have been responsible for most of the world's economic activity and investment.

In 1990, the United States and the European countries that now form the European Union (twenty-seven countries) were responsible for 55 percent of all manufacturing, 57 percent of all exports, and 59 percent of all world economic activity. The majority of investment—52 percent—was made in Europe and America too.

This was in itself a remarkable achievement of two centuries of economic growth. Nations that today represent little more than 10 percent of the world's population accounted for much more than 50 percent of the world's production, manufacturing, output, exports, investment, and, of course, consumption.

Even in 2000 the dominance of America and Europe was just holding. But since 2000, the balance of economic power between the two first industrialized continents and the rest of the world has been shifting fast.

By 2010, America and Europe accounted for only 45 percent of manufacturing output and for just 47 percent of exports. Today, most of the world's additional growth is not American or European but comes from the rest of the world—and so we are tipping over from an old world where America and Europe accounted for more than half of all world economic activity to a new world where it is much less than half. The latest figures suggest that America and Europe will soon be investing less in their future than the rest of the world. As a share of world investment, America and Europe's share is falling even faster and will fall further by 2015.

Yet with less than half of world trade output and investment, America and Europe still consume much more than half—more than 60 percent—of the worlds goods and services.

The rapidly rising *production* in Asia had not been complemented by similarly rising *consumption* in Asia.

So for the first decade of the century, one side of the economic equation—production, investment, exports, and manufacturing, and the other side—consumption in these two parts of the world—have been moving in different directions. Globalization has generated opposite gravitational poles of production and consumption, and today the world arrangements look unbalanced and unsustainable.

6

These changes not only reflect but arise from this uneven development of our global economy. This is a direct consequence of the global sourcing of goods and services—the first defining characteristic of globalization—and, second, the global flows of capital. No nation has the ability to navigate on its own in a world that has grown more and more interdependent. The global sourcing of goods and services has led to cheaper Asian goods, which are out-pricing traditional American and European manufacturing. The global flows of capital have made it possible for American and European consumers to borrow from Asian producers. So instead of the shift from American and European production to Asian production matched by a shift in consumption to Asia, we have seen a shift in borrowing with Asia, especially China, lending to America and Europe. We might have expected a world in which the high income industrialized countries were net exporters of capital to the emerging markets; instead the biggest emerging market economy is itself the biggest net exporter of capital. Never in human history, as Martin Wolf puts it graphically, has one superpower lent so much to another. These new economic arrangements could not have happened without the global sourcing of goods and the global flows of capital. Put simply, the uneven development I am charting could not have happened without globalization. That is why I call it the first crisis of globalization. But the policy question is not whether we retain globalization—globalization is a fact—but whether we manage it well. This is what this book is about.

At the heart of the crisis was a failure intrinsic to unregulated global markets, an instability that resulted from the manner in which increasing flows of capital around the world happened and impacted the economy. As economies became more interconnected and global finance more entangled, regulators and governments have failed to keep pace and increase coordination.

* * *

For more than a decade, up to 2007, globalization—global flows of capital and global sourcing of goods—had expanded, but in an uncoordinated way. In 2008 we saw, one by one, commodity markets subjected to such volatility that they put growth in the world economy at risk—with sharply rising oil prices, then booms in industrial metals, then rising food prices and volatile currencies.[4] But the imbalances that globalization had created had also made possible a flood of excess liquidity. And the search for the highest yield had taken banks not just into new areas of risk, but had pushed them into using new risk-laden instruments too. These activities, combined with the high leveraging of bank assets, created a race to the bottom by encouraging people to take risks they did not understand, by selling assets the banks wouldn't properly value, all without the capital to support them and with perverse incentives to do the wrong thing.

The bubble in American home prices and mortgage-backed bonds had started to burst as early as 2006. By the time the world discovered a word previously unheard outside banks and trading floors, *subprime,* hundreds of billions of dollars' worth of assets backed by American mortgages had been bundled up, rated as rock-solid Triple A investments, and sold around the world, often to investors who had no real sense of the value (or lack of it) of what they were buying. Included in those mortgage bundles were those sold at high interest rates to the poorest and most likely to default.

The financial innovations that allowed this to happen, and how the impact of what happened at the bottom of the American housing market was felt throughout the financial centers of the world,[5] are described in part 2 of this book.

The crisis continues to unfold, and without action of the sort I describe in part 3 that could mean low growth and high unemployment in Europe and America for a decade. It could also mean millions more around the world condemned to lives of poverty.

Avoiding that outcome will require governments across the world to make the difficult long-term decisions I detail in part 3. Everything I recommend will be underpinned by my lifetime commitment to fiscal responsibility, keeping deficits and debt as low as possible. Addressing low growth and high levels of world employment and poverty are the biggest long-term challenges today, so policies for fiscal consolidation must support growth and jobs and not destroy them or put them at risk.

Even more than the ability to act boldly, I believe, this crisis calls for the ability to reason morally. I believe the most stunning revelation of the crisis was this: despite the financial market's infusing every aspect of everyday life, the ethical values that matter in everyday life had never infused the financial markets. On the eve of the London G20 Summit I addressed religious, civic, charity, and business leaders at St. Paul's Cathedral and put it this way:

> You know in our families we raise our children to work hard, to do their best, to do their bit. We don't reward them for taking irresponsible risks that would put them or others in danger. We don't encourage them to seek short-term gratification at the expense of long-term success. And in Britain's small businesses, managers and owners are the enterprising people our country depends on and we rightly celebrate. But they do not train their teams to invest recklessly or behave in an underhand way or keep their biggest gambles off the books.
>
> Most people who have worked hard to build up their firm or shop understand responsible risk taking but don't understand why any company would give rewards for failure or how some people have grown fabulously wealthy making failed bets with other people's money. So it is absurd for those on the extremes to blame the private sector for our problems. What we actually need is the practice of most of our private sector to be adopted by all of our private sector.
>
> And our task today is to bring our financial markets into closer

alignment with the values held by families and businesspeople across the country.

The argument underlying both that speech and this book is that while moral hazard was a serious issue in the bank recapitalization, there was an even wider, deeper, and more urgent moral question which the behavior of the banks created. While the manifestation of bank failure may have been undercapitalization, the true cause was much simpler: recklessness and irresponsibility all too often created by greed. Money that should have capitalized the financial system went instead directly to excessive rewards. Money that savers put into banks on trust was gambled—and not for the savers' security, but for the benefit of the traders themselves.

It was as if we had forgotten, as I said at St. Paul's, "that the virtues we admire most and the virtues that make society flourish—hard work, taking responsibility, being honest, being enterprising, being fair—are not the values that spring from the market but the values we bring to the market. They don't come from market forces; they come from our hearts, and they are the values nurtured in families and in schools, in our shared institutions and in our neighborhoods. Markets depend upon what they cannot create. They presuppose a well of values and work at their best when these values are upheld."

The operation of the financial market had presupposed—but at the same time actively undermined—precisely those values that are needed to create trust and maintain both a good society and a strong economy.

Just as the crises of the 1970s raised questions about the proper limits of government, so now this crisis raises questions about the proper limits of markets, for every day the crisis worsened it became clearer that much of the economic orthodoxy was irrelevant to the conditions we faced.

Under orthodox economic theories, markets "clear" continuously, wages and prices adjust in a flexible way, an economy's resources are then fully put to use, and any systemic shock will bring about a further adjustment of wages and prices to the new realities. Even when we know that there is imperfect information and imperfect players, it is assumed that markets are optimally self-regulating in the absence of government interference.

But the crisis has shown us that orthodox microeconomics does not give the full picture. Financial markets are in fact capable of the most spectacular self-combustion. In these conditions the basic issue for public policy is this: Can we agree that markets are in the public interest but cannot be automatically equated with it? If markets can be guided not just by rational judgment but by what Keynes called "animal spirits"—risk-averse one day, irrationally exuberant the next—and if globalized risks cannot even be properly managed with the best mathematical models in the world, then it is in the public interest to ensure a proper balance between the role of markets and the role of government under which both markets and government are tamed, in order to ensure that they reflect the values of the people and meet their needs.

So the question I want to pose is this: Do markets, like states, need their own constitution—an explicit statement of ethics and rules—to be debated, discussed, argued about, redrafted, and agreed on? I will revisit this point later, but for now my argument is that, in each generation, the norms and workings of our economy are forged in a set of relationships that are established among individuals, governments, and markets; and the settlement many governments had reached by the 1980s and 1990s proved wholly inadequate for the global problems we have had to address in these past three years.

But we are even more at risk from another market failure. The mirror image of the microeconomic problem is a macroeconomic one. Ever since Keynes and the experience of the 1930s, we have understood that demand can fall short of supply. Now, in 2010, we are facing the same kind of decisions the world faced then, with at least 200 million people around the world idle and 100 million more poor people already pushed into extreme poverty.

In the 1930s, when markets failed, governments had to step in, and so the modern relationships between government and markets resulted from the New Deal in the 1930s. The postwar welfare state in Britain is one example. By the 1970s, with problems of corporatism, producer-vested interests, state inefficiencies, and the revolt against collectivism, we realized that government itself could become a vested interest. But it is true to say that, instead of reforming the relationship between governments and markets, the dominant paradigm became one of "efficient markets"—a view consistently challenged by thinkers in the tradition of Keynes and, more recently, behavioral economists and George Soros, with his influential theory of "reflexivity."

And now in the first decade of the twenty-first century we have come to realize again that markets too can be shaped by vested interests, that economic players are not always rational, that markets are not self-correcting, that employment does not automatically recover, and that a wholly deregulated, passive model of capitalism and of absentee government cannot cope with extreme fluctuations and shocks of the sort we saw in the banking crisis.

Most of all, we have found that such problems are not lessened but magnified by globalization. But, as I will suggest, the answer is not to reject markets or to reject government action. Instead, recognizing that both markets and the state can fail, the answer is to find a new way for individuals, markets, and governments to work together.

We can no longer say that markets do not need morals while governments do, or that markets must be unbridled because it is government—but never markets—that can be shaped by vested interests. Nor should we say that markets can never be moral but governments can.

So I will test what I think is the most far-reaching conclusion from this crisis: that ending that age-old battle for territory between private and public sectors, between the role of markets and the role of governments, does not happen just with a cease-fire. Its resolution must be founded not upon a mechanical compromise—just agreeing to public-private partnerships or a tactically driven line of demarcation—but upon a moral foundation of a shared commitment to the public interest.

In my view we should test the argument that if both markets and government can get things wrong, then it is best that they both be underpinned by values that reflect the desire for fairness and responsibility as well as the need for competition and enterprise. For me this is the only sustainable basis for the trust on which markets and governments depend. The twentieth century was dominated by a sterile battle between markets and states, between public and private sectors. In the twenty-first century markets and states must both subject themselves to a greater force: the values and the best aspirations of people themselves.

I now believe, more firmly than ever, that we need a shared ethics for globalization that goes far beyond the interests of a few large global companies and financial institutions, and instead supports a new global order in which, in the approach to economics, the environment, and social justice, each new policy direction we take will be founded not just on the common interests that arise from our interdependence, but on the shared beliefs that arise from our common values. When we look at possible model relationships between markets and government for the way ahead, I will suggest that we can build on two truths we have discovered amid the crisis. The first truth is that as a society we have many more weapons available to us to deal with market crises than we had previously thought. The second is that, where appropriate, these weapons can be most effectively deployed when coordinated at a global, and not just a national, level.

When asked at a *Wall Street Journal* conference for one piece of advice that summed up the lessons I had learned from the crisis,

I replied very simply, "Global problems need global solutions." This is true not only of the financial market, but of terrorism, climate change, nuclear proliferation, global health pandemics, development, and mass migration. Perhaps the clearest expression yet of a growing internationalism among the peoples of the world is the awareness of extreme poverty, with a whole generation who watched Live 8 and signed up to campaigns like ONE proclaiming that the gross inequities between rich and poor nations cannot endure forever.

Of course, we will always be proud to be British or American or Russian or Chinese or Indian citizens. But we cannot deal with any of this by thinking of ourselves just as British citizens or as only American citizens or simply as Russian or Chinese or Indian citizens. Unless American, British, Russian, Chinese, Indian, and many other citizens and their governments work together to address those global problems that can be solved only by coordinated international action, then we will have failed.

In writing this book I have tried to address what I consider to be the defining test of our generation: whether we are prepared to make globalization work for people and not the other way around. In my speech at St. Paul's I recalled a placard I had seen at the Make Poverty History rally in 2005, which humbles me still: "You are G8. We are six billion."

Billions of people around the world are in need of and are demanding a better globalization. It is the nature of *power* that you always leave tasks unfinished when you leave office. It is the nature of *politics* that the argument must continue. This book is my warning of a decade of lost growth and my answer to that fear with a call for a better globalization. It is an explanation of a pattern in the numbers that points to an enormous opportunity to alleviate poverty, create jobs, and grow. A future of low growth, high unemployment, decline and decay is not inevitable; it's about the change we choose.

PART ONE

CHAPTER 1

"All I Need Is Overnight Finance"

Looking back now, the shocking run on Northern Rock in September 2007 was the first sign the British people had of the global banking problems that would eventually overwhelm our largest banks.[1] But behind closed doors, back before I became prime minister and while I was still Chancellor of the Exchequer, a lot of us in the Treasury felt it right to ask questions about how the financial system would respond to bank failures. The timing was not dictated by any particular bank event; at that time, no one had reported an institution in danger, and no one was telling us that risks had substantially worsened. But we always liked to plan for any eventuality, and so we thought it would be very useful to play through the scenario of a bank failure.

In this spirit, Ed Balls, the brilliant former Chief Advisor to the Treasury and then City Minister, led the Treasury, the Bank of England, and the Financial Services Authority (FSA) in conducting a Britain-only simulation exercise of what might happen in the event of a bank failure in Britain itself. Would the fall of a bank or a building society raise systemic issues? Could we allow such a bank or building society to fail? What was the point at which such a collapse became a threat to the entire system?

Always thinking of the global impact, I approached Hank

Paulson, U.S. Treasury secretary, and told him what we wanted to do. He readily agreed to participate in a joint transatlantic project.

Normally, the only simulation tests that the U.K. conducts with the United States are military exercises. As far as I know this was the first joint exercise focused on financial matters. Fortunately, all the American authorities agreed to participate. Besides Hank Paulson, we brought together by videoconference Mervyn King, the governor of the Bank of England; Callum McCarthy, head of the Financial Services Authority; Ben Bernanke, head of the Federal Reserve; and all the major regulators in the United States—nine different regulatory bodies, including the Securities and Exchange Commission and the New York Fed.

The question raised by the simulation exercise quickly focused our minds: Was the financial institutions' problem one of illiquidity, or were they insolvent? If they were insolvent, could a rescue of a building society be justified? What moral hazards—what expectations that the government would absorb future risks—were we creating if we acted?

Most who joined our financial "war game" started with the view that there would be moral hazard if a rescue was undertaken. After much discussion, most ended with the view that in at least some circumstances rescues would have to be undertaken. No one imagined that in our modern economy there would be queues around the block with runs on banks.

But it has struck me subsequently that we were asking only some of the questions that needed to be raised. For obvious market sensitivity reasons, no private sector participants were in the room, but it might have been better if we had simulated potential private sector responses. The question we could not definitively answer in a simulation was, of course, whether the private sector would be prepared to come to the rescue without government funding—a private sector subsidy was, of course, the question we had to deal with immediately after Northern Rock had gone bust.

Most important, at the time, the simulation was not set up to ask what might happen if a combination of banks might be in difficulty. With the exercise bound around the fate of one institution, there was no detailed discussion of the increased entanglement of institutions with each other and the dependence of many institutions on the shadow banking system—and what they would do if an off-balance-sheet entity had to be brought back onto the balance sheet.

Modern capitalism needs leverage to flourish. Of course we knew of the historical tendency for credit booms to happen and for the system to become overleveraged. We also knew that at the peak of a cycle extra capital will be needed when there are greater risks in the system. So I had never taken the view that the kind of global financial regulation I had been fighting for since the Asian crisis was, somehow, in 2007 and 2008 now irrelevant but that, at this point in time, it was impossible to achieve.

However, although I had fought internationally post-Asia for a proper monitoring of risk and an early warning system, I had to accept that I had lost the argument and that the best we had been able to achieve was a Financial Stability Forum with responsibility for, but little power over, financial stability. In the meantime we had to continue to press the economic leaders of the world for stage-by-stage improvements in the monitoring of systemic risks and vulnerabilities.

Of course with a leveraged economy, there would always be risk. But I and others felt that if there was a diversification of risk spread across many institutions and through many instruments, we were in a better position. I now believe that this was the biggest and most far-reaching mistake I and others made.

I was assuming that risk had indeed been dispersed across the system. The very new, very diverse range of institutions and instruments implied that the failure of one institution did not necessarily lead to the failure of some or all. But the world of finance was operating without the benefit of the global financial oversight I had been pressing for—and also without any comprehensive global picture of the full scale of the shadow and formal activities of the financial institutions and of their entanglements with each other. According to the pre-crisis assumptions, if there was a diversification of risk across the financial system, then the leveraging of financial institutions was less a systemwide threat than a matter for risk management in the individual institutions. Regulators could then focus more on the individual bank than the systemic effects from the behavior of the institutions. Such a diversification of risk implied that there were unlikely to be huge spillover effects and contagion if one institution was in difficulty. I recognized that by failing to develop both an early warning system and an effective crisis prevention and crisis resolution system in the world economy, we were at a disadvantage. There was no global system. Nationally we had a tripartite system of the Bank of England, the Treasury, and regulators assessing risks regularly. And internationally the International Monetary Fund and the international Financial Stability Forum joined the banking regulators in scrutinizing the global picture and pattern of risk.

But underlying the view that risk was diversified was the obvious conclusion that everyone assumed was right: that, as our experience after the Second World War had shown, the main threat to stability was high inflation. The economic priority was therefore to keep inflation low so that with low interest rates homeowners and businesses who borrowed would not have the kind of repayments at 15 percent interest rates we saw in the 1990s.

In the financial innovation that had happened, I saw the benefits for homebuyers (because the competition and innovation had created lower mortgage rates and the wider provision of mortgages) and for businesses that needed investment funds.

It wasn't until later that we saw what none of us had bargained for: the sheer scale of the shadow banking system that would create a race to the bottom and co-opt mainstream banks to their practices. They had not, in fact, diversified much risk, and their entanglements threatened all financial institutions.

We were to find that almost all the banks would have too little capital to cope with a mispricing of the American mortgage market. The entire world failed to fully understand the new financial instruments. But so, it transpires, had those who devised, bought, and sold them. Banks were both too big and too interconnected to fail.

Contrary to our expectations, and long-held economic wisdom, the problem the world was to face was not, in the end, high inflation—the cause of every Western recession since the Second World War—but overleverage and undercapitalization, leading to huge financial instability. Few had reckoned that there would be a complete market failure in a large part of the mortgage market in the United States, or had anticipated the breadth of the impact that would have because of the numbers who had bought subprime mortgage securities. Everybody seemed to want and to have a part of the action. What had appeared to investors to be a virtuous circle instead became a chain of destruction that led straight from the unemployed homeowners walking out on their risk-laden mortgages in Florida to the collapse of some of Europe's biggest banks. The first public sign of this in Britain was what happened with Northern Rock.

On September 14, 2007, televisions across the U.K. broadcast the story. In one day, Northern Rock depositors withdrew £1 billion in the first run on a British bank since Overend, Gurney and Company collapsed in 1866, some 141 years before. Most people watched in complete disbelief as our TV screens showed hitherto unbelievable images of a bank run in a modern economy. I was at Downing Street watching long queues outside branches of a

British main street bank. It was like a scene in a film or a picture in a history textbook, but not something I had ever expected to see in my lifetime or under my watch.

It was a disastrous outcome after what should have been a straightforward bank rescue. During August and early September, intensive discussions had taken place with Northern Rock about its problems, focusing on its access to liquidity and the state of its balance sheet. On September 13, Northern Rock asked for and received Bank of England support in its role as "lender of last resort."

Under Alistair Darling's leadership the Tripartite group went to work on a plan to rescue Northern Rock, but somehow the BBC's business editor, Robert Peston, got hold of it. On a prime-time news program he announced that Northern Rock had gone to the Bank of England because it was in trouble. "But," he added, "no one should panic."

But, naturally, people do panic when they believe their savings are at risk of being wiped out. For me, it was frightening to see such a physical manifestation of the frailty of modern economies. Because of the manner in which the information was leaked, people were terrified they might lose everything, and our main job was to make sure that the British public felt safe and was kept safe.

At 7 a.m. on Friday, September 14, Alistair announced that he had authorized the Bank of England to provide a liquidity-support facility "to help Northern Rock to fund its operations during the current period of turbulence in financial markets while Northern Rock works to secure an orderly resolution to its current liquidity problems." He went on to stress, "The FSA judges that Northern Rock is solvent, exceeds its regulatory capital requirement, and has a good-quality loan book."

Alastair and I were, as usual, in constant touch. As the bank queues grew longer and the public panic more intense, it became more and more obvious what needed to be done. The Bank of England's liquidity-support facility to Northern Rock, against appropriate collateral and at an interest rate premium, hadn't stopped people from overwhelming bank branches to get their deposits. Consequently, over the next two days, the Treasury worked on an even more radical plan: to guarantee all Northern Rock deposits and, if necessary, those of other banks that were imperiled by the run. It was imperative that we stop the panic. We did not want Northern Rock infecting any other banks. Fortunately, the guarantee did quell the panic and put a stop to the run.

After addressing the most obvious sign of the crisis we next had to look for the solution to the problem of a failed British bank. Here I intervened. I was against nationalization, especially of a failed bank, and at that stage I would not let it be considered. I favored a private sector buyout of the bank, partly because I believed we could isolate Northern Rock's problems and partly because, ever since the 1970s, the Labour Party had been losing elections on the question of economic competence. Tony Blair and I had spent twenty years building New Labour on the foundation of market competition, private enterprise, and economic stability as the path to growth and I was not prepared to undermine that painstaking work with one instant decision.

Northern Rock was the first British lender to fully embrace mortgage securitization. This meant it no longer held its loans to customers for the fifteen or twenty years it lent, but instead parceled them up, sold them, and used them as collateral for further funds.

By the end of 2007, 50 percent of the outstanding mortgages in the U.K. had been sold off in securitization vehicles. But no other bank or building society had been as aggressive as Northern Rock with so little capital behind it in pushing for a larger share of the British housing market. No other bank had relied so much on cheap debt. And no other bank was so dependent on short-term cash. As the Financial Services Authority concluded, "Comparison would have shown Northern Rock, relative to its peers, as having a high public target for asset growth (15–25%

year-on-year) and for profit growth; a low net interest margin; a low cost:income ratio; and relatively high reliance on wholesale funding and securitization."

What exposed Northern Rock was the reckless way it came to depend not on its depositors but on overnight and short-term borrowing from the markets, paying low interest rates to fund long-term mortgages on a scale that grew at a phenomenal rate. Its business model could succeed for a time, but Northern Rock had no Plan B for when the short-term financial markets dried up.

In June 2007, only weeks before its interim results of July, Northern Rock had announced a profit warning. The first sign of its reliance on a stable overnight funding market was thus revealed.

Northern Rock's problem was not liquidity, but its entire business model, which bore little resemblance to the old building societies, whose mortgages were covered by their deposits. In fact only 20 percent of Northern Rock's outgoings were covered by retail deposits and mortgage payments.

Northern Rock's problem was not simply that without adequate capital it was in no position to withstand the freezing of short-term finance in the marketplace; further compromising its position, from 2005 onward—and in its pre-crisis 2006 accounts— the mortgage bank was issuing false figures for mortgage arrears. Three senior executives have now been fined, since they admitted hiding hundreds of mortgages that were in arrears in the months before the bank failed. The Financial Services Authority's report into the failure said that staff felt "under pressure" to produce attractive arrears figures. As a result the mortgage bank issued arrears figures that were half the industry average, and then, in their reports to investors, publicly congratulated themselves on their success. The true repossession figures were, in fact, 300 percent higher than reported.

The executives at Northern Rock had pursued the model beyond its ethical conclusion and stretched their capital to the

limit to provide the highest returns to executives and shareholders. The view I held at the time has been confirmed by events: this
was more than a breach of regulatory rules. If there is no criminal law and thus there are no criminal prosecutions to deal with
these and other companies' flagrant abuses I identify later, there
should be.

Throughout October 2007 the Treasury held discussions with
putative private buyers. We looked at all the options, including
holding an auction to find a private buyer, but interest in a deal
was conditional on the government taking over all of the firm's
debts. The government was being asked to take on all of the firm's
risks but would receive none of the benefits; that would have
nationalized the losses and privatized the gains. But in these circumstances nationalization started to look like the only option.

Meanwhile the American market began to show evidence
of the impact of subprime lending: UBS announced losses of
$3.4 billion from subprime-related investments, and Citigroup
unveiled a subprime-related loss of $3.1 billion. By the end of the
month Merrill Lynch's CEO, Stan O'Neal, had resigned after the
investment bank revealed its $7.9 billion exposure to bad debt.
By December it was becoming clear that the subprime crisis was
having a major impact on the willingness of banks to lend to each
other. The European Central Bank and central banks of the U.S.,
the U.K., Canada, and Switzerland coordinated offering billions
of dollars in loans to banks to try to get money flowing through
the system again.[2]

I spent the Christmas break as usual with Sarah and the boys
in Scotland. This was my first Christmas as Prime Minister,
and I had been looking forward to getting back home to Fife
to relax. Instead I was hugely troubled as to why, despite many
commentators concluding that the problems were starting to
ease, the market seemed to have frozen. I became worried that

the cause of the freeze was the existence of toxic assets and that the freezing of interbank lending would spill over into the rest of the system. Because this was a global and not just a national problem, I was also worried about the lack of international coherence in our approach to these problems, and about banks' levels of transparency all around.

JANUARY 2008

As we returned for the New Year I set about trying to rectify these problems. I began by arranging a meeting of the European heads of government in the G8 in London for the end of January and started drafting an article for the *Financial Times*. It appeared under the title "Ways to Fix the World's Financial System." I argued that "if the manifestation of the problems was an under-pricing of risk, the source of many of the problems was *a deficit of transparency*. That transparency deficit needs to be addressed—from within organisations, their auditors, the credit rating agencies and through regulatory requirements, leading to an increased understanding by firms, investors and regulators."

As credit dried up the Fed took further action to try to ease things. On January 22 it announced a surprise interest rate cut of three-quarters of a percent, to 3.5 percent, followed on January 30 by a further half-percent cut. At the same time, consumers were getting very anxious about the standard of living they could expect in the coming year. Commodity prices were already spiking by this point.[3] They were to remain hugely volatile throughout the year.

The annual World Economic Forum, held in Davos, Switzerland, in January, had for years been a celebration of financial success. I had often attended since becoming Shadow Chancellor in opposition in the early 1990s. When I spoke there in early 2007 I had argued forcibly that people power—expressed anew through the Internet, email, and the emerging forms of social networking—would change forever the way political decisions would be made. But this year, 2008, I went with a far more urgent message: I wanted to warn that the scale of the banks' losses, unless addressed, could threaten a recession, and to argue that we would need new rules for banking in the future and that we had to be bold with both monetary and fiscal support for our economies.

Later that month, on January 29, I welcomed the European members of the G8 (President Nicolas Sarkozy of France, Chancellor Angela Merkel of Germany, Prime Minister Romano Prodi of Italy, and President José Manuel Barroso) to discussions in London. While Romano Prodi—a long-term friend with both a great intellect and a passion to help the poor—was about to leave office, the other three of us were to keep in regular direct touch by phone, videoconferencing, and meetings during the crisis. I admire Angela Merkel as thoughtful and brilliant, always able to see the way to a consensus, and a superb summit leader. Nicolas Sarkozy is also a friend who is a force of nature, and as his European Union presidency demonstrated and as his joint presidency of the G8 and G20 will soon show, is unrivaled in his sense of purpose and action. José Manuel Barroso should receive more praise than he gets for holding Europe together from crisis to crisis without ever losing sight of his vision of a fairer, more prosperous continent. We were to be a good team fighting these first stages of the crisis. The meeting started in the Cabinet room and then, after an hour, moved to a small dining room on the first floor of Downing Street. It would be a chance, I hoped, to relax a little together and to develop some informal understandings about where each of us stood.

My starting point was that we needed the banks to start lending, and we could not go on as normal if the banks did not demonstrate to us that they had rid themselves of their impaired assets. No one now believed them when they said they had cleaned up their balance sheet. I argued that to restore confidence, we had to determine a timeline within which overdue change had to happen. Everyone agreed that pressure on the banks had to be intense, but I sensed that even now my European colleagues believed this was America's crisis alone, and that the U.K. was affected because it has the same Anglo-Saxon financial system. They were not alone in hoping that the rest of Europe might escape the worst of the crisis.

Upstairs, in the more informal atmosphere of a small dinner party, we exchanged views about future cooperation. Everyone agreed the G8 could not be the sole vehicle for economic coordination, and discussion ranged from a G8 plus 5 or 6, to a possibly wider group. The debate about the optimal forum in which to discuss these issues was to continue right up until September, but my main objective—opening channels of communication and seeding the idea with European leaders that this was not an American issue but a global one—had been achieved.

FEBRUARY 2008

On February 6, 2008, I talked at length to President George Bush about working together to develop a more effective joint plan to reduce marketplace uncertainty. This was followed by an agreement that weekend, when Alistair led the meeting of G7 finance ministers in Tokyo to call for the prompt disclosure of losses. I thought that if we could only get the banks to declare their losses we could restore the trust necessary in the interbanking market, which would in turn ensure that the banks fulfilled their role in the economy for businesses and households. There was to be a slow but gradually dawning realization that the assets were so impaired and the losses so great that the banks did not actually have enough capital to declare these losses. Over the next few weeks I had a videoconference with Chancellor Merkel, phone calls with a number of world leaders, and meetings with my European colleagues (on February 21 with President Sarkozy and Prime Minister José Luis Rodríguez Zapatero of Spain), and each conversation increased my certainty that the declaration of losses was going to be a precondition of restoring confidence.

Meanwhile, in the midst of our general worries about the financial system, Alistair and the Treasury team led by John Kingman were now also meticulously considering the detailed alternatives for the future of Northern Rock. We had averted total collapse in 2007, but the bank needed to be put on a stable footing for the long term. Despite ten private companies having expressed an interest in buying the bank in October, in November Northern Rock had announced that all of those offers were below its share price (leading its share price to drop a further 20 percent). By February 13 only two bidders remained: Virgin and the Northern Rock board. Alistair and I met to discuss them both. We felt that the board's offer would disadvantage the government, while Virgin's bid was conditional on three more years of liquidity support.

By February 17 the Treasury's view was that a period of temporary public ownership was, of all the options available, the best value for money for the taxpayer. All options would require a degree of effective public subsidy in the short term; in the case of public ownership, to offset this subsidy the government would secure the full value released by any future sale compared to only a very small share of any upside with a private sector solution. Given the current market conditions, it seemed extremely unlikely that significantly better terms could be secured from one of the private sector bidders through negotiation. I accepted with an incredibly heavy heart the reality of the choice the Treasury presented me with. I had no idea that six months later I would be the one initiating the government's buying into the biggest banks in the country.

At 4 p.m. we announced that Northern Rock would be nationalized and "managed on arm's length terms, as a commercial entity."

MARCH 2008

It was against this backdrop that Alistair had to deliver his annual budget. We had just nationalized a bank, and rising prices for food and oil were still creating huge pressures on family finances, so as we dealt with the problem of financial confidence we needed also to focus on consumer confidence and to reassure the public that their standard of living would be protected.[4]

The first real sign of the massive underlying vulnerabilities across Wall Street was the acquisition of Bear Stearns by JP Morgan Chase. A year earlier, Bear Stearns had been worth $18 billion. Now it went for $240 million.

It was just one more sign of the accelerating crisis. By the time I met President Sarkozy at No. 10 on March 27 I was convinced that the comprehensive response we needed was so urgent that further steps had to be taken immediately. We made a direct reference to the need for immediate write-offs of toxic debts. Our communiqué from that meeting said we needed "greater transparency in financial markets to ensure that banks make full and prompt disclosure of the scale of write-offs." But we also called for wider economic reform: cross-border financial supervision, the management of financial crisis situations, and the reform of the IMF so that in concert with the Financial Stability Forum, it would have the ability to provide a credible and authoritative early warning system for the world.

APRIL 2008

On April 8 the IMF confirmed all this when it issued its twice-yearly Global Financial Stability Report. It said losses were spreading from subprime mortgage assets to other sectors, such as commercial property, consumer credit, and company debt. But by far its most revealing finding was the sheer volume of losses involved: "Adding other categories of loans originated and securities issued in the United States related to commercial real estate, the consumer credit market, and corporations increases aggregate potential losses to about $945 billion." The number shocked me.

Alistair asked Sir James Crosby, the Deputy Chair of the FSA, to provide advice to the government on options for improving the function of the mortgage finance markets. I was very supportive because I knew that unless we could get the mortgage market lending again, we were heading for a major recession, if not worse.

At the meeting of G7 finance ministers and the IMF meetings in Washington on April 11 and 12, much of the focus was rightly on the scale of impaired assets. When Ben Bernanke, chair of the U.S. Federal Reserve, was pressed, he suggested that total U.S. write-downs would be $250 billion. That worried me, because it implied that less than half of what was needed had been declared. What about the rest of the $700 billion in bad assets? Where were they? Representing Britain, Alistair emphasized the challenges of valuing some asset-backed security products and suggested that we had to go further than simply making more liquidity available.

April saw a wave of non-U.K. rights issues. I thought that, finally, the banks were coming clean and we at least had a fighting chance of the losses being declared and a restoration of the markets. We were expecting rights issues from the Royal Bank of Scotland (RBS) and the Halifax Bank of Scotland (HBOS), but I knew they still had insufficient liquidity and were not lending. Lending by banks was rapidly becoming my obsession. On April 15 I called British bank leaders together. All the banks there except HSBC asked for liquidity to be provided to the whole system. Andy Hornby from HBOS sounded very worried—the others appeared to be suffering a quiet anxiety—but I was becoming increasingly impatient because there seemed to be very little self-analysis of their problems and only limited focus on the broader issue of lending into the wider economy.

Immediately after the meeting I gathered together Yvette Cooper (then the formidably able Chief Secretary to the Treasury and representing Alistair, who was in Washington), Shriti, Jeremy Heywood, Tom Scholar from the Treasury (who had been my private secretary in the Treasury as well as No. 10 and had excellent judgment), and Gus O'Donnell, the head of the civil service and an eminent economist (and previously my Permanent Secretary in the Treasury), to discuss work the Bank of England had been doing on liquidity. Banks were not lending, so we agreed in that meeting on the basis of a new special liquidity scheme and the possible terms on which support would be given.

Later that day I flew to the United States to give a lecture at the Kennedy Library in Boston. Before the lecture, I called a meeting of leading American bankers in New York and asked them to explain why it was so difficult for the losses to be declared.[5]

The next day, in Washington, I explored this issue further with Alan Greenspan, then with the three presidential candidates (Barack Obama, Hillary Clinton, and John McCain), and finally that evening with President Bush himself, first in the Oval Office and again later, when our wives joined us for dinner. The next morning at breakfast I had a final discussion with Ben Bernanke before flying home to London with an ever stronger sense of what had to be done. Three days later, on April 21, Alistair launched the £100 billion Special Liquidity Scheme, which allowed banks and building societies to swap for up to three years some of their illiquid assets, including mortgage debts, for U.K. Treasury Bills.[6]

When I gave the Kennedy Lecture in Boston I talked about a declaration of interdependence under which there would be far greater international coordination for dealing with exactly the problems we were facing; this included cooperation on dealing with bank failures as well as coordination of economic policies.

The following day, when I returned to Britain, Alastair and I immediately met with the Multi-National Chairman's Group and we talked about these very issues. Given my continuing questions about the scale of bad debts, I felt that Stephen Green, the HSBC chairman, summed it up well. There was now a new scheme in place offering the banks billions in liquidity. It would test whether the crisis was fundamentally a problem of liquidity or solvency. HSBC could of course afford to watch and wait; they were a provider of liquidity to the market and did not need the Bank of England's facility.

As if to emphasize that the problem was one of solvency, on April 22 the Royal Bank of Scotland announced a rights issue worth £12 billion—the biggest in British corporate history—and on April 29 HBOS went for £4 billion. Barclays announced its rights issue of £4 billion on June 14, underwritten by Qatar's state-owned Investment Authority and a number of other foreign investors. In this period, a total of £20 billion of capital was sought in rights issues by four British banks.

Finally, I thought, what I had been pushing for was happening: capital that would allow banks to come clean and declare their losses. And if they came clean, we could have the restoration of the banking markets. I worried it was too late. It took longer for me to understand that it was too little. That the biggest rights issue in British history was simply not big enough was simply mind bending.

MAY–JUNE 2008

Throughout these months volatilities other than the financial also dominated my discussions with global counterparts. I could see that rising food prices, highly volatile energy prices, and the disruptions on the stock markets and in bank lending were not isolated events. It should not be forgotten that a series of problems intrinsic to the workings of our global economy were converging. They were all telling us something about the uncoordinated nature of our new global economy.

One way forward was to bring greater stability to oil and gas prices. I spoke by video and telephone with the Saudi, French, Australian, and German governments and on video link and then in person with President Bush. I addressed other European leaders at the European Council meeting on June 19 and oil producers and consumers at the Jeddah oil summit on June 22.

The oil summit, held at my initiative, took place when oil was trading at record-high prices; by May 10 it was at $125 a barrel, by May 21 at $130, by May 22 at $135, before soaring to its peak of $147 in early July. When we met in Jeddah we did secure a small victory via an agreement on more supply of oil production, so that oil prices were to peak at $148 a barrel two weeks later, before falling by 75 percent by December. Although we agreed on a second conference for January, events in the wider economy were moving even more swiftly.

Problems that looked like problems of liquidity were now appearing to be problems of solvency. On May 14 Bradford and Bingley launched a £300 million rights issue, but by June 2 they had to change the terms of the rights issue halfway through, after admitting £8 million in losses in the first four months of the year. Jeremy was working around the clock to monitor events for me; I sometimes wondered if he ever slept. The Treasury and the Tripartite group had their hands full managing the increasing volatility of events.

In these circumstances—low lending, a poor housing market, and deteriorating economic position—interest rates would ordinarily have been falling fast. But they weren't.

JULY 2008

Throughout July, it was clear that the U.S. housing market was getting into ever more serious trouble. On May 22, the Office of Federal Housing Enterprise Oversight House Price Index fell by its largest ever quarterly (−1.7 percent) and largest ever annual (−3.1 percent) amounts, and now Treasury Secretary Hank Paulson was having to negotiate with Congress for support for Fannie Mae and Freddie Mac (which together either owned or guaranteed $5 trillion worth of home loans). In Britain's housing market the Council of Mortgage Lenders announced on July 18 that lending had declined by 32 percent from June 2007. These figures made my blood run cold. I knew what they meant: people and businesses stuck without credit and possibly a bad recession. Already the Blue Chip consensus growth forecast for Q4 2008 had moved from a January 2008 forecast of above 2.5 percent to a July 2008 forecast of growth of below 1 percent. This wasn't predicting a recession in the technical sense, but the removal of credit was happening very suddenly, and I realized I had not been thinking out of the box enough. I had expected to push and nudge the system back to order, but it was not happening.

The market then dealt us a further blow. On July 21 underwriters had been left with more than two-thirds of the HBOS rights issue unsold.[7] I interpreted this as meaning that the markets did not believe that HBOS had come clean on its toxic assets and future write-offs. At the same time, the RBS share price was at 197.6p, while its rights price was at 200p, and the Qataris had been left with most of the Barclays issue, as there was only a 20 percent take-up of the issue. The whole market was simply walking away. They did not believe the banks; neither should I.

The collapse in credit and its consequences for Britain's and the global economy was the question that obsessed me throughout our summer holiday in Suffolk. It was always great to be out of London and spending private family time with Sarah and the boys, and as usual I tried to read widely in a way that simply wasn't possible when Parliament was sitting and each day was a full diary of meetings. It was then that I picked up and read Ben Bernanke's essays on the Great Depression.

I asked Shriti to visit us so I could argue through my latest thinking with her.

I was by now deeply worried that the swift withdrawal of credit from the global economy could tip us into another Great Depression, and so I wanted to talk through ideas of possible solutions. I discussed with her Bernanke's ideas for quantitative easing, and we talked about Japan's experience in the past two decades. How do we avoid a depression? How do we avoid our banks becoming like the Japanese banks, which were left still sitting on bad assets?

Since the IMF's report on projected losses, the market appeared to be concluding that not only did the banks need a lot more capital than they had raised, but also that the banks hadn't yet been honest—or simply did not know—about where their losses were. The failure of the rights issues of the three British banks was proof that bank investors certainly felt that. Shriti's bleak assessment was that we now had to consider the risk of a looming and much bigger problem: that the banks were in such serious trouble that some of them may well fail.

There was of course another problem: if new capital was needed, where would it come from? Could Sovereign Wealth Funds step in? Or were there any other sources of private capital around the world? Or could we do a JP Morgan–Bear Stearns, with stronger banks taking over weaker? The options seemed rather limited, but it would depend on how much was needed and by whom. When Jeremy Heywood arrived in Suffolk to join the discussion, we agreed we should get a clear assessment from the Tripartite group about the losses and the need for capital.

Shriti argued persuasively that the historical relationship between lending and recession was so strong that serious consideration needed to be given to finding ways to unlock the frozen funding markets, so that banks themselves could borrow medium-term money, without which there would be very little new lending. Alistair had already commissioned Sir James Crosby to look at the mortgage-backed market. I agreed with Alistair that Shriti and Tom Scholar should be jointly tasked to examine the merits of the interim report from Sir James Crosby on the mortgage markets and for any other solutions and report back to Alistair and me at the end of the summer.

AUGUST 2008

My underlying worry was what I now felt to be a huge double risk: banks that weren't lending and consumers who had stopped buying.

The more I explored the lessons from the past and cross-referenced them with the data from the present, the more it became clear that a huge fiscal stimulus and substantial quantitative easing would both be necessary, but they could work only if the rest of the world joined in. I started to bring together evidence which showed that the cumulative effect from all countries doing similar things would be to achieve twice the impact in each individual country. But quantitative easing and a fiscal stimulus were a necessary but not sufficient condition for recovery. The banking problem first had to be addressed at its source.

Shriti and Tom reported that guaranteeing mortgage-backed securities was problematic, but more important, it was not going to solve the problem. Certainly not on its own. It was becoming increasingly clear that the issue really was about capital and the lack of confidence in the underlying state of the assets held by the banks. Shriti sent me a long set of her email exchanges with Tom and others exploring the issues, which she entitled "Is it capital?" The net was closing. Jeremy assured me the Treasury was doing some technical work on contingency planning. The unthinkable was starting to have to be thought about. I started to call some of the leaders in the Middle East.

Throughout August I was also working on my speech for the Labour Party conference in Manchester in September. The month when most of Britain's politicians and civil servants go on holiday was always also the month my indispensable adviser Kirsty McNeill worked the hardest—crafting lines, imposing discipline on the creative process, and arguing through the big themes as I prepared for what is always an important occasion for any party leader. This speech in particular was very high pressure and had high stakes, as there were strong rumors that I would be challenged for the Labour leadership at the conference itself, and much of the political discussion that summer was dominated by whispers about a "coup" to remove me. By September 1 we had what we both considered to be a good draft to deliver in the weeks to come and felt reasonably confident that its argument and announcements were strong enough to move our party forward. Nobody realized just how much the political context of Britain, or the economic reality of the world, was to change before we got to Manchester.

SEPTEMBER 7–18, 2008

In London on September 11, I talked to President Bush by phone. We had a lot to discuss, as the U.S. market had had a very difficult few days: on September 7 the two mortgage giants, Fannie Mae and Freddie Mac, were nationalized after they had lost $14 billion in only one year. In changing attitudes to intervention we were starting to see a huge psychological shift for America in general and the Republican Party in particular. On September 10 the long-established and highly respected banking house Lehman Brothers posted three-month losses of $3.9 billion—an announcement that shook not just Wall Street but world markets.

We knew the storm was brewing and was certain to come rolling across the Atlantic toward Britain. One investment bank, Merrill Lynch, was already being taken over. At the start of what was to be an extraordinary weekend, I heard privately through Shriti that Bank of America was not going to bid for Lehman and that Barclays was possibly interested. I told Alistair that we ought to support the U.S. as much as we could without risking our own stability; he agreed, but was rightly concerned that we needed to ensure Barclays was strong enough and was adequately supported by the U.S. government to take this on.

It wasn't until quite late in the process on Sunday that Hank Paulson called Alistair.

But by late Sunday, September 14, it was clear that both the Bank of America and Barclays were pulling out of any rescue operation. On September 15 Lehman Brothers filed for bankruptcy, and a Wall Street institution that had survived two world wars and the Great Depression was no more. On Friday night there were four big independent Wall Street firms; on Monday morning there were two.

SEPTEMBER 16–24, 2008

The next day the U.S. Federal Reserve announced an $85 billion loan to AIG in exchange for an 80 percent stake in the country's biggest insurance company. This came on top of huge pressure now going from Lehman and Merrill to Morgan Stanley and Goldman; their share prices were plummeting and CDS spreads ballooning. It was bringing issues to a head in Britain too; HBOS was most under pressure. There was still a private sector solution: Lloyds had been interested in acquiring HBOS for many years, but competition considerations had always been a problem. Now both banks were talking about it, and they each approached us separately, asking for a waiver.

The Bank of England and FSA were asked to give their opinion, and the Treasury and the Business Department issued clearance for a takeover to go ahead on September 18. This seemed to me a good deal for taxpayers because we knew from the United States that contagion was the issue; if we were forced to national-ize HBOS, there could be a domino effect and the focus would switch to other banks. The chaos in the United States was at the forefront in all our minds. By now we were all watching the markets anxiously, and the atmosphere was tense. Every time Jeremy said he wanted to update me on something, I expected another piece of bad news from the markets.

As the same time, the FSA also acted to undermine the contagion by taking the lead and banning short selling. I had no argument with the practice in principle, but its impact on financial stability was by this stage acute. Our actions eased some of the pressures on U.K. banks but, I assumed for ideological reasons, were not followed by the U.S. administration.

The day after the Lloyds takeover of HBOS was made public, the U.S. Treasury announced its intention to seek congressional approval for a $700 billion fund to purchase impaired assets (the TARP scheme, as it was to become known).

Although we were surprised by the announcement, my team was concerned because it was a plan to buy assets, not a plan for capital. However, I did recognize a critically important component to the TARP plan: it was a systemic solution to the problem. This was not a one-by-one, bank-by-bank approach but intended as a once-and-for-all solution. It also attempted to underpin a market in these assets, and we considered that might be something that needed to be done. Unfortunately it was, in my view, expensive, difficult to implement, and not going to the heart of the matter quickly. I was not sure it would work, at least not in the U.K.

Buying the bad assets off the books was too roundabout a way of injecting capital and at a subsidized rate to allow losses to be taken. If we were to step into the banks in any way I wanted the government to be compensated in full, with ownership of a stake, even if it took a long time for us to be paid back.[8]

The proposal was difficult to implement because it needed the assets to be valued in a market where there was no price at present. Valuing assets and buying them up would take time and involve controversy, and yet the need was to restore market confidence now. In my view, and that of Shriti, Jeremy, and Alistair and his team, TARP was not for us, but it did provide crucial leadership in opening the door to a comprehensive, systemwide solution. And it did put liquidity and new funding into the banks. The sale of assets to the U.S. Treasury would release liquidity directly to the selling banks. But if we were to support the banks I wanted to ensure that there were changes to the banks. I was not prepared to subsidize the existing management of banks that had been irresponsible and negligent in their risk-taking.

Nevertheless, given the instability of the system that had already claimed HBOS, I wanted TARP to succeed. But because I did not think it likely it would I asked for the wider work I had commissioned on capital to be accelerated, and I focused on getting through my own big political test in Manchester.

When I spoke to the Labour Party conference on September 23, it was in a world different from the one I had known when I started drafting the speech in the summer. As I said to the delegates, "Insuring people against the new risks and empowering people with new opportunities is the mission of the hour. Those who say that governments should walk away when people face these risks and need these opportunities will be judged to be on the wrong side of history. . . . This is a defining moment for us—a test not just of our judgement but of our values."

The coup that had been speculated about throughout the summer did not materialize. My mind, in any case, was now firmly on other things.

All the time the scale of the economic threat was growing. As the conference closed, the day after my speech I boarded a plane for New York to attend the UN General Assembly. The world leaders in the world's financial center were doing something different from what I had in mind. Was I missing something? I wanted to see firsthand what was going on.

SEPTEMBER 24, 2008

When we landed in New York I was given briefings on the state of the markets and headed straight into an evening meeting at my hotel.

I had asked Stewart Wood, an outstanding Oxford don turned political strategist who advised me on both Europe and America, to bring together some of the best economists in the world, including two Nobel prize winners who came to discuss these matters with us at very short notice. There was total consensus in this group about the scale of the impending crisis and the need for massive fiscal stimulus (and they turned out to be wholly right). There was growing support for bank recapitalization.

SEPTEMBER 25, 2008

Lehman Brothers had been the biggest banking collapse in history, but was not to remain so for long. On September 25 Washington Mutual, with $307 billion assets, became the largest bank failure ever recorded. It was seized by the FDIC, and its $188 billion of deposits were sold to JP Morgan Chase.

The successive events and failures that together constituted the crisis were mounting up: Merrill Lynch had been taken over by the Bank of America, and now household names like Morgan Stanley, UBS, and RBS seemed to be hovering on the edge.[9]

Worse was to follow. Thursday, September 25, was the day it became clear that the economic powerhouses of the world were all pulling in different directions.

I began with a breakfast with American investors and led a conversation about TARP to try to ascertain whether they thought it would solve the problems and restore confidence. It was a tricky conversation, because they were investors, and I couldn't let them know that we were looking at our banks' capital. Shriti teased out of them a view that was enlightening: they didn't think TARP was the solution; they saw the problem as the banks needing more capital.

Then I met with Tim Geithner, who was then president of the New York Fed. We agreed that Hank Paulson's initiative—that the government bought up diseased assets and, by doing so, cleansed the existing banks of their bad assets—was a good one. But I explained why I didn't think it would do enough. I asked him if there was any way he could see that the U.S. government could inject capital directly into the banks. He told me that within the TARP legislation there would be a proposal that allowed direct purchase of bank shares if that became necessary. He was not able to answer if the administration and Congress would really consider such an action, but I came away from the meeting feeling far more hopeful than before. It might not be probable that the U.S. would do a recapitalization, but it was possible. If Britain were to consider a more radical path, there might be no legislative barrier to prevent America from joining us.

Buoyed by that revelation, I called Alistair and asked him to speak to Paulson about whether they were looking at capital at all. But Alastair reported that Hank was not giving much away.

Some leaders, among them President Bush himself, had already left New York. But I had leaders to talk to who were still around, and even if it were an incomplete group we could at least sound each other out on the kind of action that was needed. As well as the banking problem, I was concerned to use the time to build momentum for fiscal stimulus and quantitative easing. So I told Tom Fletcher, the resourceful young Foreign Office star who was my foreign affairs private secretary, that I wanted an appointment with President Bush the next day. I announced to my long-suffering events team that there had been a change of plan, and we would have to divert our plane from New York to Washington the next day.

At about 6 p.m. I brought together an impromptu gathering of world leaders, the main heads of government who were still in New York. I wanted to test whether there was a common approach to the financial crisis, whether there was a chance the world could come together in one forum, and whether a G20 meeting or any other arrangement could command consensus.

Brazil was the current chair of the G20, so I asked President Lula to be present. At the meeting were José Manuel Barroso, head of the European Commission; José Luis Zapatero, Prime Minister of Spain; José Socrates, Prime Minister of Portugal; Jan Peter Balkenende, Prime Minister of the Netherlands; Anders Fogh Rasmussen, then Prime Minister of Denmark; Jens Stoltenberg, Prime Minister of Norway; and Kevin Rudd, Prime Minister of Australia. I had felt that not just Latin America but Africa should be represented too, so I invited President Jakaya Kikwete of Tanzania, the retiring president of the African Union, and had a long conversation with Prime Minister Meles Zenawi of Ethiopia when he arrived.

We met together in the UN building, in an out-of-the-way room off one of its quietest corridors. It had been chosen carefully. Along almost every other corridor there always seemed to be an endless stream of keen but raw journalists, all looking for a politician who might say something unwise or controversial enough to make a young reporter famous. In possibly one of the dingiest rooms ever to be visited by such a company, we gathered around one end of a bleak, oversize table and discussed our next moves.

We discussed how we might work together as a group to deal with the crisis. We agreed that we had to decide how concerted action could be made to work. We all agreed that the G8 was too limited, because it excluded all the main emerging markets that were at the heart of the crisis. President Sarkozy and I had previously considered proposing jointly that we model a leaders' meeting on the G20 group of finance ministers. So I put our suggestion on the table, then President Lula helpfully proposed that the G20 finance ministers' chairmanship, which Brazil then held, should be passed to the United Kingdom in advance of the allotted date of January 1, 2009.

As we spoke, I found myself worrying about the infamous 1933 London conference, where leaders had failed to agree and gone off home, leaving the rest of the 1930s as lost economic years crippled by protectionist action. A failure like that had to be avoided at all costs. So at this stage we were also in contact with Chancellor Merkel and making approaches to Premier Wen Jiabao of China and Prime Minister Manmohan Singh of India. Having met with my fellow leaders, I was able to tell President Bush the next day that everyone shared the view that an urgent meeting of the leaders of the world's largest economies was necessary, and that we hoped he would find a way to support an international gathering as soon as possible.

SEPTEMBER 26, 2008

Addressing first the United Nations and then the Clinton Global Initiative, I laid out the arguments I had first formulated during my hours of reading in Suffolk in the summer. In every forum, my theme was that the financial crisis reflected a global problem that could not be resolved by one nation alone but needed a global solution. I recalled that the institutions of the global economy had been created for a different world—of sheltered economies—and that they had to be adapted to a new era of global finance.

But as I stepped off the podium I was still going over the previous night's conversation in my mind. I knew that the consensus we had reached then was important, but I also knew that without American buy-in it wouldn't be enough.

I reached the White House around 5 p.m. President Bush, who was always enjoyable to talk with, having a ready joke and good humor, was in remarkably good spirits. He listened to me attentively and, as always, with great courtesy. I explained that Hank Paulson's toxic assets plan was a good idea but that I didn't think it would be enough, and I suggested we consider a more direct approach: taking equity in the banks. I told him that, in my view, the crisis had moved from appearing to be a liquidity problem to what it now clearly was, a bank capital problem, and that nobody believed the protestations of the banks anymore. He said he would speak to Hank, but obviously his first priority was to get the troubled assets program through the Congress.

I had two additional matters of substance I wanted to discuss with the president. I wanted to persuade him to agree to have a G20 meeting, as I had discussed with other leaders in New York. There we had agreed that I would pitch the idea to Bush first, and that Sarkozy would follow up. Bush was not against a meeting in principle, but said it could not be a meeting simply to talk. I said that there were many financial sector issues that could be resolved only if leaders came together, and that if he supported a meeting I would take responsibility to ensure an agreed policy. I also reminded him that G20 already existed at the finance ministers' level, so we were not talking about creating a new forum. He had one other stipulation: during the presidential handover he would not travel; if the meeting was to take place it would have to be in Washington.

The other matter of substance was trade. I pointed out that making progress on the Doha Development Round of trade talks would signal that the world could come together to solve its problems, that America and India had to examine whether they could resolve their differences. After many conversations with Prime Minister Singh about the issues I felt able to stress the potential for agreement. I believed that India was prepared to move from its entrenched position that it had to be able to cut off food imports if they were to rise substantially. I felt that there was an accommodation that America and India could reach. The president called his trade specialist into the meeting to discuss what might be possible, but it became clear that the real issue was the political hurdle to a deal involving cotton in advance of the U.S. elections.

As the meeting in the Oval Office finished up I was told a fax had come through from No. 10, and that I also needed to have an urgent call with Alistair, so I went into an anteroom to talk to him. He said that our last remaining mortgage bank, Bradford and Bingley, was going under, and that there was no alternative but to nationalize it. He and I approved the policy, and then I picked up the fax, which contained the figures I had requested from the Treasury on our estimates of the losses and capital needs of our banks; and figures from Mervyn King on capitalization.

SEPTEMBER 26–27, 2008

As I got on the plane back to London and started reading the latest analysis of the capital problems of our banks and Mervyn King's letter, I sensed the urgency and sheer scale of the decision we faced. The only answer to the structural problem was for governments to buy into the banks.

For too long banks had argued that they had a liquidity problem and denied that their real problem was deeper. Now they were so undercapitalized and overleveraged with unimaginable losses from toxic assets that many could not, in our view, survive in their current form. This was reflected in the collapse in their share prices and the stress in the interbank market.

I was turning the question Hank Paulson was trying to answer on its head. He, and we, knew the banks had bad assets. We now knew also that the banks were not sufficiently well-capitalized to deal with these impaired assets and their other problems. So instead of buying up diseased assets that in any case could not be quantified or even properly priced for sale—and still leaving people in doubt as to whether the bad assets had been removed—why not do things the other way around?

Instead of the government buying assets from the banks, why didn't we recapitalize the banks that needed capital, and, with them now for the first time in years properly financed, make sure that they cleaned out their bad assets immediately?

I was now convinced that TARP by itself couldn't solve the real problem and that recovery from recession depended utterly upon us getting the banks to lend again. We knew that, even with interest rates at zero, the interest rates at which banks lend, and their additional charges, would remain high. The availability of credit was what mattered. Small and medium-size businesses were wholly dependent on the ability and willingness of banks to lend. The temptation for the banks was to become risk-averse and to preserve their capital by simply not lending. If the banks were to be able not just to deleverage, but to lend again, we had no alternative but to recapitalize the banking system.

On the flight back to London, I remember asking, "If we go out on our own, how does that solve it?," and then answering my own question with "But do we really have a choice?"

I talked about the risks of acting alone, that it might not be enough to gain the confidence of the markets and might put the U.K.'s own credit at risk. But we were now sure that, if we as a government did nothing, at least two of the world's biggest banks could collapse within days—and soon others would come tumbling down. The U.K. economy would face a depression if RBS and HBOS both failed. The choice was clear: either we had to step in and accept all the associated risks, or simply leave the free market banking system to collapse.

The United States, which had already embarked on TARP, had Congress to contend with. I still had a chance to persuade the

Europeans, albeit it would be difficult. They fundamentally did not believe they were as exposed as the U.S. and the U.K. Should the U.K. go it alone?

I was clear that this had to be a moment in which a line in the sand was drawn with the market, and that would mean comprehensive action to deal with the problem. While capital should eventually lead funding markets to open, Shriti argued we needed to include some type of solution on funding, which she and Tom had looked at over the summer. I asked her to make sure we had a comprehensive plan that covered all the bases and reduced the risks of a negative response from the market. I told her I wanted to announce it the following week. Never easily daunted, she didn't blink.

As we debated, I had come to a settled view: we needed a comprehensive plan centered on capital, and, if necessary, Britain would have to go it alone. On that overnight flight I knew that the path we were choosing could be a lonely one.

But I also felt a wave of relief that I had thought it through and was convinced it was the right path. Whenever I am faced with a huge issue, I do three things. First, I read as widely as possible about it; I had begun that process back in Suffolk in the summer. Second, I consult with the smartest people I can find; I had done that inside the government, but I also talked with economists and investors. Third, I try to think about where the decision I have to take will lead in the short and long term. After doing all these things, I make a decision, and then want it executed as quickly as humanly possible.

I asked Mike Ellam, the Downing Street director of communications, what story the press was filing from the back of the plane. We joked, "They're probably trying to find a way they can say the meeting with the president was short enough that they can call it a snub."

My team, who had gathered around my seat, laughed, and I went back to work with my big felt-tip pen.

SEPTEMBER 27, 2008

As I arrived back in London on Saturday morning I went straight into the office to meet Alistair, who was preparing to announce the nationalization of Bradford and Bingley, the one remaining demutualized mortgage bank in Britain, whose assets would end up alongside those of the other failed demutualized mortgage bank, Northern Rock.[10] Alistair and I talked about the overall position of the banks, and I could see that we were coming close to similar conclusions about the bigger issues of recapitalization. Together we set in motion a series of inquiries that would identify the scale of the structural problem and the size of the recapitalization that would be necessary. I knew that a lot of arm-twisting lay ahead, but my mind was made up. I could see no other way forward.

SEPTEMBER 28, 2008

On Sunday, September 28, Hank Paulson announced more details of his $700 billion bank rescue scheme, which would buy diseased assets. He then began his heroic work to get it through Congress.

Throughout the day, Alistair and I continued our discussions about how to provide the best outcome for the taxpayer from the Bradford and Bingley deal.

SEPTEMBER 29–OCTOBER 14, 2008

The next day, Monday, September 29, Wachovia, with $447 billion of deposits, was sold to Citi by the FDIC (in the end, Wells Fargo bought it), and Morgan Stanley sold a 12 percent stake to Mitsubishi UFJ. The stock market took another lurch downward. The panic selling was a response to the Republicans in Congress voting down TARP, and it saw a record one-day point fall on the Dow Jones Index: with 770 points wiped off the value of Wall Street. The contagion quickly spread to Asia and across Europe.

Then on Tuesday, September 30, the Irish government announced it would guarantee all deposits in the country's main banks for two years. The president of the European Central Bank announced that he had not been consulted on this move, and I phoned the Irish Taoiseach, the country's leader, to ask him to extend the guarantees to foreign-owned subsidiaries.[11]

We discussed whether we could bring forward our recapital-ization plan. We agreed that the lesson to learn from the United States was to be totally prepared. The Tripartite group was still working on legal issues and numbers, and we were waiting for its advice. I asked how it was going, and Shriti said she thought she had an outline in her head but was speaking to some market peo-ple to consider all the risks and implications and ensure we had a workable plan. By the time I thought to ask if that risked leaks, she had gone. She consulted people whose discretion we trusted: former colleagues Robin Budenberg, now head of United King-dom Trade and Investment, and David Soanes of UBS. She was also in touch with Michael Klein, formerly of Citi, to test how the plan would be received in the United States. She said she had wanted to stress-test with a U.K. bank how recapitalization would work in reality, but she couldn't go to any of the banks that needed the capital, or to HSBC, which was a direct competitor with all the other banks. That left Standard Chartered.

She had arranged with Peter Sands, CEO of Standard Char-tered, for him to host a secret meeting with her group and Peter's finance director, Richard Meddings. Tom Scholar, with whom she had privately been working very closely, was going to be there.

The result was a note on Thursday, October 2, with a three-pronged strategy to offer to provide capital, enhanced liquidity, and government-guaranteed medium-term funding, but for the latter only if the bank recapitalized to a level individually assessed by the FSA from private or government sources. It would be implemented in two phases—the public offer to the banks followed by a bank-by-bank agreement. It was not too dissimilar, but more practically worked through, in the capital piece at least to what had been worked on and discussed inside the Treasury and in No 10 for some time. I spent that day—in between phone calls to Alistair, Mervyn King, and completing my plans for a Cabinet reshuffle—considering the advice. In parallel, Tom Scholar was working through the proposal in the note with Alistair. During these days, Mervyn King and I met and talked on a number of occasions and we were totally at one on the need for a substantial recapitalization.

Before meeting with Mervyn King and Adair Turner, Chair of the FSA, Alistair and I insisted that an agreement to lending be added as a condition. Mervyn and Adair had been asked to consult the banks without providing any detailed information about our thinking, and their report was not encouraging; the banks were still in denial about their capital needs. But that simply strengthened my resolve to forge ahead. It was now clear we could no longer trust some of the banks to judge their own interests, or those of the public.

On Saturday, October 4, I went to Paris to meet President Sarkozy, Chancellor Merkel, Prime Minister Silvio Berlusconi, President Barroso, and Prime Minister Jean-Claude Juncker, the president of the Euro Group. This mini summit, while a welcome chance for all of us to share our concerns, was inconclusive. I sensed that most of Europe still considered the problem essentially an American one, even in spite of everything that was happening across Europe. For example, Fortis, Dexia, once a European financial giant, had the week before been rescued by the German, Luxembourg, and Belgian governments, and the Dutch government was working with the French to join the rescue effort. And in Germany Dresdner Bank had merged with Commerzbank at the start of September. These European policymakers did not believe that they had as big a potential banking and financial fallout as the Americans and the British, and that if European banks were under pressure it was not because of anything they had done wrong but because of contagion from the U.S.

For my part, I knew differently about British banks, and I was fairly sure that similar problems existed in France and Germany. I argued that European banks were more highly leveraged than banks in the U.S., and I argued that concerted European Union action was vital. It was only later that all of us realized that half of the securitized U.S. assets, including mortgage-backed securities, had been sold to foreign investors, most of them European, and that hedge funds had placed high-risk bets on subprime securities.

During the meeting and in light of what was happening in Ireland, I posited the idea of a joint guarantee on bank deposits. People had different opinions on the idea, but everyone seemed at least interested.

The next day, Sunday, October 5, Chancellor Merkel made the public case for a guarantee of German bank deposits,[12] and I received an early-morning phone call from President Sarkozy, who was calling to relay the message that Chancellor Merkel had not intended this to be a public announcement of a specific guarantee, but merely to provide a "political guarantee" to reassure her market. She called me later with the same message.

But elsewhere a series of events had already been set in motion that would be difficult to halt.

Out of the blue news came through that the Danish government wanted to announce that they were guaranteeing all their banks. I spoke to Prime Minister Rasmussen, who said he would make an announcement on Monday as part of a decision to set up a liquidation fund. He told me he had acted because there was no response from Europe.

This was also the day I announced the appointment of city financier Paul Myners as a minister at the Treasury to work under Alistair on the execution of the recapitalization plan and to take through the Lords the banking reforms we needed. Peter Mandelson had become business secretary two days before. I am full of admiration for how they both took on the challenge from the very first hours of their appointments. I met with Alistair, Paul, Shriti, Jeremy, and Tom that evening and agreed that the first phase of the plan would need to be executed by Tuesday or Wednesday, October 8, at the very latest.

Paul, Shriti, and Tom went to Jeremy's office next door to the Cabinet Room and appointed advisers to help for the following three days. They picked the two UBS bankers because they were already up to speed on the plan and also David Mayhew of JP Morgan because, as Shriti argued, if we were about to take an unprecedented step that would be seen as forcing the banks to capitalize we should have at our side one of the most respected men in London's Square Mile.

That group, with the FSA and Bank of England and led by Treasury officials, worked around the clock for the next two days, then began a comprehensive operation involving the full Tripartite and advisers. I talked to and met Alistair several times during each day, and together we met with Mervyn King and Adair Turner daily to review the results. As agreed, the plan would be executed in two steps. First, we would announce the availability of capital, funding, guarantees, and liquidity, with overall numbers. Second, as each bank came to us, we would advance individual proposals based on the FSA's assessment of the needs of each bank.

At all times we were absolutely sure of one thing: we were going ahead regardless. That is why our bottom line was no funding support without recapitalization.

As we worked throughout that Monday, October 6, I phoned President Sarkozy and told him the problem was no longer confined to one country and that confidence could be restored only if banks were in a position with sufficient capital to convince people they could both write off bad debts and lend again. We agreed on a text to issue that described our discussions from the weekend:

> The leaders of the G4 on Saturday made clear that each of them will take whatever measures are necessary to maintain the stability of the financial system—whether through liquidity support through our central banks, action to deal with individual banks or enhanced depositor protection schemes. We reiterate that, because of our actions, no depositors in our countries' banks have lost any money. And we will continue to take the necessary measures to protect both the system and individual depositors.

Prime Minister Zapatero and I also talked during lunchtime, and we agreed to coordinate further announcements about guarantees. While he worked through all the details of bank capital, on Monday afternoon Alistair announced (after consultation with our European colleagues and in advance of the European Union finance ministers' meeting the next day) changes to the compensation limit for retail deposits, from £35,000 to £50,000.

Alistair traveled to Europe to get support. On the afternoon of October 7 the European Union finance ministers announced two big steps forward. First, after days of confusion, with one country after another jumping the gun, finance ministers agreed on minimum guarantees across Europe for bank deposits. Second, they stated that systematically relevant banks should be prevented from collapsing. They were determined to avoid a European Lehman Brothers.

We were making some progress on the international response to the crisis that I had discussed with colleagues in the dingy meeting room in the UN building only a few weeks before, but the pace wasn't fast enough for the markets. The pressure was on, and escalating throughout the day. In most centers the stock exchange fell on October 7, in some places by nearly 10 percent. Despite all the initiatives we were taking to stem the tide, I could see nothing but a chain of destruction at work, necessitating very big decisions that could not be avoided any longer. The two remaining independent Wall Street investment banks, Goldman and Morgan Stanley, applied to become bank holding companies so that they could have access to the facilities of the Fed, the lender of last resort.

In a further sign of increasing cooperation the world's leading central bank governors were deciding on a coordinated assault on interest rates. They were planning that on Wednesday, October 8, they would announce—simultaneously, and for the U.S., the U.K., the Euro-zone, Japan, and Switzerland—the first-ever fully coordinated interest rate cut. The fact that these countries were prepared to cooperate on interest rates made me even more hopeful that they could eventually cooperate on recapitalization.

But, to everybody's considerable annoyance, it became clear that somebody had again been leaking information to Robert Peston, business editor of the BBC. Ordinarily leaks and political briefings of this sort are irritations you simply have to accept when lots of egos are involved in a government, but of course the point of the plan was to reassure markets with a decisive, clear, and completed intervention at one stroke; if they saw it coming in bits, the impact on market confidence would be blunted.

I called the governor of the Bank of England at 1 p.m. on Tuesday, October 7, because I wanted the recapitalization package to be backed by liquidity and for the Royal Bank of Scotland to get through to the end of the day. If we were able to achieve that, we could still launch in a structured way in the morning, and not with some desperate evening announcement to stop the RBS from going under.

I then met Alistair and Mervyn King, to be joined by Adair Turner later. In the meantime I also spoke to the Qatari Prime Minister, urging him to consider investment in recapitalization of our banks, something he later did by buying further into Barclays. When the meeting with Mervyn and Alistair resumed, we came to an agreement on the need for the package to contain specific constraints on excessive risk taking and therefore remuneration. Privately I had determined also that just as there would be no recapitalization without changes in remuneration, there would be no recapitalization without the resignation of the leaders of the banks at the center of the crisis.

By now Britain's own plans for a bank recapitalization were as fully developed as they could be, but we were watching events in America to see whether there was still any scope for simultaneous and coordinated action on recapitalization. However, because Hank Paulson had had to use all his political energy convincing Congress to support the purchase of banks' impaired assets, this was now looking difficult. I wanted to try one last time, so I phoned President Bush and Hank. If we weren't able to bring them on board, I at least wanted our American friends to know in advance what we would be announcing the next day.

The Tripartite members had decided that Alistair should see all the bank CEOs that night to explain the plan.

After his meeting Alistair called to tell me the banks were incredibly unhappy. The most vulnerable banks said they did not need the capital, nor did they want it, because to accept it would publicly signal a further downturn in their prospects. But we were in no mood to compromise, and I was determined to drive the plan through in its entirety. Alistair asked if I would speak to Stephen Green of HSBC directly, because HSBC was clearly not going to need government capital; it had higher levels of capitalization than other banks, and its banking activities were mainly in the Far East, which was relatively immune from recent developments. Still, HSBC needed to be supportive: we were worried that HSBC might act to make the contagion for the other banks worse because they themselves did not need immediate capital. So I spoke to Stephen, and he gave me his assurance that he would raise a token amount of private capital in due course and would support the plan. We already knew that Standard Chartered was supportive because of their previous involvement, so the last key conversation for me to have was with RBS.

When I spoke that evening to Tom McKillop, the chairman of the Royal Bank of Scotland, he told me he was worried about the immediate financial position overnight and wanted me to make our announcement of new liquidity immediately. I assured him that Mervyn King was aware of the problem and that he would be able to survive overnight. So that there was no doubt about it, I immediately telephoned Mervyn to confirm this position and repeated that I would not make an announcement until the morning. But what worried me was that some of the bankers at the very center of the storm still did not accept or would not admit, even now, that their problem was a structural one and not just a liquidity issue.

"All I need is overnight finance," I was told.

I was simultaneously furious and shocked; it was clear the banks didn't have a clear idea of what was happening.

After they finished their meeting with Alistair, the bank CEOs had a final late meeting, where the details of the plan were disclosed to them by Paul, Shriti, Tom, and John Kingman. They were shocked by the £50 billion figure we were suggesting and tried to halve it. Alistair and I refused the compromise and told them the deal was final.

I went to bed at midnight on Tuesday, October 7, with my mobile phone next to me in case of any further disasters. Alistair and I had decided on a 7 a.m. announcement and that we would phone leaders and finance ministers immediately before and after.

We had to rely on other countries seeing the logic of what we had done. I felt we had done all we could, in the days and weeks before, to bring the leaders and finance ministers of other countries around to our view that this problem went so much wider than liquidity or toxic assets.

The case was, I felt, compelling. But it was clear now that Britain would have to act first, though I hoped not alone. No one country was able to take the initiative alongside Britain. America could not act because of its TARP scheme, and Europe could not act immediately either, because so far only a few of its banks were openly sending their governments the signal that they needed help. I sensed that if no one acted, a total collapse was imminent.

The information I had been looking at in the past weeks was as stark as it was serious: we were facing a situation that risked becoming worse than 1929. No one trusted anyone in the banking system, and people were predicting not a recession but a depression. People were panicking, asking which would be the next bank to collapse. The financial system was looking over an abyss.

If no one else could lead and we could not act together, Britain had to act on its own, and it had to be now. I knew that if our announcement did not work, then with every day that passed another bank could go under.

People have asked me subsequently how I slept that night.

The reality is that I've always been a sound sleeper, even more so when my mind is made up. And on this, it was. Yes, there was a chance it could fail, and if it did I would need to resign as Prime Minister. But I was also confident that this was the right thing to do by the British people. This wasn't a last throw of the dice conceived in haste and desperation, but a coming together of thinking I had been doing for months. I had started, much to my family's irritation, to read great tomes on the bleak 1930s during a sunny summer holiday in Suffolk, and I had been refining my thinking in each of the daily conversations I was having with other world leaders, their top advisers, and my own.

I believed that there was space within TARP to include my plan for recapitalization. And the fact that banks were failing in Europe meant that at some stage the Europeans would see the risks and would have to join. So even if for a while Britain would stand alone, I believed it was a chance worth taking to stabilize the banking system and rescue lending and to stabilize the economy, which I feared would be in freefall soon.

Everything in my bones told me it had to happen, and happen now.

When I went to bed Sarah was already asleep. So it wasn't until the morning that I warned her that we might have to move out of Downing Street in a matter of hours.

At 7 a.m. on Wednesday, October 8, just as markets opened, Alistair announced a comprehensive bank plan: capital, funding, and liquidity, not just for one bank but for the whole banking system. We were offering more money than any British government had ever offered: £50 billion of public money in capital, £250 billion in guarantees of funding by the banks, and £100 billion more for the Bank of England's Special Liquidity Scheme.

At 9 a.m. Alistair and I held a joint press conference to answer questions from journalists still trying to get their heads around the breadth of the measures. Then, in quick succession, I phoned President Sarkozy, Chancellor Merkel, and Prime Minister Berlusconi to ask them to consider making their own comprehensive bank stabilization. Afterward I went over to the House of Commons, as I did each Wednesday, to answer Prime Minister's Questions.

This session, known as PMQs, is an important weekly session where members of Parliament from all sides can question the Prime Minister about their concerns. It is an important moment of accountability for and to the whole House of Commons, but it is also a high-profile and widely covered political session, because a set number of questions are reserved for the leader of the opposition.

So in a day of high pressure and complex announcements, it was an added twist that the governor of the Bank of England called me twenty minutes before I got to my feet at Question Time to confirm that at midday, precisely when the session would start, the Bank of England would be announcing an interest rate cut to 4.75 percent as part of a globally coordinated rate cut that he had secured.[13]

Much more had to be done to win European support for our action, so I also spoke to President Barroso, who was worried about maintaining a common front. I also took time to speak to the Finnish prime minister, who was about to come to London to visit me, as I wanted to send him our condolences over the tragic shooting of schoolchildren in his country. He thanked me and congratulated me on our announcement. He told me that Finland had dealt with its own banking crisis in the early 1990s in exactly the same way we were now proposing, and he wished me luck.

We had made our choice. We had identified that at this moment in time the markets couldn't sort things out for themselves and we had to intervene by offering to take unprecedented stakes in the largest banks in the country.[14]

We had now moved on to the next stage, and the response of the banks became the issue. Having protested the night before that they did not need capital, only "overnight finance," RBS called the Treasury, and then Fred Goodwin, RBS's chief executive, spoke to Shriti to say he thought that maybe taking some capital would be prudent. He said he didn't want to shock anyone but that his needs might be as high as £5 billion or even £10 billion. When she recounted the call to me she told me her reply: "I am shocked—not by how high your estimates are, but by how low."

The Treasury now needed to form detailed agreements with each bank.

RBS came to the Treasury and started negotiations immediately. In fact they did need overnight funding, as at that point they were no longer able to fund themselves. When HBOS realized that RBS would be taking up the offer, they knew they would be under serious pressure from the market—despite the merger they had agreed to with Lloyds—so HBOS came in, leaving Lloyds no option but to follow.

We ended up with three banks and their financial advisers, the Tripartite, Treasury financial advisers, and all of their lawyers in the Treasury that weekend, agreeing bank by bank on numbers and terms with the Treasury team. Some of the individual dramas that unfolded have been recorded, but I am sure many more are still to be revealed.

The Treasury was worried about Barclays withstanding the pressure. In discussion with them it became very clear that taking government money was anathema, and they were prepared to pay the price for capital from elsewhere to avoid that. That led to a lot of concern from the Tripartite about systemic risks. But Barclays had luck on its side. It had been to see some Sovereign Wealth Funds for capital quite recently to fund the Lehman acquisition, so they had some ready investors lined up and decided to go to them instead. As far as I was concerned, the less government money used, the better.

Alistair was in Washington for the annual meetings of the World Bank and IMF but still directing operations remotely, while I made my second trip in a week to Paris, on Sunday, October 12. I had been asked by President Sarkozy to attend the first meeting of the new Euro Group of fifteen political heads of state. That meeting was extraordinary for two reasons: first, because finance ministers had always jealously guarded their control over policy for the Euro member countries, and this was the first time policy would be discussed at the level of heads of government— the most intensely political level of all for what was in reality the most intensely political decision; second, because Britain was not, of course, a member of the Euro area. I know that some of President Sarkozy's colleagues complained bitterly about my presence because of the latter point. He took a personal risk in forcing my involvement because we both believed that the raw urgency of the task meant we could dispense with ordinary protocol.

Prior to the Euro meeting I met with Sarkozy, President Barroso, Chairman Jean-Claude Trichet of the European Central Bank, and Prime Minister Juncker of Luxembourg. I told them I now believed European banks held around $2 trillion of U.S.-originated assets, of which around $400 billion were toxic—with probably a similar amount in the shadow banking system. I said also that European banks were more highly leveraged than American banks.

So when the full Euro Group met I was able to explain why I thought the problem was capital, and why Europe should not confuse the origins of the crisis—which came out of America—with its severity and its still-growing consequences, which made it now a firmly European crisis too.

I left the meeting after I spoke and was pleased to learn later that there was unanimity on their position. One by one, countries in the Euro area and beyond decided to recapitalize their banks, and they would design common European rules for a credit guarantee scheme like ours.

But as I told the Europeans, America had to act too. If the Americans did not agree to recapitalize it was difficult for me to see how stability could be restored. The U.S. Treasury had won Senate approval for its toxic assets plan, but by Hank Paulson's own account, the administration had accepted by this point that the toxic assets plan would not in itself calm the market. "Here we were," he wrote, "worse off than ever." And, as I had already sensed from my meeting the week before, Tim Geithner was also saying recapitalization was essential. Indeed he also wanted to guarantee the liabilities of financial institutions.

Hank also reported that the next day, October 12, he and President Bush had a telephone call to prepare for the G7 and G20 meetings that weekend. The British recapitalization had, of course, already been announced. And they talked about recapitalization. As Paulson records, "He [the president] pressed me about the capital program and asked, 'Is this what it's going to take to end this thing?' 'I don't know sir,' I admitted, 'but I hope it's the dynamite we've been looking for.'"

Helpfully also that week, Alan Greenspan made a telling intervention in the debate. He demonstrated that the capital requirement models of the banks had been faulty in that they had underestimated the need for higher capital requirements. And he said, "Had the models instead been fitted more appropriately to historic periods of stress, capital requirements would have been much higher and the financial world would be in a far better shape today in my judgment."

By that weekend, as the G7 met, Hank Paulson had already approved a paper for the G7 that said we should balance the goals of stabilizing the system while protecting the taxpayers. He wanted the banks to get much-needed capital without raising the specter of nationalization. Thanks to Alistair's heroic efforts, the communiqué went even further, by including bank recapitalization by governments if necessary. One of the five specific paragraphs of agreement was to "ensure that our banks and other major financial institutions as needed can raise capital from public as well as private sources in sufficient amounts to re-establish confidence and permitting them to continue lending to households and businesses." At the meeting of the IMF timed to coincide with the G7, IMF Managing Director Dominique Strauss-Kahn announced that he too was supporting the plans.

U.S. officials worked through the weekend to get the U.S. capitalization plan up and running. On Sunday, October 12, and in great secrecy, Paulson, Bernanke, and Geithner met to detail a recovery plan involving capital from the government. Paulson then personally called all the major bank executives. He asked them to meet him in the Treasury at 3 p.m. on the following day, Monday, October 13.

And so on that Sunday evening, as I returned from Paris, President Bush phoned to give me the news that now some of America's TARP funds would be used for recapitalization of the banks.

The formal announcement was to come two days later, on Tuesday, October 14, but before that the banks had to agree the terms with the administration.

While America prepared to announce its first decision on recapitalization, we had to make our announcement of the details on ours. It had taken a weekend of careful and detailed negotiation involving the Treasury's top officials, led by civil servants John Kingman and Tom Scholar, and the ministers Paul, Shriti, and Alistair himself. No one seemed to have much time for sleep in the Treasury.[15]

I was working every minute at the leaders' level to try to translate the technical interventions into a confidence-building plan. It was grueling, and after my day in Paris, my calls with President Bush, and further conversations with officials, I went to bed at 1 a.m.

At 5 a.m. I was suddenly wakened by a noise at the door of our bedroom. I thought it was our young son, John, who often woke up and came through to our room, and Sarah shouted out, "John, seriously, not tonight, you need to go back to bed and let Dad sleep."

The reply was a whispered "Sorry, Sarah, it's Shriti. The Treasury have come up with new numbers which Alistair wants Gordon to see."

Overnight the Treasury had been working on the final offers we would make to the banks. The figures now added up, but in a new way. Alistair wanted me to be aware we were definitely going to own a majority of RBS. But I had been well prepared by Shriti for that probability. Alistair and I had to approve in advance the offer we were going to make, so we met at 5.30 a.m. and concluded our proposal.

On Monday morning, October 13, as markets opened, we announced a £37 billion recapitalization of RBS, Lloyds, and HBOS. We would take a 57 percent stake in RBS and a 58 percent stake in HBOS, with a 32 percent stake in Lloyds subject to their mergers. The detailed terms of our £250 billion credit guarantee scheme was also announced, along with new arrangements for dividends and remuneration and a commitment to keep credit flowing.

I had long felt that we were dealing not only with a technical failure, but a moral failure too. So for me, a crucial part of the announcement was that some degree of justice was secured: remuneration was cut back, dividends were canceled, and the chief executive and the chair of RBS both tendered their resignations. And the CEO of HBOS would not be working for the merged entity anymore.

On the same day, Germany announced €400 billion in guarantees and €100 billion in capitalization; France €320 billion in guarantees of medium-term debt and €40 billion for capitalization; Italy €40 billion in capitalization and "as much as necessary" in guarantees. Holland added €200 billion in guarantees, and Spain and Austria €100 billion each.

That day saw a 10 percent rise in the European stock exchange, the biggest rise ever.

At no point in history have governments ever injected so much money into buying up assets in the banking system, with capital and guarantees running into trillions. When officials gave me a list of all the countries that had followed Britain's lead—Germany, France, Spain, Denmark, Portugal, the Netherlands, Austria, Switzerland, and America—I knew that we had come through this in one piece. The patient was out of the emergency room and into intensive care.

PART TWO

CHAPTER 2

The Problem Foreseen:
Lessons from the Asian Crisis

For many years before the most recent crisis I had been warning that globalization was outpacing our national capacity to shape it for progressive ends.

I believed, and still believe, in globalization. But I match that belief with an equally passionate conviction that accepting globalization's benefits—growth, jobs, and greater freedom—should not mean tolerating its negative consequences: climate change, financial instability, inequality, and risks to security without attempts to remedy them through global cooperation.

My critique had, in fact, become so familiar to other international politicians that my friend Jens Stoltenberg, the Prime Minister of Norway, left me both flattered and embarrassed at the Progressive Governance Summit in Chile in 2009 when he followed my remarks by saying, "You know, I've been a friend of Gordon's since we first started attending events like this a decade ago, and every time since I've heard him give exactly the same speech!"

He was right. My fixation on global financial cooperation had begun some ten years earlier, when considering the fallout from the Asian crisis. The Asian crisis is worth analyzing in some detail, for it is there that we find the roots both of the banking crisis I described in part 1 and the global imbalances I will tackle in part 3.

As far back as 1998 it seemed to me that the issues that had emerged during the Asian crisis were serious enough to justify speaking out about them and recommending a set of changes in the world financial system. In a speech I gave that year at Harvard University I spoke about how the Asian crisis should be a profound reminder that our fortunes were being made not just in local and national economies, but in a new global economy. The crisis made clear that we needed choices beyond a network of wholly deregulated financial systems or an overly interventionist approach. We needed a middle ground, but with an explicitly global component.

Rereading my speech now (it is included here as an appendix), my regrets are deeper than ever that I was unable to persuade more decision makers to accept its recommendations for new systems and norms of global cooperation. We failed to fully appreciate and then apply the lessons from Asia, with consequences for people everywhere that are easy to see.

Since the crisis of 2008–9 I hear too many people speaking as if the thirty years before the Great Recession had been stable. Those who talk of the Great Moderation often forget that over those three decades there were a total of one hundred banking crises. According to Barry Eichengreen of the University of California at Berkeley and Michael Bordo of Rutgers University, financial crises are twice as likely now as they were in the period before 1914.

I remember vividly my meeting with the late governor of the Bank of England, Eddie George. It was Christmas Eve 1997. As usual he lit up his cigarette before he came to the point. His message was blunt: South Korea was bankrupt. This was for me an immediate and consuming priority because in 1998 Britain held the presidency of the G7 group of nations: Canada, France, Germany, Italy, Japan, the U.K., and the U.S. As the newest finance minister, I would be chairing the G7 finance ministers' and bankers' meetings, which throughout that year would examine the Asian crisis and its repercussions.

I first went to Asia in September 1997, visiting Thailand and then going on to Hong Kong for the annual meeting of the IMF on September 25. Then in 1998 I made a longer trip, traveling widely across Asia to meet its leaders. But I also made a point of visiting cities, towns, and villages to see firsthand the devastation the crisis had caused: unemployed people begging on the streets; schools half-built and left to crumble; children left to beg above open sewers.

It seemed that the progress of decades in Asia had been thrown into reverse in a matter of weeks. I saw on that trip a chain of destruction that was not dissimilar to the events we have just seen in the West since 2007. The key elements were all there: a boom in property; asset prices rising to record and unsustainable levels; foreign investment chasing this and rising accordingly; a rush for the highest yields; and huge amounts of credit on offer from institutions that became very highly leveraged.

Prior to the Asian crisis, Asia was attracting half the total capital going to emerging markets and developing countries. But at some stage productive investment shifted into a speculative bubble.

All the neighboring economies—Thailand, Malaysia, Indonesia, Singapore, and South Korea—were growing at 8 to 12 percent a year, and people talked of a new Asian economic miracle. But this time it was hot money that was inflating an already serious bubble and magnifying the impact of excessive property speculation.

Investors were reassured by these regimes' determination to maintain an exchange rate fixed to the dollar, but Thailand's rising current account deficit reflected an excessive exposure to risk in both the financial and corporate sectors. Then in 1997, as

U.S. interest rates rose to deal with America's domestic conditions, money flowed back to America, and as the dollar also rose, Asian exports became more expensive. As exports fell, asset prices started to fall too, and individuals and companies began defaulting on their repayment obligations.

Raising domestic interest rates turned out not to be enough to prevent currencies collapsing, and although the central banks used their foreign reserves to purchase domestic currency at the pegged exchange rate, the scale of withdrawals was so big that it could not work. Simultaneously, and with disastrous effects, these higher interest rates were pushing the economy into recession and the central bank was hemorrhaging foreign reserves, forcing the Thais and others to float their currencies. Soon, with its property market overwhelmed with foreign private debt that was now falling in value, Thailand was technically bankrupt. Foreign credit withdrew and domestic credit froze up amid further bankruptcies. The collapsing currencies of Thailand and other crisis countries threw the global markets out of kilter. The actions of key central banks to defend their currencies were designed to forestall the consequences of the crisis. Instead, they may have made things worse.

All these factors contributed, but it was clearly the real estate bubble that was the root cause, with Indonesia and South Korea as badly hit as Thailand, and Hong Kong, Malaysia, and the Philippines badly affected too. In a number of instances and to varying degrees, corruption added to the problem.

In 1998 I met President Suharto of Indonesia a few days before he was pushed out. After thirty years in power he was both old and tired, and I found him unable to fathom what was happening around him. On the face of it, Indonesia, in contrast to Thailand, had low inflation, a billion-dollar trade surplus, a not bad banking sector, and $20 billion of its own foreign exchange reserves. But Indonesia had followed Thailand in floating its currency, the rupiah, which then fell dramatically to an almost unprecedented

20 percent of its original value. Because Indonesian corporations had been borrowing in U.S. dollars, their costs rose as the rupiah fell, and many made the position worse by selling rupiah, causing it to fall even further. All this exposed Indonesia's poor financial management system, and with it the corruption at the top.

When I met Suharto his explanation of the current problems—"the university students"—told me just how much he had lost touch and how vulnerable his position had become. Then the army leader, Wiranto, allowed students to occupy the Parliament building and reported to the President on May 20 that he no longer had the support of the army. Within a day Suharto had been ousted.

He was not alone. Throughout Asia politicians everywhere were falling victim to the financial crisis. I visited Malaysia and met Finance Minister Anwar bin Ibrahim. He was well-respected in international circles, and when I had spoken with him in America at a meeting of business leaders he confided to me his worries about his own position. Anwar said that staying on meant he would have to fight damaging though unfounded allegations about his own personal behavior, but to walk away would set Malaysia back in its commercial links with the world. A few weeks later he was forced out by Prime Minister Mahathir bin Mohamad. Mahathir then ushered in a new regime of capital controls that gave Malaysia short-term protection against the crisis.

During that autumn the arguments between Mahathir and financier George Soros over the causes of the crisis were heard all over the world, but Malaysia got its response right. For a short time at least, controls on capital can prevent, or at least reduce, the uncontrolled flow of short-term funds across borders.

The example that most inspired me, however, was that of Hong Kong. I talked regularly to the Hong Kong chief executive, Donald Tsang, because like everyone else we were worried that, despite the assurances that had been given at the time, the handover of Hong Kong to China would lead to a less open Hong Kong market. Donald convinced me of his determination not only to keep Hong Kong an independent financial center, but to make sure the promises of an open society would be upheld too.

When the crisis hit, it was to be Donald and his team who surprised everyone with their brilliantly innovative tactics. In what was called a "Hong Kong double play," speculators had simultaneously sold short both the currency and shares in the Hong Kong stock market. They expected Hong Kong to raise interest rates to protect the currency, which would force stock prices lower. They had worked out that if Hong Kong failed to raise interest rates, their short on the currency would be profitable; if Hong Kong did raise rates to save its currency, their short on the stock market would create huge profits.

But the Hong Kong government outflanked them. As well as raising interest rates it bought shares to support stock market prices, purchasing at least 5 percent of every stock traded on the Hong Kong exchange. It became the largest shareholder of some of those companies, taking a 10 percent share of their biggest bank, the Hong Kong and Shanghai (HSBC), by the end of August, and eventually owning a total of $15 billion worth of shares.

The speed with which they acted sent shock waves through the markets. They had outwitted the financiers and demonstrated, to me at least, that it was possible to stand against speculative forces with a clear, coordinated plan of government actions, and to win through. In due course they turned a profit of $4 billion on the shares they had bought.[1]

I drew a different conclusion from the experience of Japan. I had visited Japan on many occasions, first when it was in the ascendant and still seen as a model for the world to come, and then on a number of occasions when it was falling victim to a depression not just in its economy but in its own view of itself. I had been in Australia in 1992 and heard the Japanese ambassador there giving what I thought was a quite incredible lecture to the

Australians that as a nation they were too lazy and unenterprising. I was even more surprised to hear him threatening that Japan would desert Australia and withdraw its investments there if the Australians did not run their economy like the Japanese.

But as things started to go wrong in Japan I found less willingness to act collectively or even to recognize the depth of the problem. Incentives to spend abounded, stopping not far short of handing out money in the streets. It was almost as if they had adopted Milton Friedman's famous advice to drop money on the population from helicopters. Still, Japanese consumers, worried about their savings and their pensions and provision for their future, were unwilling to spend.

I learned some hard lessons, and fast. Japan looked to me like a classic case of what Keynes called "the liquidity trap": once recession takes hold, it cannot easily be reversed by monetary policy alone. With his invention of the term *balance sheet deflation,* Richard Koo of Nomura Research Institute has described such an economic trap in which credit stops growing, not because banks do not want to lend, but because companies and households do not want to borrow. The conclusion is that when the private sector has a surplus that it will not invest, the government has to become the borrower of last resort. With such a combination of corporate surpluses and low demand, only running a public sector deficit can stop a recession from becoming a depression.

As I look back, the biggest lesson I have learned from Japan's long-running recession is to never allow an economy to sink so far that a recovery becomes more and more elusive. And the lesson from Hong Kong is that determined and clear-thinking governments can win even when big market forces are aligned against them. They proved that the markets and the speculators, even at their most determined and devious, could be faced down.

As for domestic policy, the Asian crisis confirmed my view that we had to prevent inflation from ever again getting out of control, and we had to keep interest rates low. In Britain the new

Labour government had already understood that Britain's unique high-inflation culture needed a commitment to low inflation, which is why, on coming into office, we had (controversially, and with no notice at all) torn up our old established monetary rule book and made the Bank of England independent.[2] We had tried to learn from the best of Keynes and from the best of the anti-inflation school led by Friedman. The new paradigm of the 1990s had been to think of just one target for monetary policy, inflation, and just one instrument, the interest rate. We took the view that, if we did what was right and kept inflation permanently low—something we had been unable to do as a country for fifty years—the gap between potential growth and actual growth was likely to be small. For two years Ed Balls and I had planned independence, and in the week before the election, unknown to anyone, we had submitted a large dossier to the Treasury. We were therefore in a position to announce the entire policy within a few days of taking power. The original plan, written by Ed, remained intact.

Too often politicians have fallen at the first hurdle. They set out with good intentions to keep inflation low, but then fail to make the tough decisions on interest rates when action has to be taken. The independence of the Bank of England was, for me, the essential signal we had to send to show that it was the long term that mattered—and that never again would there be short-term manipulation of the macroeconomic position for political gain.

Beginning in 1997 we were fortunate that in Britain we did eventually succeed in avoiding the inflation cycles of the past. Inflation not only came down; it stayed down. Historically, because of our wage bargaining system, Britain had always suffered a second wave of inflation whenever inflation started to rise. But by keeping inflation expectations low—and helping people to understand that an inflationary spiral would benefit no one— we kept wage rises at an affordable level. In the 1970s British price inflation had averaged 15 percent; in the 1980s, 12 percent;

and in the 1990s, 6 percent. But, during the time I was Chancellor of the Exchequer, it was 3 percent.

The second lesson the Asian crisis reaffirmed was that systems of national financial regulation had to evolve to cope with the new complexities of international finance. In 1998 the British government set up the first comprehensive Financial Services Authority in the world, with far-reaching powers to end the old self-regulation of financial institutions and to deal directly with their individual supervision and regulation. The Financial Services Authority, distinct and separate from the Bank of England, replaced myriad self-regulated institutions that had no public accountability whatsoever. We agreed to form a Tripartite committee of central banker, regulator, and government that would meet regularly, measure risks, apportion responsibilities, and take action together in an emergency.

But the third and the most critical lesson I learned from the Asian crisis was that capital markets were now global, and therefore without adequate *global* financial supervision the world remained unstable. That was the argument I made at Harvard, and continued to make in many forums for many years.

In the wake of the Asian crisis, if we were to be capable of dealing with shocks transmitted through an interconnected banking system, we had to have a set of global crisis-prevention and crisis-resolution measures. I proposed a twice-yearly convocation of regulators, central banks, and finance ministries to act as an early-warning system for the world economy and that there be transparency all around, with the biggest financial companies supervised for not just their national but their worldwide activities. I wanted global agreement on banking standards and the opening up of the various tax and regulatory havens to proper scrutiny.

I also proposed radically different ways of crisis resolution where there were solvency or liquidity problems, and in order to do better at crisis prevention, I suggested we reexamine the whole structure of economic government for a new global era. I made recommendations for the reform of the IMF, to make it more like an independent central bank, similar to what had been proposed by Keynes when he negotiated for Britain in the 1940s. In particular I argued for new standards of transparency and openness for all financial institutions and governments. We had to have informed markets—or at some point there would be market mayhem.

In coming to each of these views I had discussions with people such as Alan Greenspan, Robert Rubin, Larry Summers, and Tim Geithner and my European and Asian colleagues. They didn't always share my analysis or agree with my prescriptions, but they were unfailingly generous with their time and expertise.

We debated what exchange-rate regimes might look like and what we should do if there were ever liquidity or solvency crises and how we could spot the difference. We also discussed at length the problem we have now been facing in earnest in the past two years: how we could avoid moral hazard while at the same time intervening to prevent and resolve crises.

I pursued these arguments not only at Harvard and in private discussions with economists, but each time there was a meeting of policymakers where it could be forced onto the agenda. Most of the proposals that Britain made—for a system of crisis prevention and crisis resolution, for the free flow of information, for proper risk management, for the global coordination of supervision, and for an early-warning system—reappeared on the table beginning in 2007, and most of them are now being examined or implemented in the reforms of our financial system.

Yet the end product of these discussions in the years before 2000 was a compromise, made possible with the welcome support of the governor of the Bundesbank, Hans Tietmeyer: an agreement to set up a milder but more easily achievable version of my original proposal, the Financial Stability Council.

The compromise was a half measure, and I have to take my share of responsibility for its failings.

I wanted an early-warning system, and I also wanted the financial regulators to work together at a global level as an executive, so that they understood the true scale of risk and could act upon it. I asked the IMF to prepare in advance of each meeting their study of the new risks and uncertainties in the world, so that we had a clear idea of what was likely to be ahead of us. But once the Asian crisis seemed over, I had only limited success in persuading the governments of the day that the early warning system and a new system of global financial regulation were still of critical importance. I will forever regret my failure to bring other countries onboard or persuade them of the urgency of action. I can see with hindsight that this was not because the problem had gone away, but because it was impossible to build an international consensus.

One innovation that did emerge from the Asian crisis that was very much in line with Britain's ideas about enhanced global cooperation was the American proposal for the formation of the G20. Its first manifestation was a meeting of finance ministers called by President Clinton in 1998 at the instigation of many concerned people, notably Paul Martin, later the Prime Minister of Canada. I remember as Britain's Chancellor of the Exchequer detailing the agenda for radical financial system reform in a speech at the first meeting.[3] The new forum (which, as we shall see in chapter 4, was, as a leaders group, to prove so crucial to averting a great depression) had a difficult start. It involved only central bank governors and finance ministers. There was resistance from some European countries that had been denied membership, and the role for the European Union had not been thought through. Some people asked why Argentina, a country beset by complex economic problems, should be there, but not Spain or the Netherlands.

The truth is that, in its original conception, the G20 was an attempt to bypass the IMF, and at the same time to balance the group toward Asia, where the economic crisis was then raging.

When I took over in 1999 as the chairman of the IMF committee, I sought to get the balance right between the G20 and the IMF: the G20 would take a strategic role and look at long-term issues, and the IMF would deal with the more immediate problems that required decisions to be made. The process of financial sector evaluations was set in motion,[4] and later a group on capital markets was set up.

However, an initiative by the IMF to deal with global imbalances fell by the wayside. Too many countries, it seemed, were not prepared to move on. I had restructured the IMF's twice-yearly ministerial meetings so that they would begin with a survey of the risks the world economy faced. I would ask the chairman of the Financial Stability Forum to report on financial risks. The process was an improvement on what had gone before, when ministers simply read prepared statements,[5] but the brutal assessment is that all the long-term studies of the G20 and the IMF yielded more diagnosis of the growing imbalances and the financial risk but little action.

So my overriding feeling, emerging from the Asian crisis, was that the case for global cooperation was growing stronger, but, as the crisis receded, the political will to deliver it grew weaker.

Economists I admire were quick to draw similar lessons about the financial system from the Asian crisis. Asia, Joe Stiglitz argues, represented a failure of global financial markets: the effect of asymmetric information in the financial markets, which in the end led to a run on the banks, inadequate government and international responses, and then a recession made worse by a fiscal austerity program. So the root of the Asian crisis was not just the irrational exuberance of investors and the herd instincts of markets, although that played a part; nor was it simply the result of new market methods and new technologies. The Asian crisis arose from inherent problems in the global financial system: people taking excessive risks but with inadequate capital.

The Asian crisis not only offers some lessons that, if we had learned them, could have helped if applied before the current financial crisis, but it also has some complete and direct parallels with it.[6]

Revisiting the events of 1998 now, it is clear to me that the world's failure to deal adequately with the Asian crisis is one reason for the huge imbalances of the past ten years, because it prompted Asian central banks to build up massive reserves. During the crisis, the IMF ordered countries without adequate reserves to retrench. Higher interest rates than they needed were imposed on them, together with spending cuts that were excessive. As a result thousands of jobs were lost unnecessarily.

Asia learned that they could rely only on their own resources because the penalties imposed by the IMF were simply too high to be paid by their people again. Because there was no global coordination that could support Asia through the adjustment, Asia's response was to protect itself.

These countries have now accumulated around $8 trillion of reserves, with, today, $2.4 trillion in China alone. As long as that money is saved in that way and not spent in others, Asia will contribute to the long-term imbalances and lack of aggregate demand, which I will argue in part 3.

That suppressed demand, along with the fallout of the recent crisis, could combine to contribute to a decade of high unemployment, low growth, and falling prosperity.

Whether it does or not will depend on whether policymakers now accept the need for a better global framework to promote supervision and transparency in global finance. Whether, in other words, we finally learn the lessons from Asia.

CHAPTER 3

The Problem Revealed: Capitalism without Capital

"We are only just beginning to understand the risks that we have been taking." That single sentence, coming in a moment of frankness from a senior banker who normally personified confidence to the point of arrogance, summed up for me what had gone wrong.

The story of bankers whose approach to risk-taking became so complex and obscure that only very few people could fully understand what they were doing has yet to be fully told. The story is all the more difficult to follow because of a language problem within finance, in essence a cryptic, acronymic jargon virtually incomprehensible to the layperson.

In part 1, we saw how the story of bank failure and bank rescue unfolded. In the previous chapter we traced its roots in the Asian crisis. Now I want to explain how a new and largely unregulated global financial system developed in the twenty years before the crisis and demonstrate how, in a risk-laden world of finance (in which excessive financial remuneration was at the expense of the equity capital that banks needed), we had created a wholly new economic phenomenon: capitalism without capital.

If I had said in 1990 that global flows of money, then around

$2 billion a day, would double as the world economy grew, people might have believed me. But if I had said these flows would rise by more than 2,000 percent few would have thought it possible. In fact something much bigger happened: a *6,000 percent* increase in global financial flows, so that by 2008 there were flows of $130 billion *per day*. Finance went global, far outstripping growth in the rest of the economy, and became the biggest industrial-scale moneymaking machine the world has ever known.[1]

While its surface manifestation took the form of the main street banks and the investment banks, underneath, as with an iceberg, there was much that was hidden. Submerged beneath the surface was an unseen, unregulated shadow banking network that grew in volume to become more than half the entire system. Gradually this global banking system became overleveraged, undercapitalized, and excessively laden with risk.

One of the main benefits of open and free global markets is the wide number of available products, which should lead to a dispersal of risk across many institutions and instruments. But the new global derivatives, which developed first in the shadow banking system without proper mechanisms to monitor and manage them, swamped the potential benefits of diversification. They facilitated huge entanglements between banks; by 2007 more than one-third of all global financial transactions were deals between finance companies entangled with each other. At the center were lots of derivatives built on poor-quality assets that had minimal capital allocated to them because they were treated almost as if they were risk-free. When those assets started to lose value and become toxic, the losses cascaded through the system precisely because financial institutions were so entangled with each other. And as I stated earlier, the diversity of institutions, instruments, and financial centers did not in the end spread the risks to those most able to hold them in the way that had been assumed.

The roots of the recent growth in the shadow banking system lie in the aftermath of the dot-com bubble and the Internet boom. Although the packaging-up and then selling on of blocks of mortgages had already started in the 1980s, it moved to a new level at the turn of the century as investors moved out of the new Internet stocks.

Literally trillions of dollars' worth of new mortgages of variable quality were packaged up, securitized, given Triple A status, and sold. Indeed this mortgage-based business quickly moved to become one of the primary sources of activity and the principal source of income for many of Wall Street's major firms. These Triple A bonds were enticing because they sometimes could pay up to 3 percent, and often at least 1 percent, over the risk-free rate. That was more in interest than Triple A corporate bonds were earning.

Upon this shaky foundation of risk-laden mortgage-backed securities came the collateralized debt obligation, or CDO, a derivative that was, in turn, divided into new tranches and sold to investors. Derivatives had started as hedging instruments, a means of protecting yourself against a real risk. But in the new shadow banking system, derivatives themselves were little more than the vehicles for speculative activity. Instead of being the hedge against risk, they became the risk. American mortgage bonds with a Triple B credit rating were used to build collateralized debt obligations, which then gained a Triple A rating. And all this was justified on the grounds that such diversified portfolios exposed individual investors to less risk.

Shadow banks, or parallel banks, were finance companies, asset-backed commercial paper conduits, limited-purpose finance companies, structured investment vehicles, credit hedge funds, money market mutual funds, securities lenders—all defined by the fact that, unlike formal banks, they had no access to central bank liquidity or public sector credit guarantees but had built up huge liabilities.

This new shadow banking system divided up the simple processes of deposit-funded, hold-to-maturity lending conducted by traditional banks under one roof, into what some call "a daisy chain" or "vertical slicing." That meant separating out these traditional bank processes into the origination of loans, their warehousing, their structuring into and then pooling of asset-backed securities, and the issuance of collateralized debt obligations into separate transactions. The purpose of all of it was to transform risky, long-term loans, such as mortgages, into what were presented as risk-free, short-term, and desirable instruments.

By 2007 the shadow banking system had outstripped the size of the traditional commercial banking sector.[2] The total volume of credit intermediated by the shadow banking system was close to $20 trillion, or nearly twice as large as the volume of credit intermediated by the traditional banking system, at roughly $11 trillion.

Why does all this matter? After all, if a few hedge funds and structured investment vehicles had gone down, there would not necessarily have been a global financial crisis. There were no implicit or explicit guarantees from any government or central bank that if they failed they would be rescued.

The reason the explosion in shadow banking mattered was because its sheer scale and pervasiveness had created a race to the bottom. In order to compete, practices and instruments that had grown up in shadow banking were now also being copied and used almost as extensively by the formal banking system. Instruments that had grown up free from regulation but also free of any government guarantees were now being used either directly or in structured investment vehicles by some of the world's leading banks, whose fate did pose systemic risks to the system.

Of the approximately $1.4 trillion total exposure to subprime mortgages, around half of the potential losses were borne by U.S. leveraged financial institutions. Worryingly, banks had not just invested in subprime market securities directly; this was a comparatively small part of the story. They had backup credit lines for special-purpose vehicles. Because these banks were already highly leveraged, they were also at greatest risk.

Another practice, selling short, is, of course, better known right across the system. It has long been possible to sell shares you did not own but had borrowed—and to keep the profit when they fell. But the CDO market took it one stage further; it didn't even require you to borrow a security.

So I began to see why mortgage securities and CDOs had become so attractive to the markets. When there were not enough of them to go around, "synthetic" CDOs—even more intricate derivatives—were created, with no gain whatsoever to the real economy. I like the way Nouriel Roubini, coauthor of *Crisis Economics,* described what had happened to much of our financial system. In most of the cases we are dealing with, he wrote,

> the purchaser didn't have to own any portion of the asset. And, worse still, he had an incentive to make the default happen. . . . Worse even than that, buying the insurance without owning the underlying asset is not only akin to insuring a house an investor does not own, but leaves the insurance holder with a direct interest in seeing it fail. As CDOs developed they became like buying insurance on a house you did not own and then setting fire to it. And there was little or no regulation to prevent or deal with the fire.

So investments could be easily created by a series of synthetic derivative contracts. Nowhere is this better shown than in the now infamous "Paulson scheme."

John Paulson bought the insurance that enabled Goldman Sachs to package a collateralized debt obligation known as Abacus 2007-AC1, most of it at a Triple A rating. Within six months the referenced assets of this synthetic collateralized debt obligation—already sold on to, among other banks, the Royal Bank of Scotland—were worthless. Paulson had made $1 billion on shorting on the mortgage-backed securities and then picking up the insurance. Goldman Sachs itself denies wrongdoing; they say that these were market transactions based on information widely available.

But too many companies had bought loan originators and at the same time created instruments that bet on the collapse of the subprime mortgage market. That has been described as "like a salesman who knows the product he is marketing is not what he says it is, but strikes a deal with an unwitting customer whose interests he knows are put at risk through the sale."

The Paulson case highlighted another feature of the new system: its interconnectedness. The real problem became not so much the size of one individual bank but that the fortunes of each bank were so tied up with those of the others. So when eventually instability took hold, it had a vast and widespread impact, a tsunami effect that rolled around almost the whole world. We now know that in 2008 an astonishing $50 trillion—*more than the entire annual income of every family in the world*—was pledged between financial companies, contracts that were wholly private and undeclared. One company, AIG, had signed a trillion dollars' worth of insurance contracts and not made any provision, and British and European banks had bought half of the subprime assets sold from the U.S.

While I had spoken, at various times over these years, of an interconnected global financial system, no one had the detailed information we now have about how dependent financial institutions were becoming on each other, and how risky these new entanglements had become. Lacking a significant global supervisory oversight, the world had no proper understanding of the true nature of the growth happening below the surface not so much in trading between banks and businesses, but in banks trading with each other.

It was reasonable to expect individual financial institutions to take responsibility for managing their own risks, but when institutions are entangled with others, some with guarantees and others without them, there are clearly large public consequences, particularly when the positions being taken are not known and the effects are not adequately reflected in the price system.

The more rigorously we look behind the events of the time, the clearer the picture emerges. It starts with an enormous and unfathomable shadow banking system operating far outside normal rules and procedures. Those practices then spread to the mainstream banks, and soon everybody knew the priority was, in Chuck Prince of Citibank's famous words, "to keep dancing" as long as the music was playing.

The reason governments had to step in during October 2008 was not, therefore, because government action had itself caused the problem,[3] but because the music stopped. It was one of those moments when markets did not automatically come to a safe equilibrium in the manner the familiar old textbooks suggest.

There are good reasons for this, some of which serious neoliberal thinkers happily accept, and which I rehearse here simply because they have been so willfully obscured in some of the less serious domestic political debates.

First, although the economy is global, global markets are not yet deep enough or mature enough. We still have gaps in information, weaknesses in institutional capacity, restrictions on the mobility of labor, tariff barriers to trade, and, even more significant, nontariff barriers to the flows of goods, services, and capital. In a very real sense the global capital flows and global sourcing of goods and services that characterize globalization are not complemented by the institutions and culture of a global market that functions sufficiently well for us to gain all the benefits of market disciplines.

Second, in another very real sense we have a global market that, though imperfect and not yet matured, exhibits and exaggerates some of the worst failings of markets: externalities, inadequate supervision, and no procedures for dealing with shocks.

Third, and perhaps most important, the marketplace was characterized by massive asymmetries of information. Wages and prices do not adjust as flexibly as theory would suggest because interest rate adjustments—based on imperfect information—often occur too slowly. Global consumers operating in global markets are thus not, and cannot be, individuals making perfect judgments in perfect markets. With inequalities in the availability of information even greater on the global stage, vested interests emerge stronger and can be a risk to the public interest.

These three conditions combined on the eve of the financial crisis to create what Alan Greenspan has since called "a fundamental flaw in the edifice of market economics." As a consequence of the events of 2007–8, and in an act of quite stunning intellectual honesty which is why he is to be respected as a man of integrity, Alan confessed that much of what he had thought and argued for his whole career had turned out to be wrong. With management manipulating their control of information to run their business neither in the shareholders' interest nor in the public interest, but instead only in their own interest, the whole foundation for market trust was gone.

While Alan had thought that the risk of reputational damage would ensure that executives retained some sense of business ethics, he later admitted that he was thinking back to the old world of business partnerships. He, like the rest of us, had not fully appreciated that moral norms were not constraining the behavior of those competing across complex and interlocked global entities that covered both shadow and formal banking systems.

The consequence, put simply, is a persistent mispricing of risk, and therefore a consistent failure to hold enough capital to offset it. In the pages to come I consider the implications of what happened with three practical examples that illustrate the problems of capitalism without capital. These examples were foremost in my mind when I made my speech at St. Paul's Cathedral, arguing that markets need morals. I have chosen these examples because together they illustrate the failings whose elimination must be the basis of a reformed financial system.

First, we will find that some of our most important banks put their savers and depositors at risk without having sufficient over-all capital or viable assets to cover them. When they should have increased their own protection by raising their capital ratios, they preferred to take the risk or, as it happened, impose their risk on others. We have to insist that in future all financial institutions have capital to cover their risks and also have their leverage and liquidity levels controlled.

Second, we find that when banks should have made sure that the products they were selling on were not toxic, many used the "originate and distribute" model of securitization to wash their hands of any responsibility for the product. In future we must make sure that every originator of risks everywhere takes some continuing responsibility for that risk.

Third, many in the formal banking system used their protected position to create off-balance-sheet vehicles, which themselves became part of a race to the bottom in financial standards. In future the informal banking system must be regulated alongside the formal system, and a free exchange of information across reg-ulatory regimes must make possible global financial supervision of all major companies.

Fourth, we will find that some banks had done more than take speculative risks on their own account. Without the knowledge of savers, and without proper protection of these savers, banks bet ordinary savers' deposits on speculative activities. This raises the even bigger question of executives putting their own interests above those of their savers and the proper balance in the alloca-tion of revenues between capital, the remuneration of employees and shareholders, and the recognition of the costs to the public in taxation. The reward to the public for both the profits and the risks from the activities of banks and financial institutions was nullified. In the past decade revenues went principally to top employees at the cost of capital; that remuneration was not cost-free, but came at the cost of the very stability upon which financial institutions' stability depends. In future we have to get the balance right between dividends, capital, and taxation.

What happened to Lehman Brothers illustrates each of those four problems of global banking in the past decade.

LEHMAN BROTHERS

In September 2008, like almost everyone else, I was surprised by the news of Lehman's problems and the rapid sequence of events that followed: its huge losses, its frantic attempts to secure a rescue, and its final bankruptcy.[4] As the news broke, I asked myself three questions: Why should a firm that had just been reporting apparently healthy results—record earnings, three-quarters of a trillion dollars of assets covering its liabilities, and a quarter of a trillion dollars of capital—be in such terminal trouble? Lehman's assets were predominantly long-term, while the liabilities were largely short-term, but did Lehman have a liquidity problem or a solvency problem? And was there any case to justify the government's stepping in?

The answers to these questions would fully emerge only with the publication of the Valukas Report, which, though now questioned by Lehman's then chief executive, gives an in-depth, month-by-month analysis of what actually happened. In it I read that in 2005, just two years before the beginning of the financial crisis, Lehman changed its strategy and its business model with devastating effects.

For a century and more, Lehman was a brokerage firm. It did not for the most part use its balance sheet to acquire assets for its own investment; rather Lehman acquired assets (such as commercial and residential real estate mortgages) primarily to move them by securitization or syndication and distribution to third parties. But in 2005, in a shift from this lower-risk model of being a brokerage firm to a high-risk, capital-intensive banking model, Lehman committed its own capital to buying commercial real estate, leveraged lending, and private equity-like investments.

This, in itself, was one part of the race to the bottom. Convinced that other banks were using their balance sheets in the same way, Lehman thought that their decision was in line with the rest of the market. But even in 2005 this business model was already a risk because of the firm's high leverage and small equity base. Buying up commercial real estate, levered loans, and other principal investments consumed more capital and entailed more risk, making Lehman less liquid than it had been in its traditional lines of business.[5]

Lehman funded its plan through the short-term "repo" markets, in other words borrowing millions of dollars each day from counterparties just to be able to do business.[6] Of course that meant that the moment counterparties to repurchase agreements were to lose confidence in Lehman and decline to roll over its daily funding, Lehman would be unable to fund itself or to continue to operate.

When did Lehman know it had a problem? A draft presentation on the firm's assessment of its equity and its adequacy has been found. Dated October 2007, it states that the firm's capital adequacy over the previous five to six quarters had "materially deteriorated" and was "at the bottom of its peer range with respect to the regulatory requirement of a minimum 10% total capital ratio imposed by the SEC."[7]

From August to November 2007, Lehman posted the lowest total capital ratio in the industry, and the firm was at or near its SEC-imposed 10 percent requirement for six months during 2007 and 2008.

We now know that on three separate occasions, Lehman had admitted to themselves their concern that the total capital ratio would fall below the 10 percent requirement. But while the Securities and Exchange Commission expected notification if it did indeed fall to or below 10 percent, Lehman failed to admit to them that it had.

Of course the contributing cause for the rapid decline in Lehman's equity position was the shift to illiquid assets, including real estate, high-yield loans, and principal investments. In just one year, from November 2006 to August 2007, the firm's illiquid holdings grew by 72 percent, while their "Tier 1" capital grew by only 26 percent.[8] The reason they were able to manage their stretched position was that they had been using an accounting device to manage their balance sheet: temporarily removing approximately $50 billion of assets from the balance sheet at the end of the first and second quarters of 2008. Normally such deals are accounted as "transactions," but by adding some cash to the transaction, Lehman was able to call them "sales," and the balance sheet was pumped up.[9]

Known within Lehman as "Repo 105," the assets were transferred through the company's London operations so that the Repo 105 deals could be conducted under English law. Then, at the beginning of a new quarter, Lehman would borrow more money and repurchase the assets to put them back on its balance sheet. It was, says the Valukas Report, "balance sheet manipulation," and it allowed Lehman to mask the perilous state of the bank's finances before its catastrophic collapse in 2008.

Throughout 2008 Lehman continued to claim that it had sufficient liquidity to weather any foreseeable economic downturn, failing to disclose its repurchase device or that it now owned a heavy concentration of residential and commercial real estate that would be difficult to turn into cash quickly. The Valukas Report describes a board obsessed with growth, surrounded by executives who said openly that they did not want to hear "too much detail" about the risks they might face in case it held them back from making the high-risk deals on which the biggest bonuses depend. Lehman did not disclose its use, or the significant magnitude of its use, of Repo 105 to the U.S. government, to the rating agencies, to its investors, or to its own board of directors. Their auditors did not question Lehman's use and nondisclosure of the Repo 105 accounting transactions.

The Lehman case reveals that right at the heart of the world's biggest banks was a culture of unethical financial practices that were, right up to boardroom level, connived at, condoned, and rewarded.[10] It was nothing short of chronic recklessness powered by unchecked greed. I was furious to discover that other major banks too were recklessly using their customers' own money to speculate. In February 2010 the securities arm of JP Morgan was fined just under $50 million, the largest fine ever levied by the U.K. financial regulator, because its future and options business was keeping up to $23 billion in institutional clients' money, inextricably mingled with its own funds, in an "unsegregated" account at the securities division's parent branch.

ROYAL BANK OF SCOTLAND

People will rightly ask why we did not know earlier of the fundamental weakness of RBS. The simple answer is: we were misled. The story on paper was of the world's most successful growing bank: making huge profits, paying high dividends, able to acquire new assets, one of the first into China, and on its way to becoming the world's biggest bank. It was already the tenth biggest company in the world and one of the few British banks that also had the legal power, normally reserved to central banks, to issue its own banknotes.

Its investment bank business focused on foreign exchange and fixed income, but to the general public in Britain it was a dynamic retail and commercial bank with links to some of the most trusted names in Britain. After all, that was how the RBS presented itself on just about every advertising board in the country. Every year £1 million was paid out to each of what were called their "global ambassadors," who included Sir Jackie Stewart, the former racing car driver, the golfer Jack Nicklaus (with its power to issue new notes the bank had already brought out a £5 note with Nicklaus's face on it), and the tennis player Andy Murray (who to his credit, once the government had bought into RBS, immediately volunteered a cut in his payment).[11]

So when RBS collapsed, the British government, which owned a majority of the shares, inherited these million-pound deals with sports stars along with a top-of-the-range private plane. As part of the estimated £200 million sponsorship budget, large contracts for up to five years had been agreed just weeks before the bank crashed.

I had known the bank from my early days as an MP serving a constituency near its headquarters in Edinburgh, and I remember visiting their new offices before they were officially opened. The new HQ was like a small town in its own right, and my first impression was that this was an institution with endless ambition for itself; the headquarters was built on the assumption that, having doubled in size, the bank would inevitably double again.

Fred Goodwin, the RBS chief executive, was a self-made man. I admired the way he had worked his way up from a working-class background by training as an accountant. But over the years I saw him change. Whenever I met him he always had a complaint about something the government had failed to do for him, whether it was about access into China (which he secured) or about critical reports issued by the "Treasury Select Committee" in Parliament (over which I, of course, had no control).

I recall a conversation with him that should have alerted me to the RBS's likely capital problems. While I was still the Chancellor of the Exchequer I met Fred at his Edinburgh office and asked him about what were called "orphan assets." These were assets held on banks' balance sheets but owed to deceased customers who had died without leaving any instruction about what should happen. In some cases these customers had passed away a century ago or more, but their savings were held by the bank and accruing interest. I believed that, morally, this was money that the banks did not own and that it should be put to community purposes, such as building new youth centers or funding education in financial literacy. I was planning to introduce a policy to redistribute these assets and had found other banks, if not overjoyed about change, at least receptive. Fred was the most skeptical, for reasons that at the time I couldn't work out. I can only now imagine how delicate the capital position of his bank was. The Royal Bank of Scotland had a low capital base, so its defining failure was the decision to proceed with a leverage and risk-laden bid to take over the bank ABN Amro at a price of $60 billion. That was a vast sum to pay for one bad bank.

At the time the deal, which was engineered by a business consortium including Santander and Fortis, was seen as a bold stroke: the first hostile cross-European bid for a large bank, the first breakup of a bank into its component parts, and at a record price.[12] The trouble was that they bought without checking properly whether this Netherlands-based bank was riddled with subprime and impaired assets. I was told of an email that gave the order to get on with the signing, leaving them to deal with the assets and liabilities later.

The inquiry into this should be a matter for the regulator, the Financial Services Authority, who is looking at the roles played by former members of the executive board and is also still examining the bank's 2007 acquisition of ABN Amro and its capital-raising in early 2008. The review is about how much risk was on RBS's books and whether management should have been aware that its £12 billion rights issue, launched six months after its ABN Amro acquisition, would not be enough to allow it to cope with its toxic debt mountain.

In just over a year, from mid-2007 to late 2008, RBS had doubled its debt and interbank borrowings to £500 billion. Even after their rights issue in 2008, their capital ratios were still low, at only 6 percent, and by this time the bank was also weighed down by losses, having had to take back ownership of £2 billion in German properties, bought at the market's peak and now almost worthless.

So, during 2008, as cash flow became even more difficult, the clock was ticking for RBS. With too little capital in the first place, with a vast and serious error over ABN Amro's toxic assets, and with other mistakes in Germany, America, and later Eastern Europe, funding had started to dry up.

HALIFAX BANK OF SCOTLAND

The mistakes that brought the Halifax Bank of Scotland to collapse were quite different from those seen in the RBS story, but they led to the same disastrous conclusion.

At both banks, credit committees were formed on an ad hoc basis, with risk managers sidelined wherever necessary. But the cardinal mistake at HBOS, the one that resulted in the surrender of their independence to Lloyds TSB and then necessitated a wholesale government rescue, was to stake everything on rising prices in the property market.

The bank operated a set of fundamentally unstable arrangements with a series of property speculators. A few got out before the crisis began in earnest, one it is alleged with £2 billion in profit from his property deals. Those left standing when the music stopped personally lost millions, though not as much as the bank lost.

In February 2009 the Lloyds-HBOS chief financial officer, Tim Tookey, went to speak at the UBS Global Financial Services Conference in New York. As the new finance officer of the merged Lloyds-HBOS he gave a slide presentation entitled "Understanding the HBOS Loan Book." This revealed an astonishing figure: 40 percent of the Halifax Bank of Scotland's £432 billion total loan book was what he called "outside Lloyd's appetite"—a curious phrase, which meant that these loans should never have been taken on.

He made it clear that of the £255 billion lent by HBOS in retail mortgages and other consumer loans, £86 billion was lending he would not have done. Of their £61 billion of international lending, he would not have done £20 billion. But the worst—and for HBOS the fatal—part of the story was the conclusions he reached about the biggest loans on their books, the £116 billion of corporate lending advanced by the Bank of Scotland Corporate unit: £80 billion—more than two pounds in every three loaned—was, he repeated, "outside Lloyds TSB's risk appetite." Half of that £80 billion was loans to construction and property companies.

Later, at a meeting of a House of Commons committee, an angry Member of Parliament asked the chairman of the Halifax Bank of Scotland, Dennis Stevenson, "Your highest paid banker, your head of corporate lending, Peter Cummings, was lending £40 billion of your £100 billion loan book to construction and property companies?" The reply: Yes, the corporate lending unit had, said Lord Stevenson, "lent too much. We made some mistakes and that is the bottom line."[13]

In April 2008 the bank revealed another damaging failure: its exposure to U.S. toxic debt through the £7.1 billion tranche of Alt-A mortgages on its books. From then on it was crisis management, and by September 2008, with a £120 billion gap between its lending and its deposits and with wholesale markets frozen, HBOS was effectively bust.

On September 18, 2008, Lloyds TSB announced that it had reached an agreement on the terms of a "recommended acquisition" of HBOS. And the "bottom line" the chairman talked of—the prime cause of the failure of HBOS—was the huge lending misjudgment on property-related deals.

When I look again at the story of HBOS it is not only the scale of what they assumed was their one-way bet on property that shocks me; it is also the sheer aggression and presumption of the bank in its practice of playing the markets not just as a moneylender but, in the same deals, as a property owner too. This is a business model enjoying the innocuous label "integrated finance."[14]

After the year 2000 the bank did more than a hundred integrated finance deals and bought into sixty businesses, issuing debt to companies in exchange for equity. The bank also amassed a £4 billion unlisted equity portfolio, with many of the stakes in house builders and other property-related companies.

The bank continued to support high-priced, some say overpriced, property purchases just as the market started to falter. In 2006 HBOS joined with an investment fund to pay £1.1 billion for the retirement homes builder McCarthy & Stone, trumping rival bidders; then in March 2007, just at the peak of the property bubble, the same duo spent £750 million on the house builder Crest Nicholson. In May 2007 the bank took a 50 percent stake in an overstretched property developer, Kilmartin Holdings, and even as the bank was forced into a £4 billion emergency fundraising, it was embarking on an equity and loan deal with Britain's largest privately owned house builder, Miller.

But the emerging problems were not restricted to domestic property markets. HBOS had been taking on subprime too—six billion pounds' worth. In August 2007 the HBOS head of treasury, Lindsay Mackay, admitted that Grampian Funding, an off-balance-sheet "conduit" of the bank, had $36.1 billion of debt outstanding, and that investments mainly in Triple A–rated securities were effectively toxic assets. The only way to deal with such a debt was to add around £14 billion of risk-weighted assets to the bank.

But the bank did not see what was coming. At an awards ceremony the HBOS head of corporate banking defended the bank's decision to continue its risky policy toward the commercial property sector. He said, "Some people look as though they are losing their nerve—beginning to panic, even—in today's testing property environment. Not us." But the bank was later forced to deny rumors that it had to seek emergency funding from the Bank of England, and accused short sellers of spreading false rumors.

But there were problems. When in 2004 the FSA conducted a risk, or Arrow, assessment, the bank was told to "strengthen the control infrastructure within the group." The regulator also commissioned a report from PricewaterhouseCoopers on HBOS's risk-management framework. HBOS's head of group regulatory risk, Paul Moore, warned that, without a change to its sales-obsessed culture and inadequate internal controls, the bank would collapse. HBOS, he said, was "going too fast" and was "a serious risk to financial stability and consumer protection."

So what do we learn from the tortuous and troubled histories of RBS and HBOS? These histories confirm what we know of other banks elsewhere: that there was too much leverage and a system-wide shortage of capital. But they confirm also that risk-taking was given priority over and above the imperative of protecting the capital of the banks.

In addition, pay and bonuses too often took precedence over the need for capital. I know that many actions I found abhorrent were well within the law. Mario Cuomo, the former governor of New York, once said, "Every time I've done something that doesn't feel right, it's ended up not being right." In that sense, an awful lot of what was going on wasn't right. HBOS was a case in point. Just as the company was collapsing, the board awarded payment to at least one employee most implicated in the failed commercial property deals that brought it down. An extra £600,000 was paid out. This unjustified and, I believe, illegitimate payment was not simply an example of a technical failure; it was also a moral failure.

Inadequate models for evaluating risk were complemented by a perverse system of incentives that maximized rather than minimized these risks. Short-term incentive structures, which relied excessively on self-regulation, aggravated rather than contained the recklessness of risk-taking. As we have seen, management's rewards depended less on long-term returns than on short-term share prices. Indeed there was an incentive to drive up short-term shareholder returns by moving risks to off-balance sheets and increasing short-term turnover through increased fees, profits, and bonuses. In the case of mortgage derivatives, incentives were focused on the quantity of mortgages originated, not the quality. There was little or no knowledge on the part of the ultimate buyer or, as often, even the seller of mortgage-backed securities of the creditworthiness of the mortgage holder. It was the inevitable result of a system that put short-term remuneration before the real long-term capital needs of the banks.

In conventional business manuals, the constraint on bad behavior by bankers is considered to be a loss of reputation for being trustworthy. But the worry about losing one's reputation with others depends on others knowing what is going on. With globalization and securitization in particular came even greater gaps in the information available to the investor. And so with a race to increase remuneration even at a risk to the capital needs of the company, and with information skewed in favor of the executive, no one could automatically equate the bankers' pursuit of their own self-interest with the interest of the company or the more general public interest.

George Akerlof and Robert Shiller raise similar but more general ethical questions about behavior in the marketplace in their book *Animal Spirits*. They seek to demonstrate the more general case that our economy cannot be understood by looking exclusively at economic motives. In the true spirit of Keynes, they suggest that we need instead a "detailed understanding" of the "real motivations of real people." They bring forward evidence that a number of what they call "non-economic forces" are at work in the marketplace, and suggest that economic decisions do not depend entirely on economic rationality. Individuals, they write, can go through waves of optimism and pessimism (which causes big changes in economic demand). Behavior is also influenced by judgments about what is fair and unfair, which means that wages are set not just by economic forces, but also by social forces. Corruption and demonstrations of bad faith are everyday realities. Individuals can easily confuse the nominal value of money with its real value, and individuals can be moved to act not just by the power of reason but by the power of stories. "Animal spirits" therefore play a crucial role in explaining why depressions occur, why saving is so variable, why stock markets fluctuate so widely, and why there are large bubbles in the housing market. Over time no system can endure if it is not underpinned by values that try to harness people's animal spirits for the public good.

For me, the conclusion is that, underlying and at the core of both markets and governments, there must be a set of commonly accepted values that emphasize enterprise and competition but also elevate fairness and responsibility. These are values that can guide us in developing the right relationships between the public interest and market forces, and can help us reset the post-crisis relationship between markets and government at a global as well as national level. I will deal with this in my conclusion, because it is part of a global compact for growth.

JUSTICE AND BANKERS' PAY

Well into the crisis, in late 2008, I had a conversation with one of the country's leading bankers who told me all I needed to know about the gulf between his profession and the rest of society. I had questioned the need for the huge bonuses he, his board, and many of his senior people were taking, even as the consequences of their poor judgment and decisions were coming to light. "But they'll leave the country," he responded. I refrained from offering him the response that ordinary members of the public would have given him.

The motto of the old order in the City of London was "My word is my bond," but the financial crisis revealed a culture quite alien to that heritage, a culture whereby the stewards of people's money were revealed to have become speculators with it. Bankers have experienced near-unprecedented income growth over the past decade. (According to analysis from the Centre for Economic Performance at the London School of Economics, the highest-paid workers are taking home nearly a third of the U.K.'s total wage bill; big bonuses paid to bankers and traders accounted for most of those gains and drove Britain's rising inequality over the past decade.)[15] Yet many of them seemed quite oblivious to how public tolerance for the excess had changed in light of the bailout.

The bankers' key argument—that they took big risks on their own shoulders—was being exposed as illusory. It was not the bankers who took the risk, but the government—and the people—who had had risks thrust upon them, often with little prospect of reward. Even as taxpayers all around the world were losing out as a result of their recklessness, the bankers continued to claim that the grotesque rewards they enjoyed were essential to the banking sector and the public interest.

Their reluctance to face up to reality was exposed again in November 2009 when we introduced a one-time levy on the bonuses of the banking community. We knew that we had to pre-empt problems in January 2010, when the bankers would again be reporting huge bonus rewards in companies where we had the most shares.

There were of course bonuses that were legally binding, and these were contractual obligations governments had to meet. Then there was the familiar counterargument: that if Britain acted on remuneration and America failed to act, then whole companies would relocate. Switzerland became a much-quoted option for bankers faced with tax changes not in their favor, and, as the Swiss told me, there were no plans there for changes in its remuneration rules. But when Alistair Darling bravely demanded from the banks a 50 percent tax on their bonuses, the outcry from the financiers was in my view a disgrace. Certainly no one could have argued that there was any public support for them in their self-interested campaign.

Support for the plan that banks would contribute to small-business lending at the high-technology end was then suddenly withdrawn. I had conversations with one company before the tax was introduced and was told that making money was their business, and that taxation was solely a matter for government. They would accept what government did, a position that was maintained only until we announced the tax, when they, with others, threatened to leave the country.

We were under daily pressure to modify the tax, and to his credit, Alistair refused to back down in any way. We were right to press on, and the eventual net gain to the public purse from the tax was £1.2 billion. However, in this form it had to be a one-time boon; by now the banks have restructured their remuneration packages in order to avoid having to pay a similarly constructed tax in future.

Deferral of bonuses and bonus claw-back have been introduced across the G20 to move remuneration from short-term deal making to longer-term success. So far, since the banking collapse, we have seen a welcome reduction in the proportion of the revenues global investment banks have paid out in bonuses. Deutsche Bank's global compensation fell to 40 percent of revenues in 2009, from nearly 60 percent in 2008. Similarly, Goldman Sachs' global compensation ratio fell to 36 percent in 2009, down from nearly 50 percent in 2008.

But the reason bankers' pay is absolutely crucial to the wider story we have been examining has nothing to do with the unacceptable politics of envy (to punish wealthy people for the simple act of being wealthy), nor even to do with an unacceptable politics of retribution (wanting to make bankers suffer for wrongdoings). Instead the issue of pay assumes an importance because there is a very particular relationship between actions taken by one person and consequences suffered by everyone. Excesses in remuneration are not cost-free.

We can now detail in the most precise of terms the cost of excessive remuneration at the expense of adequate capitalization. We now know that if British bankers had paid themselves 10 percent less per year between 2000 and 2007, they would have had more capital, some £50 billion more, to help them withstand the crisis. The extent of the undercapitalization of our banks was £50 billion, and was exactly the sum put up by the taxpayers for the emergency stabilization of our banking system.

So one great issue that needs to be resolved internationally is the right balance between the capital that banks need, the dividends they pay, the remuneration they give employees, and the contribution they make to the public for the economic and social costs of their risk-taking.

But there is also a prize waiting to be grasped that I was still pursuing in the final weeks before I left office: a globally coordinated levy on the banking sector. Some might ask: Why should governments charge a levy? Part of getting the balance right between dividends, pay, capital, and tax is assessing the public interest, not just for its reasonable share of the profits earned but because of the risks the public takes. For example, using credit ratings to help quantify the implicit support that banks enjoy from the government, Andrew Haldane of the Bank of England estimates that over the past three years the U.K.'s largest lenders benefited from an average taxpayer subsidy of £55 billion a year. Using an alternative approach, looking at the relative funding costs of big and small banks, he suggests the annual subsidy should be £30 billion. Banks, I argued in front of the G20 finance ministers and bank governors, are a strategic sector of the economy, one that had to be treated differently for the purposes of government guarantees. In return we would expect that the banks should contribute to paying off the consequences of their past failings.

But I believe that without all financial centers involved, a bank levy will be difficult to apply in some cases. And the first response to my call for a global financial levy was not encouraging. With President Sarkozy's and Chancellor Merkel's support, we inserted into the G20 statement at Pittsburgh the request for an IMF report by 2010 on a financial levy, and at the G20 finance ministers' meeting in St. Andrews in Scotland in November 2009 I made my first major speech on the type of global financial levy we might consider. I explained the conditions under which I would support a global levy: it had to be universal; its purpose had to be in line with supporting competition and openness; and it could not work unless all the major economies supported it. I outlined options for how we could deal with the relationship between banks and society, and thus put that relationship on a more defensible path: we could have an insurance levy for the future, contingent capital, a better resolution mechanism, or a levy, perhaps a transaction levy. I made it clear that we had to look at all four options; that any final settlement would have to meet my key tests: and that the tax had to be universal, in line with competition rules and not harmful to enterprise.

But just the mention of a levy on transactions attracted great publicity. Quickly, but wrongly, people assumed it was the so-called Tobin tax on all transactions. Immediately after I spoke, the U.S. Treasury secretary, Tim Geithner, announced that he opposed a transactions tax. Dominique Strauss-Kahn, the head of the IMF, said he thought a transactions tax unlikely but, though he said he supported action on a levy, the only press coverage on his comments was on his direct questioning of the Tobin tax. The response from Europe was no more encouraging. I had gone into the lion's den and been mauled. Newspapers assailed me. I was said to be out of touch and to have lost international support. My intervention, people said, undermined the achievements of the chairmanship of the G20. I could see a rocky time ahead as we continued to promote the global levy, but was in no mood to give up.

Over the next day or two I telephoned all who had criticized the tax and asked them to look again at all the options. I left them in no doubt that I would be stepping up my campaign and would seek to win public as well as government support for the levy. We could not stand still, act as if nothing had happened, and leave the banks to pick off governments one by one, with the inevitable result that no action would follow.

By the beginning of 2010 what had seemed a wayward idea started to gain more support. I was grateful to Tim Geithner for telephoning me to explain the new American proposal for a ten-year levy. We agreed that we were working on parallel tracks, but with the same motivation and eventual destination.

I talked to Chancellor Merkel directly, and she agreed that Germany would move in line with an agreed proposal. Because of the amount of state banking in Germany, much of the levy would become a transfer within the public sector, but she saw the logic of global action. President Sarkozy had always been a strong supporter of a global levy, and so France, Germany, and Britain were pushing forward in Europe with the support of President Barroso and also the new Spanish presidency of the European Union, led by President Zapatero. There were even suggestions that Europe could move ahead on its own with an all-European-banks tax.

In March I met privately with Larry Summers. We agreed on what the shape of a tax applied in a similar or parallel way in the main financial centers could look like, and we talked also on the ranges for its scale. After the Summers meeting I phoned President Obama. It was clear we were working on parallel tracks and could be expected to deliver a similar base for a parallel tax in Europe as in America. When the IMF reported in April it came out in favor of a dual tax system, which I found easy to support.

During my final weeks in office I continued to push for agreement on the global levy, but with the British general election looming, it was a race against time. I planned to announce the U.K.'s target figure in April, but in the time available before the general election we could not secure the final details of an agreement. This is part of the unfinished business of the G20 I will discuss in the next chapter. I am pleased that the new British government has now accepted the argument for such a levy and hope it can take up where we left off and work with the other countries to get it agreed and implemented. In my view, however, it must be an agreement of the major financial centers of the world. From a reluctance on the part of the international community to talk about these issues at all we now find ourselves in a position where a deal is there to be struck and signed.[16]

THE CASE FOR A BANKING CONSTITUTION

So we cannot write off the failures of the financial system as mistakes in just one sector by a few individuals, and thus, because of laziness in our analysis, leave ourselves wholly unprepared for the next crisis.

But even now there can be no return to high levels of employment and growth without finding a way of harnessing finance's creative energies to allocate resources and risk so effectively that it spurs and speeds economic growth. We must never forget that credit, and the need for securitization too, is at the heart of a modern financial system. It should not be just tolerated as a necessary evil, but nurtured as one of the keys that unlocks opportunity. Access to credit is critical for companies that make and do things and in the process create decent work that enables people to get ahead and not just to get by. The answer to problems in the credit and securitization markets is not to ban securitization but to root out the abuses—and create the conditions through sensible reforms, by which credit can best contribute to the public good.

So the solution is neither some ill-thought lurch leftward that ignores the importance of lending; nor can it be a return to the old neoliberal versions of the Washington consensus, a now bankrupt ideology that died with bankrupt banks.

I believe the best way forward is to agree on the objectives and basic rules of a global constitution for the banking system, because it is upon a foundation of strong banking and reliable finance that we can build real wealth. I am convinced that in a global financial system the rules can no longer simply be national but have to be global too. When I talk of a constitution for the global financial system I mean a codification of principles, rules, and standards that are then universally applied across all major financial centers, with a process of surveillance and supervision through international colleges of regulators, bankers, and, where appropriate, finance and business ministers.

I believe also that securing a better and fairer reconciliation between the rights of shareholders, of executives, and of the general public—between capital, pay, dividends, and tax liabilities— can also best be addressed internationally. Only by reshaping the structure of incentives and the flow of financial information on a global basis can we avoid a new race to the bottom. There is an argument, on economic efficiency, for establishing price-based incentives to encourage important parts of the financial system to avoid extreme systemic risks, making it more expensive for institutions to take reckless risks with other people's money. The alternative is outright quantity constraints on positions, the size and scope of activities, or even limits on the types of instruments that can be purchased or sold.

We have identified the central miscalculation of governments as a failure to recognize that the highly leveraged institutions were not spreading risk to those most able to handle it. Instead there was a reckless mismanagement of risk. In time we discovered that leverage was even higher than had been reported, thanks to a lack of transparency in some of the financial instruments, and, in addition, the ratios of leverage used for regulatory purposes often did not adequately incorporate some risks or even understand the dangers at the top of the cycle. But when overleverage happens it is invariably doubly dangerous. Not only do you have too little capital to survive a loss, but the chances of loss rise as the leverage increases. As leverage builds, the newest bought assets are inevitably of a lower quality because the search for yield drives lending to higher risks. At some stage in the top of the cycle the system is inevitably exposed to very bad lending decisions, and maybe even to fraud. So if the regulatory mistake was to think that risk had been widely spread and taken on by people who could afford it, we must, as a priority, rectify this by bringing all players within the supervisory net and making sure systemic banks do not have liabilities obscured in another shadow system. And we must monitor and set standards for comprehensively identifying and managing risk not just in one institution but across all entanglements around the world.

An operational framework for macro-prudential supervision based on globally applicable principles is still evolving. It has to take account of the size of institutions, their entanglement with each other, the nature and complexity of their risks, and their vulnerability to cycles (so that both upswings and downturns are not amplified by regulations or market practices). In working out the policies that flow from this, there will have to be further big changes in capital regimes; more rigorous focus on accounting practices, risk management systems, and compensation. As demonstrated in the article "Capital Regulation after the Crisis: Business as Usual," written in July 2010, capital requirements remain too low and their increase under Basel 3 may post-date the next financial crisis. Martin Hellwig of the Max Planck Institute is blunt in stating that "The current system has no theoretical foundation, its objectives are ill-specified, its effects have not been thought through, either for the individual bank or for the system as a whole." His conclusion is persuasive that "objections to substantial increases in capital requirements rest on arguments that run counter to economic logic or are themselves evidence of moral hazard and a need for regulation." At the same time, the IMF, the Financial Stability Board, and the Bank of International Settlements must enable authorities to identify systemically important institutions, markets, and instruments. Not all big banks failed, and not all small banks were successful. Both retail and investment banks went under. A simple separation of retail and investment banks or a breakup of big banks is not sufficient: all financial institutions will have to hold substantially more capital, to link that capital on a sliding scale to their risks, and to have in place resolution systems, or what are called "living wills." And all will have to divest parts of businesses where there are potential conflicts of interest. We will have to work out systems for addressing the new moral hazards, but in a financial system still too leveraged up for the risks being taken, reform cannot be avoided or postponed. As the IMF has pointed out in their Financial Stability Report of October 2010, stringent bank capital and liquidity requirements must apply far beyond a subset of the financial system to hedge funds, insurance companies, and non-bank institutions that are a systemic risk, and if we are to have the buffers we need to cushion the system against failures without aggravating moral hazards, then we must examine capital surcharges and levying fees rated by risk—preferably with international agreement.

I believe a global banking constitution is a huge prize to reach for, and I believe that just as we did for other international issues—from the Millennium Development Goals to third world debt and the ban on cluster munitions and land mines, and then with the global fiscal stimulus—it is possible to create a worldwide coalition for change. But first, at the beginning of 2009, the world had to come together to prevent a great recession from becoming a great depression.

CHAPTER 4

The Problem Assailed:
The One-Trillion-Dollar Plan

On the afternoon of April 2, 2009, I closed the London G20 meeting and took to the podium to announce that my colleagues had agreed to a $1 trillion rescue plan for the world's economy. It was the biggest economic support program ever agreed on, and that evening, our final press conference had a TV audience of one billion people that reached around the world.

After seeing the stock market fall two months before, on March 9, to levels unseen since 1997, all the leaders were determined that with this latest statement, our overstretched and volatile markets would hear a message from all of us that was firm, bold, and unequivocal.

In my speech I spoke of the sheer urgency of the crisis. I explained that prosperity was indivisible, that growth had to be shared, and that our financial systems had to be strengthened and better regulated, with international action to overcome this crisis and to prevent future crises. Then, to the surprise of hardened journalists, I was able to announce that there would be $1 trillion available to underpin the global economy. It was simple: the G20 had delivered, with a sum approaching the total yearly output of countries like Britain, France, and Italy.

I set out where the guarantees would come from: new money from the International Monetary Fund and World Bank, new guarantees from countries on trade credits, and a new issue of the IMF "currency"—Special Drawing Rights. But I also set out their purpose: to prevent a great depression and to bring the recession to an end. I was able to say that there was now a plan. We had formed a consensus that would ensure that any country in difficulty could be helped. Crucially for me, we had also set aside money to lessen the impact of the financial crisis on the poorest countries of the world. And we had agreed to major surgery on our international institutions to make them more relevant to this new global age.

Most important, we had demonstrated that the world's biggest countries could work together, both quickly and effectively, for a common purpose. I felt that day, and still feel, that after such an extraordinary cooperative effort, the world will never be quite the same again. This chapter tells the story of how we got there, what we decided, and why it mattered.

I have already detailed the discussions I was having with other world leaders in the fall of 2008 about the banking crisis. At the same time, I was already thinking about how we could coordinate more comprehensive action on the global economic fallout that was sure to result from the failure of internationally entangled banks.

In order to begin to resolve the issue, it was essential not just to cooperate, but to recognize the fundamental ways in which the world had changed. For forty years after the Second World War the G7 was responsible for around 70 percent of all world economic activity. Only in the past twenty years has the G7's share of world output fallen dramatically, from above 70 percent in the early 1990s to around 40 percent on the eve of the worldwide recession in 2008. This dramatic shift of economic power, from North to South and West to East, was driven by what Larry Summers has called the biggest economic event of the last thousand years, indeed bigger than the first Industrial Revolution; in just over two decades, the workforce of the global economy has tripled as an extra two billion potential employees have reached working age in China, India, and other emerging markets.

In early 2008 President Sarkozy was quick to see that this meant we could not rely simply on the G7 to deal with the crisis. He had originally floated an extended G8 meeting, but when I visited his official country house we talked alone, concluding that a G20 would be best, and we decided to work together for membership in the G20 for Spain and the Netherlands.

Later in September, at the height of the banking crisis, I met President Bush at the White House and suggested to him (mirroring my discussions with other leaders at the United Nations the night before) that there was real appetite for a G20 meeting to address not only the banking issue but what it meant for jobs and living standards more widely.

On October 18, when President Sarkozy and President Baroso met with President Bush, they considered all possible options, including an extended G8 summit to be held in New York and the counterproposal of a G20 meeting. Two days later President Bush and I talked on the phone and made some progress on who might attend what was to be the first ever meeting of the G20 country grouping at leaders level.[1] I said that there was a case for all the G20 countries being present, and that there was an additional case for Spain and Netherlands as well as better representation from Africa, which had only South Africa in the G20.

On October 22 President Bush announced his invitation to a special G20 leaders meeting in Washington on November 15.

This was a major step forward because it recognized that cooperation had to extend beyond the narrow grouping of G8 countries. The November meeting was the first chance to see if a forum of leaders on such a scale could work. While the detailed policy focus would be on getting all countries to agree to a series of measures to reform the financial system,[2] the real success of Washington lay in the recognition that there was a common interest in regular contact coupled with a shared approach.

After the American presidential election in November, the focus shifted from George Bush to the new president, Barack Obama. As Obama prepared to take over, our talks with America and other countries on the future format and status of the G20 continued. We agreed that it should emerge as the premier forum for economic cooperation.

When the chairmanship of the G20 passed to Britain for the year 2009, work was already well under way, led by sherpa Jon Cunliffe. The job of a sherpa is to lead technical international negotiations, and Jon was one of the most respected and experienced sherpas in the world. He and I worked closely with Alistair Darling and his team led by Nick McPherson and Tom Scholar and shared advice and decisions with them on everything we planned. Sir Gus O'Donnell chaired a civil service group, and we held an important seminar of major world economists. Jon was joined in his task not just by Shriti Vadera but also by some of the best and brightest advisers. Tom Fletcher (my civil servant adviser on foreign affairs, along with his very able team, including Nick Catsaras) worked tirelessly alongside his superb political counterpart, Stewart Wood, and the policy unit at No. 10. Along with No. 10 Permanent Secretary Jeremy Heywood, who was a constant source of sound advice and meticulous delivery, and Jon's team, they turned the whole focus of the U.K. government from January onward to what could be achieved at the London summit to be held in April.

I had asked David Miliband, the highly respected Foreign Secretary, to allow Mark Malloch Brown, his incredibly effective and well-connected Minister of State, to work full-time on preparing the G20. His task was to ensure that we understood what leaders all over the world, not just in the G20, needed and that they understood what we were trying to achieve. He came back with a message consistent with our analysis and other soundings:

they wanted confidence restored through global action and they needed liquidity.

At the same time, we saw from the figures on lending, repossession, business closure, and unemployment that the crisis had moved from Wall Street to Main Street, and people's jobs, homes, and pensions were at risk from the contraction in the world economy. During the banking crisis there was the risk that some banks would collapse, but it was looking increasingly as if some countries were at risk of collapse too. Financing to emerging markets, Korea, and Eastern Europe had simply dried up. Their economic activity dramatically declined. That was dangerous not just for them but for us. The world's major economies were too interconnected for the effect not to be felt by businesses and people everywhere. World trade fell by 20 percent. We might have saved the banks and domestic savers and businesses but the global economy was in free fall.

I asked my team what could be done to shore up the system: What could be done to restore confidence, what was the equivalent of the extraordinary measures we had taken at the national level for banking that we could take at an international level for the so-called real economy? I went over and over this question in meetings with Shriti, Gus, Jon, Jeremy, and Tom Fletcher. It always led back to liquidity and financing from the IMF and World Bank to substitute for the withdrawal of credit and liquidity in emerging markets. No other global institutions could readily provide the coverage and resources, and indeed their resources would need to be replenished by countries who could access liquidity.

I pushed Jon, his team, and Shriti to go through every permutation and seemingly every acronym of existing and new international financing—Special Drawing Rights, High Access Precautionary Arrangements, Flexible Credit Lines, New

Arrangements to Borrow, global trade facilities, bank guarantee facilities, capital replenishments, gold sales. Jon started testing out his sherpa colleagues, and everyone spoke and met with their counterparts at every level.

Dominique Strauss-Kahn, Managing Director of the IMF, and I spoke several times in that period. He was in the forefront of understanding the need for radical and urgent action and vocal in sounding the warning bells. We were lucky to have him and his team constantly analyzing and assessing the dangers to the global economy and supporting the G20 in providing solutions. I spoke often to him and to World Bank President Bob Zoellick. Bob was rightly concerned about the impact on low-income countries and also agreed to set up a trade finance facility to substitute for the disappearance of international trade finance.

I had been to see President Obama soon after his inauguration. He was engaged and well informed, and I was pleased he had Larry Summers, a veteran of international crises, at his side. Nevertheless, it was some time before the team in the U.S. Treasury and White House was assembled, confirmed, and able to fully engage. That made the job of building consensus doubly hard, especially as the United States holds a veto on key IMF activities.

In the process of testing the waters, the most promising idea they came up with unfortunately fell foul of legal and technical problems. At the heart of the problem was the withdrawal of liquidity and credit to emerging markets and Eastern European countries, so we thought they should get the IMF to guarantee their debt issuance. It was similar to the idea of the medium term credit guarantee scheme we had instituted for banks in the recapitalization package. It would simultaneously facilitate liquidity and credit that had dried up but also help kick-start the international bond market which had seized up. But it was not to be, and we were left with a package that maximized what we could do in a number of elements of financing for these countries.

I worried about how this package would truly create confidence and break the free fall the global economy seemed to be in. There were a lot of different measures whose effectiveness depended on them being greater than the sum of their parts. Shriti's pre-summit personal note to me set out what the whole package should look like—credits for trade, liquidity for countries that needed it, and the widest possible international safety net. Taken together, they might lift confidence. The note had a number for every element, and at the bottom of the table of numbers a total that leaped out at me which thereafter we discussed only in code: a trillion-dollar summit.[3]

I turned to Jon and said, "Let's go get it." I had pushed Jon hard over the years as my sherpa to secure more from every G7, G8, IMFC, and G20. He never failed to deliver. But when he realized the scale of what we were attempting, he turned pale; he knew just what a tall order it was. We had not discussed such a large sum and he knew how little time there was. But I knew that if any team anywhere could deliver something so ambitious, it was this team.

In the final weeks, we prepared for the summit by drafting what I thought would be the optimal communiqué with a mix of actions to underpin the economy in crisis, but also long-term actions to prevent a repetition. We then worked backward from our intended outcome to persuade countries to play their part, but kept the top-line figure a closely guarded secret.

As Jon negotiated word by word with his fellow sherpas, the weeks running up to the London summit were filled with visits made by me, Alistair, Mark Malloch Brown, Paul Myners, Shriti, and others to gain support for sections of an already drafted communiqué, as well as more high-profile public interventions. I spoke to the European Parliament, the Joint Houses of Congress, and an audience at St. Paul's Cathedral to press my case, and I visited Brazil, Argentina, and Chile as well as America and Europe.[4] By the time of the summit I had spoken to every single leader— some several times—to lay the groundwork. It was a slow and tortuous process, but I found all leaders focused on trying to find a solution.

Unfortunately, our work hit a big snag when, a few days before the G20 met, the draft communiqué was leaked to a German magazine. Luckily, the leaked version did not involve the figures that would have added up to $1 trillion. That huge total was still under wraps, because I was determined it should surprise and therefore jolt the market.

Jon and his team began rewriting immediately, and the final draft, while similar in policy to the first, was completely restructured to differentiate it from the leaked documents.

The night before the summit, the leaders of the countries of the world met at 10 Downing Street for dinner. Seated around the table were actually twenty-six national leaders, including the newly elected president of the United States, Barack Obama, and the head of the three-centuries-old traditional monarchy, King Abdullah of Saudi Arabia. They were joined by the heads of all our major international institutions: the United Nations, the European Union, the International Monetary Fund, and the World Bank.

I had personally invited Prime Minister Meles of Ethiopia and the secretary general of the African Union, Jean Ping. A few months earlier President Sarkozy and I had persuaded President Bush to add to his Washington G20 gathering, on an ad hoc basis, both Prime Minister Zapatero of Spain and Prime Minister Balkenende of the Netherlands. Now I had ensured that in London they were present in their own right.

The evening had begun with a reception given by Her Majesty the Queen at Buckingham Palace, after which all of the leaders arrived in Downing Street in the allotted order: heads of international institutions first, prime ministers next, and in reverse order of their seniority in service, presidents, and the king of Saudi Arabia. Because he had just been elected prime minister, even though it was for the third time, Italy's Berlusconi had to be the first in, while President Sarkozy, now more senior in his third year, was the last to arrive.

As we assembled for predinner drinks, I repeated the words of Winston Churchill in the 1930s: we must ensure that we could never be criticized, as he criticized politicians then, for being "resolved to be irresolute, adamant for drift, solid for fluidity, and all powerful for impotence." Colleagues agreed with me that we must not let that happen again.

I started the dinner by reminding the assembled leaders of the London 1933 conference that had met in the Great Depression to resolve trade and currency pressures and to prevent protectionism. It had failed miserably, and its failure had made the world an even less stable place. As a result, protectionism ruled in the 1930s and, as I put it, "that failure had foreshadowed all the other terrible events of that decade and the one to follow."

But these leaders did not need such grim reminders that the task they faced was serious, and that the consequences of inaction would be dire—we all knew that the next day's work would be crucial. That was the day on which we would have to agree on the details of a bold and radical communiqué. To prepare the way for that, as the dinner progressed, I invited everyone at the table to make opening comments on the world crisis. President Obama spoke first and, with both eloquence and a winning humility as the most recently elected leader present, accepted America's responsibility for the origins of the financial crisis. Then each leader in turn offered a view on what had to be done. With twenty-six of us at the dinner, that did not happen quickly, and by the time of the agreed 9 p.m. finish, not everyone had been able to speak, with potential consequences for goodwill the next day, when some, who felt their seniority meant they should have spoken before others, might demand immediate speaking rights. During after-dinner drinks I spoke to those who had been skipped and agreed with them on an order for their interventions in the morning.

As we left that evening the mood was positive and determined; serious, but not at all grim.[5]

Overnight I worked hard to persuade people to agree to the more controversial aspects of the draft communiqué. British officials worked every minute on the main areas of disagreement. The first roadblock in the way of consensus was some trepidation about the very scale of what we were proposing to inject into the economy: IMF Special Drawing Rights, World Bank Resources, and trade credits on a level unseen before.

Second, there was a strong and in the end decisive resistance to the inclusion of a number for global growth. I argued that there was no evidence that the inflationary problems of past decades were likely to hit us in the foreseeable future, so that there was, at least as yet, no inflationary barrier to rapid growth out of recession. I wanted us to be able to say that by taking all the action that was necessary, we would return the world to the pre-crisis growth path by the end of 2011. But there were one or two of the other G20 members that I could not persuade to agree to either having a target, or a figure attached to it.

After discussions the next morning with world leaders, and after some phone calls, I realized that we would likely have to compromise on a growth number, and settle simply for an "objective," with no hard figure attached. But by working through the night, we had at least drawn nearer to agreement on the crucial decision: the underpinning of the world economy. And—with extra IMF support, Special Drawing Rights, and World Bank money and trade guarantees—we were now approaching agreement on a sum that no one had hinted at before: contingency support amounting to $1 trillion.[6]

For me coordination was the truly big prize.[7] When the meeting began, I had felt a huge weight of responsibility, but also a curious lightness arising from the knowledge that this was the sort of serious and substantive environment in which I felt at my most effective and able to deliver the big changes to the lives and living standards of regular people that I believe politics should be about.

My method of chairing international meetings had been honed over ten years as chair of the twice-yearly committee of the International Monetary Fund and two stints chairing the finance ministers of the G7. But the best lessons that I had learned, and was still applying, had come long before all that. I had chaired the governing body of my university when I was still a student. Scottish universities abided by an ancient law that permitted students to elect the chair of the University Court. The Rector, as he was called, could be a celebrity (and recently often was) or a politician of stature (which had been the traditional practice). But there was nothing on the books preventing a student from assuming that position, and my fellow students had elected me to chair the Court. I took the position seriously and used the role to promote causes that were not popular with the university establishment.[8] At every meeting I had to find a way through the discordant views of academics, business leaders, High Court judges, and students, and just to survive the meetings I had to take procedure very seriously. So I had a very tough early lesson in the chairing of powerful and sometimes difficult people. I learned that you need to drive meetings toward conclusions and not simply wait for them to emerge.

Instead of inviting the usual open-ended discussions, which often, and conveniently for some, went nowhere, I would go straight to the business at hand. It was an approach that had worked in Edinburgh in the early 1970s, and which worked just as well in London in 2009. With my encouragement, we were able to agree on a draft communiqué that made its way around the table that morning. I had personally drafted the opening points, and I believe they sum up the magnitude of the tasks we faced:

1. We, the Leaders of the Group of Twenty, met in London on 2 April 2009.
2. We face the greatest challenge to the world economy in mod-

ern times—a crisis which has deepened since we last met, which affects the lives of women, men, and children in every country, and which all countries must join together to resolve. A global crisis requires a global solution.

3. We start from the belief that prosperity is indivisible; that growth, to be sustained, has to be shared; and that our global plan for recovery must have at its heart the needs and jobs of hard-working families, not just in developed countries but in emerging markets and the poorest countries of the world too; and must reflect the interests, not just of today's population, but of future generations too.

I asked the members to speak to the communiqué's specifics, and we went through it paragraph by paragraph. At times the meeting was stormy; it is no secret that President Sarkozy threatened to walk out if tax havens were not dealt with, because he saw them, understandably, as a problem and indeed a major cause of the global financial crisis. In the end the standoff was resolved only by President Obama taking President Sarkozy and Premier Wen to the side of the meeting room and putting an arm around each, urging a compromise be reached. Surprisingly, one or two emerging market countries held out against action on tax havens. Indeed, from around the world a number of non-G20 states were phoning in and asking that their voice be heard against the naming and shaming of tax havens close to them.

But I was certain that financial institutions were using them to avoid tax on a huge scale and that tax havens—which are, of course, also regulatory havens—were facilitating a regulatory race to the bottom that continually threatened the legitimate interests of more fastidiously regulated nations. However, I knew that the Organisation for Economic Co-operation and Development had drawn up its lists: a black list of noncompliant regimes, a gray list of countries on their way to compliance, and a white list of the fully compliant. To get off the black list, countries had to sign twelve exchange-of-information agreements with neighboring countries, and do so within weeks.

I wanted the G20 to signal its complete support for the outlawing of noncompliant tax havens. But not everyone could agree on this, or on how far we should go. Some wanted the black-list countries excluded from the international community immediately. Others wanted them to be given some more time. Others thought this was no business for the G20, which after all had been set up as a leaders' organization only in the past few weeks.

So, as I was chairing the meeting, I was also making phone calls to the OECD Secretary General, who was in Paris.[9] I asked him to agree to publish the list of noncompliant tax havens and wanted him to tell the G20 he would do so. Eventually we agreed on a complex face-saving formula whereby the G20 would not ourselves list the names of tax havens that were noncompliant. As a result, the text of the G20 communiqué did not name the tax havens that had only a few weeks to come into line with information disclosure; instead we referred to the existence of decisions being made by the OECD. The OECD list was, however, published at the same time as our communiqué, and it proved to be a major breakthrough.

As is more or less expected at meetings like these, there was a problem with the communiqué. But on this occasion it was not a failure of political consensus, but a failure of hardware. We had too few photocopiers, and those we had were too far away from our conference room. So the minute we changed the draft with a new sentence or an amended one, there were delays before the next draft could be circulated. Leaders who had agreed on the wording were kept waiting. I had seen it all before in international meetings; as people wait impatiently in an atmosphere that is already tense, the momentum can slip backward as issues already taken as agreed are reopened. Minor failings really can change a conference; my way through the danger of reopening the text was to press on and call a debate with new speakers on the next stage of our work.

By the time we were due to complete our deliberations, threats to walk out had changed to something much more encouraging: repeated demands for a common and united front. Most leaders around the table knew that this was a make-or-break day for the world economy, and their collective response to that challenge was best when it mattered most: as the meeting drew to its close. In only a few weeks more had been achieved in addressing the problems caused by tax havens than in several decades of fruitless discussion. Many countries were to benefit as a result. Britain received its first gain from the decision within a few months: £1 billion in unpaid taxes recovered from Liechtenstein.

President Obama, the youngest leader, was present for the first time at a G20 meeting, indeed present at his first international meeting. The whole gathering was, I believe, impressed by his calm and understanding as he persuaded people that by our unity of purpose we could demonstrate the difference that only global leadership could make. Obama's speech was an inspiring end to two difficult days that left a world still in turmoil but clearer about the direction ahead. We had taken the first steps to unite the world behind a plan for ending the global financial crisis.

First, we underpinned the world economy at its most difficult time with a multinational guarantee of resources made available through international institutions. The IMF was overstretched; its available capital, once 5 percent of the world's resources, was now just 1 percent. For years the boldest of attempts to give it the funds to do its job had not gotten anywhere. Now we cut through all this and gave the IMF new Special Drawing Rights, to be voted on by its member countries, and the power to extend its support for individual countries.[10] The World Bank was encouraged and agreed to double the funding it gave to poor, recession-hit, developing countries. The African Development Bank led the way with its own injection of additional funds to prevent recessions in a number of African countries.

Second, we also set in motion the biggest and most comprehensive reform plan for our banking system. In future, a World Stability Board would be responsible for the early warnings and the management of global risk. We set clear timetables for the global institutions responsible—the Board, the Bank of International Settlements, and national regulators—to agree on new international rules, capital requirements, new liquidity ratios, and new transparency and accountability mechanisms. If the world had moved too slowly in the past on global finance, it had to move with speed now, including bringing an end to tax secrecy.

Finally, we agreed that all of us would take what action was necessary to move us out of recession. So in addition to the $1 trillion underpinning our economies, monetary and fiscal action was to be coordinated on a level never seen before. Interest rates were close to zero; the independent central banks were now working in unison in their plans to inject new resources into the economy; the increased supply of money through quantitative easing was now happening around the world; and a very critical extension in bank-to-bank currency swaps was providing the funds necessary for each continent to address recession. One of the least reported successes of global action against recession was how quickly the Federal Reserve and other central banks developed swap credit lines with other countries. Total swap lines rose to half a trillion dollars.[11]

This package was described by the president of the World Bank as the thing that "broke the fall" of the global economy. But our ambitions were higher still.

Our shared objective, set by the London summit, was to return to trend growth, and with Prime Minister Singh's intervention we agreed that our next meeting would receive a report which I would prepare on how international institutions could work better to achieve that growth.

Without the G20 the real and present risk of a global depression might have materialized. Professors Barry Eichengreen and Kevin O'Rourke have done a great service by charting the scale of the global collapse and then assessing the impact of the measures the world decided to take together. They first published their data on the scale of collapse in April 2009, collating data that covered the years 2007 and 2008. Their initial findings were stark. "To sum up," they said about the period before April 2009, "globally we are tracking or doing even worse than the Great Depression, whether the metric is industrial production, exports or equity valuations. . . . The 'Great Recession' label may turn out to be too optimistic. This is a Depression-sized event." In their second report, later in 2009, they wrote:

> The parallels between the Great Depression of the 1930s and our current Great Recession have been widely remarked upon . . . [with] the U.S. stock market since late 2007 falling just about as fast as in 1929–30. . . . When we look globally the decline in industrial production in the last nine months has been at least as severe as in the nine months following the 1929 peak. . . . To summarize: the world is currently undergoing an economic shock every bit as big as the Great Depression shock of 1929–30. . . . The good news, of course, is that the policy response is very different. The question now is whether that policy response will work.

It did.

In both 1929–30 and 2008–9 global gross domestic product fell for five successive quarters, the fall amounting to 5 percent in both periods. In the 1930s, however, the collapse continued for a further eight quarters—two *years*. In contrast, the collapse of 2008–9 was halted in the three *months* after the G20 met.

Of course many individual actions came to bear to end the recession: national fiscal policies, quantitative easing by a number of central banks, the recapitalization of the banks. But from April 2, 2009, everyone knew the world economy was underpinned by funds collectively agreed to and on a scale never seen before.

Starting in April the world started to move forward again. That is why the years 1929–32 are known forever as the Great Depression and the years 2008–9 will be known as the Great Recession. The G20 had averted a second global depression.

As I have said, after Prime Minister Singh's intervention at the London summit I was charged with preparing a report on the way ahead for the international institutions. Some leaders, I think, hoped that I would focus simply on proposing changes in the constitution of the IMF and World Bank. Instead, I started from a wholly different standpoint: What changes were required in order to ensure high levels of growth and employment over the next few years? And how could we best use the Pittsburgh G20 to bring them about?

The basis of my argument was that we could not return to the previous status quo: American and European consumers were very likely to spend less and save more for an extended period; we could expect a rise in the American and European household savings rate; and the outcome would be a shortfall in global aggregate demand relative to the world economy's productive potential. That, for me, was not an abstract question but a profoundly moral one; to my mind it is simply wrong to leave people without jobs and the ability to build a better life for their families when there is work that needs to be done.

In the long run I said that the shortfall should be filled by an increased consumer demand in emerging market countries and in countries that were running surpluses. The longer it takes to fill this gap, the more likely the incentive to shelter your own country and use protectionist measures to capture a bigger share of global output.

But with coordinated action to expand demand in surplus countries, with a worldwide effort to resist the resort to protectionism, and with a willingness of emerging countries to reallocate resources from traditional, low-productivity activities, such as agriculture, to new industries, America need no longer be the consumer of last resort.

In August 2009, before the September Pittsburgh G20 meeting, which President Obama would chair, I wrote him a private letter.

We were both fully aware that at the G20 meeting in April we had succeeded in bringing world leaders together around a $1 trillion rescue program to stave off a world recession. But I wanted to put on paper my thoughts about how, as they moved forward from the London G20, the major economies could and should work together in the future.

In my letter I suggested to him that, while the London G20 had achieved a lot, the world's economies still faced a very rocky road ahead, and that the next few years would be a great deal worse if we did not do much more to promote common action and global coordination.

The deleveraging of the banks and the loss of consumer spending power—as Americans and Europeans necessarily saved more and spent less—would withdraw around $2 trillion from the world economy. Wiping out two trillion dollars' worth of economic activity could only mean lost growth: jobs lost, businesses gone, people's hopes for their future and for their children's future dashed. And if we failed to take the necessary further action, mortgage repossessions, business failures, and personal bankruptcies would go on and on.

Every country, I told him, wanted to export its way out of recession. But as American and European spending power was cut, Chinese and Asian imports to America and Europe could fall without any major rise in China's spending on American exports; world trade between developed and emerging markets would grow far more slowly; and the world's richest countries would then inevitably face a "lost" decade of low growth and high unemployment. We had completed the first stage of our work: preventing the recession becoming a depression. But the second stage of our work, the restoration of high levels of growth and employment, had barely begun. The one way out of this vicious spiral of less activity, slower growth, and fewer jobs—with the damage running on for years ahead—was for the G20 to agree in Pittsburgh in September on a strategy for global growth.

I then set out what I meant by a global compact to which each continent would sign up. That would require coordinated action: first on imbalances, then on currency reserves, then on monetary and fiscal policies, and then, if possible, on trade. I had no doubt as to the difficulties of securing any agreement on issues as great as these; many vested interests were at stake, and it would be even more difficult to build a consensus on a future growth strategy than it had been to put together an agreement on the $1 trillion emergency rescue plan.

But the stalling of growth, with the resultant unemployment and much of the world's economic capacity unused, are together the big issues that world leaders now have to face.

In the past we have seen investment and productivity race forward out of recessions and growth restored as successive new innovations took hold. Again and again, in economic cycle after economic cycle, we have seen new forces appear in the world economy to push growth upward. But on this occasion, did we not have a structural problem impeding a strong recovery? What could we do to restore growth to a world economy in which one part of the world wants to save (and not spend) and the other wants to stop spending (and save)?

President Obama said to me that we must work to get broad agreement before we arrived at the formal sessions. He told me he would back our ideas for growth and instructed his officials to work through a potential plan for Pittsburgh with ours.

He was as good as his word. Negotiations behind the scenes over the summer between us and the Americans—and then between America, Europe, and China—made good progress. The finance ministers too, led by Tim Geithner and Alistair Darling, were called on to reach some difficult decisions, and they too succeeded. By the time we all arrived in Pittsburgh, the G20 were prepared to accept the idea of a global growth compact.

First we agreed not to withdraw stimulus from the economy until recovery was assured.[12] Of course this was a judgment about the stage of the economic cycle, but also about the relative merits of stimulus and austerity. But the bigger plan that we agreed upon was that each continent would play its part in formal discussions on the removal of barriers to growth. And what I had called a "compact" became the Pittsburgh plan.

Even before the meeting began there was recognition from all its participants that Pittsburgh should send a clear and positive signal about the future.[13] I am pleased that in that meeting we agreed on the essentials: plans for financial regulation of the banks; the setting up of a group to examine a global financial levy; unanimity that governments' support for their national economies should continue until recovery was assured: and, most important of all, we set ourselves a growth objective for the future.[14]

Whether and how we will meet that objective is the subject of part 3.

PART THREE

CHAPTER 5

Going for Global Growth and Jobs

I look back on the successes of the two G20 meetings of 2009 as high points for international economic cooperation. But I believed even then, and I believe more so now, that the decisions world leaders made in 2009 can only be the beginning and not the end of shaping the transformation of the global economy. There is still so much to do.

In the autumn of 2010, nearly a year after the Pittsburgh meeting, more than 25 percent of industrial capacity still lies idle in Europe and America.[1] Forty-seven million workers are unemployed in the highly industrialized countries, and global unemployment is estimated at 200 million for the wider group of OECD industrialized countries. Global poverty is rising, not falling.

While China, India, and Asia appeared to be returning to higher levels of growth,[2] and Africa moving in the same direction, the two historic engines of growth, Europe and America, are still growing far too slowly to reduce unemployment quickly. Even as we examine the trends for 2011 and beyond, the surplus of industrial capacity means that the recovery of growth and jobs will be at best weak.[3] My fears of a low-growth decade are, even now, beginning to come true, with all of the consequences for individuals, communities, and whole societies which that entails. Calculations by Jorgenson and Vu suggest that while in the old G7—Germany, France, Britain, Italy, Japan, and North America—the underlying annual growth rate in the decade after 1998 was 2.1 percent, it is likely to be only 1.45 percent a year over the next ten years—slower than at any time since the Second World War.[4]

This weakening of the European, American, and Japanese growth rate also reflects the fundamental shift taking place across the world in the location of production and the direction of trade. As we examine the prospects for China, India, and other emerging market countries from the standpoint of the second decade of the twenty-first century, we will have to think beyond the familiar model—America and Europe controlling high-paid design and the intellectual property and outsourcing low-wage production—to a new industrial and business model with world-beating companies locating innovation and development centers across Asia as well. The European Commission predicts China and India will double their R and D world share to 20 percent by 2025. And with China leading the growth of south-south trade (China now the largest trading partner not just with Australia and Japan but also with Brazil and Africa), globalization will no longer be dominated by trade between today's developed countries.

But if America and Europe, for two centuries the biggest drivers of world growth, are to spend less and save more for an extended period, the outcome is, other things being equal, a shortfall in global aggregate demand and high levels of global unemployment. Before the crisis, the spending of American and European consumers accounted for 35 percent of the world's economic activity. This compares with China's consumer spending, which even with that country's phenomenal rise, is only 3 percent of the global economy.

So the world is at a critical moment. We can, if we choose, build a genuinely global society with diverse drivers of growth, diverse centers of power, and a genuine stake in the international community for every country and its people. If we make the right choices now, we can replace the lost growth of Europe and America with a new multipolar growth in which each region contributes and each benefits. If we fail, we are condemning an entire generation to an era of lost opportunities, lost jobs, and lost hope.

The following chapters are my necessarily top-line assessments of the potential contribution each region can make to the world's return to high levels of employment and growth. These are working assumptions only, based on my own reading and reflection over the past few months since leaving office. I look forward to debating them with specialists during my travels in the months and years to come, and to refining and changing my position in light of their insights and expertise.

My argument, at its simplest, is that no one country or region can, in the short term and on its own, fill the global demand gap created by the shortfall in American and European consumption. A decade from now the exit from low growth will come as a result of dramatically higher levels of economic activity in Asia, emerging markets, and developing countries.

But none of the countries and regions I will assess in the following chapters can offer such an exit today, because they cannot at this moment supply enough growth to raise the overall economic activity of the world sufficiently to reduce unemployment substantially. However, I believe that together, through global cooperation and coordination, we may just be able to generate next year and in the years to come higher levels of growth than assumed today.

I reject the view that sees global economics as a zero-sum game. There is no inherent contradiction between what the leaders of each of these regional economies want to achieve for their people and the wider needs of our shared global economy. Of course during the growth years there seemed little short-term gain to countries if they joined a global growth compact, but now both the developed and the developing countries could lose if overall levels of growth do not rise fast enough.

In the 1930s politicians failed to talk with each other about potential solutions, and there was no international institution pressing realistic programs of action. But at my request and that of other leaders, the IMF prepared its first global growth report to the Toronto G20. This identified not only a huge gap between the potential of the world economy and its actual condition today, but as we had requested, it also suggested a way of agreeing on coordinated action to deal with it. The IMF states that the difference between "good" and "bad" global coordination is of the order of $4 trillion by 2014, or a 5.75 percent higher global GDP. If they had said this would make a difference of a million or two jobs, or take a million or two people out of poverty, then it would still have been worthwhile. But this is translated into a breathtaking difference of *50 million* jobs worldwide and helping *90 million* people out of poverty.[5] Under this scenario we not only create new sources of consumer demand to replace that which has been lost during the American and European recessions, but we also advance the objective "to make poverty history" by meeting the moral imperative of removing unnecessary suffering.

Like the IMF, I believe that working through shared policies we can—and must—come to a win-win global prospectus for growth. We should not underestimate the $20 trillion contribution to growth that American and European consumer spending represented in the previous decade, nor how difficult it will be to replace its lost growth.

If consumption in America and Europe were able to grow at rates similar to pre-crisis levels through to 2015, this alone would add over $3 trillion to world output even after inflation. But at best we can expect consumption to grow by $1 trillion less than that, possibly by $2 trillion less if, as many expect, American consumption falls further, from 70 percent to 65 percent of GDP.

The other major trend of the past twenty years is how emerging economies have challenged the West in manufacturing.[6] For the four decades following the 1940s the United States, with Japan and Europe, monopolized manufacturing. Today the United States remains the largest producer, but China's output has risen above $1 trillion and is now more than the output of Britain, France, and Italy combined. The shift has not simply been in heavy industry but in high value added products, too.[7]

As a result of this plentiful supply of cheap imports, American families have been buying their cars, fridges, computers, and clothes at around $1,000 a year less than they might otherwise pay. Similarly, across Europe, as computers and electronic goods have crashed in price over ten years, the luxury goods of 2000 have become commonplace purchases in 2010. However, even at these low manufacturing prices, ordinary American and European families whose incomes have stalled have borrowed to pay for their higher consumption and for the increasing number of homes they have been buying.

The result is that we have not only trade imbalances (Asia exporting much more than Europe and America) but also imbalances in the ownership of debt (Asia saving while Europe and America borrow to spend). In addition, these shifts in manufacturing production have also seen the developed countries lose millions of jobs to Asia,[8] where even today Chinese wages are one-twentieth of U.S. wages. So while Western consumers have benefited from lower prices for manufactured goods and services, Western workers have found their jobs to be far more insecure.

In short, Asian workers increasingly produce more and more of the goods, and soon perhaps also more and more of the services of the world, while their American and European counterparts are consuming almost forty times more.[9] Even if we added the BRICs (Brazil, Russia, India, and China) and the N-11, the fastest growing of the other emerging economies, their total consumer spending—the spending of five billion people—represents just a third of the spending of Europe and America.

As I will show in the analysis of China, India, and Africa that follows, this is not a historical accident or some inexplicable political peculiarity, but a long-term problem of low consumption rooted in widespread poverty. Put simply, those condemned to live in extreme poverty will work, but not buy.

So the challenge for the world economy is also structural. A return to an American and European pre-crisis growth rate is difficult if their consumer spending is to fall; therefore a return to the high levels of global demand is impossible without a global growth plan. So here are the questions I hope to answer in the coming chapters:

- If we are to reduce unemployment in the West and poverty in the East and developing countries, what part can America now play by raising its level of growth? What role can policy reform in Europe, now weighed down by sovereign debt crises, play? How much bigger a contribution can China now make to a balanced world economy? Can India, about to see an explosion in its workforce, make a bigger impact not just for itself but by ensuring that global growth is balanced? Can the BRIC countries with the developing N-11 countries make a bigger than expected contribution to global aggregate demand?
- If none of these countries nor these continents on their own can make a big enough contribution, can the benefits of cooperative action yield results that raise levels of employment and growth? Can the world work together without blaming each other for what's wrong?

Of course any assessment of what to do next for the world economy depends very much on how that economy is viewed. Where some see recovery as the major objective, others see deficit reduction as the dominant concern, even if it means constraints on current growth and rising unemployment. Some worry that inflation might rise again too quickly, others that it will fall too fast. Where some believe that China, India, and Asia can power the global economy, others see the biggest threat to world growth in the current crises in Europe. Low interest rates, to some, are essential for growth, while others see low interest rates as carrying the threat of new financial asset bubbles.

So there is a battle of ideas now raging between those who argue that the world should end the fiscal stimulus now and immediately usher in a tough fiscal consolidation program, and those who believe that to end such support immediately would threaten recovery with the risk, at least in some key countries, of a double-dip recession.[10]

The debate also reflects an age-old battle: between those who say that the role of government is to keep deficits and inflation low and leave the rest, including the fate of the unemployed, to market forces,[11] and those who, like me, say that there are times when we need government to underpin and support the economy because the maintenance of employment and living standards is a moral imperative.

This debate transcends traditional views about national economic policies and the respective role of individuals, markets, and state. Here there is a far wider divergence of views about the future of the global economy: between those who say that it is now up to individual nations to get on with it and do their best, and those who, like me, say that just as we needed global action to prevent the collapse of the financial system, so we need now—probably more than ever—a global strategy to deal with the combination of low world growth and high global unemployment that lies at the heart of the continuing crisis.

In my view there is a more fundamental set of shared global decisions we can make together: decisions that go far beyond the necessary individual national plans to tackle high national levels of unemployment and high national deficits. Cutting national deficits is one part of the picture, but not the whole picture.

National plans for growth must include measures to tackle unemployment, yet even that is only a symptom of a bigger problem. In the coming chapters I explore the case for far bolder action than can be achieved by simply updating national growth targets and tightening national fiscal reduction plans. I do so because the blunt truth is that the high unemployment and high deficits that America and Europe now face cannot be solved without a higher level of global demand for goods and service, without a higher level of "aggregate demand."[12]

Each year that this lower level of aggregate demand continues unaddressed, we are taking the equivalent of a Britain, a France, or an Italy out of the world's overall output. It is as if the recession had already wiped one of these great countries from our global economic map, eliminating any contribution it might make to world output. And now, instead of doing something about it, we are prepared to live with it for years.

In the 1970s politicians retreated from talking the language of aggregate demand, not because it was ever a bad thing to seek, but out of the fear of rising inflation. Every time we emerged from recession, inflation threatened to return too quickly. So, rightly, we had first to ensure that inflation remained low.

In 2010, however, the industrialized world has low inflation, with even the threat of deflation. This makes it possible to take action to raise aggregate demand quickly, ensuring that unemployment comes down too. It is possible for every region to contribute to growth and employment in all regions, but only if the right decisions are made, based on the correct analysis of the unique role each can play.

The task of America at this crucial juncture is different from Europe's, which is different in turn from China's or India's or Africa's. We are each called to something different, and something better. Precisely what that is will be the subject of the coming chapters.

CHAPTER 6

The American Challenge

The American dream is one of the most powerful and enduring stories of hope that continues to inspire the world. The idea that if you work hard there is no limit to the life you can build for yourself and your children has motivated millions in every part of the world and is one of the reasons I called America in my speech to the Joint Houses of Congress "not only the indispensable nation, but the irrepressible nation."

Even today Americans are still the world's most aspirational people. In 1900 only one in five of the American workforce was in a white-collar occupation; today that figure is three in five, and America is the economic giant with the largest middle class. For my whole life America has been and is still now the foremost manufacturing country of the world,[1] and American workers take justified pride in the products, services, and inventions they deliver to the global market.

Yet despite all these considerable achievements, the two-centuries-old American dream is under new and unique pressures, with consequences not just for America but for the world. The manifestations of this are high unemployment, falling middle-class incomes, and concern about educational opportunities and upward mobility amid rising competitive pressures from Asia. The primary cause of these concerns arises, as I will seek to argue, from there being too

143

much inequality of opportunity and income in America. Because of it the American middle-class citizen, as consumer, does not now have the money to be as big a driver of future world economic growth as he or she has in the past.Nor does the American citizen, as producer, yet have what is possible: all the most modern skills supported by the educational investment to lead, as a more skilled America surely will, the next stage of world growth.

The American recession has been both deep and long; from a peak in 2007 to the lowest point before the London G20 conference, the loss of output exceeded 4 percent, making the 2008–9 recession the deepest since official quarterly data began to be gathered in 1947. To offset the decline in consumption and lending capacity, the U.S. government and U.S. Federal Reserve have committed a total of nearly $14 trillion, including loans and guarantees for businesses. As has been noted by many, the Fed has gone from being the "lender of last resort" to the "lender of only resort" for a significant portion of the economy. In some cases the Fed can now be considered the "buyer of last resort."

But, despite the huge injection of funds by the Obama administration to get the economy moving (and the saving of millions of jobs as a result), joblessness, on almost all tests we use,[2] is at its worst since the Second World War. At a minimum, America now needs to create 12 million jobs to achieve anything close to a return to full employment.

Estimates vary about how big the underlying demand gap is likely to be. President Obama said in January 2010, "Our economy could fall $1 trillion short of its full capacity." But now, as a result of the recent statement of the Congressional Budget Office that "economic output over the next two years will average 6.8 percent below its potential," a $2 trillion gap over two years has been confirmed.

In 2010, of course, as wages fell and long-term unemployment remained at a record high, economic growth has been underpinned by the restocking of inventories—about 76 percent of last year's increase—and by $400 billion of additional government spending. Before the crisis, the U.S. government spent only 35.5 percent of national income; now in 2010 it is 44 percent. That fiscal stimulus includes help for the jobless, housing support, and the measures of the American Recovery and Reinvestment Act. But to replace the lost production of $2.1 trillion, the fiscal stimulus offered only a $775 billion plan, far less than half of what is needed over the next two years. Any rebound out of recession would have to be five times what it is at present to return discretionary spending back to previously normal levels.

Usually the U.S. economy soars out of recession, but even after falling faster and farther than in any recession since 1945, the bounce-back of American growth is far slower than that from previous crises—just half the 6 percent to 9 percent growth of the upturns in the 1970s and 1980s. It is simply not yet high enough to get unemployment down fast.[3] Unless exports improve remarkably, the shift from debt and consumption to savings will simply leave America with too much unemployment.

America's international economic future depends on high productivity in knowledge-intensive global industries such as medical devices, pharmaceuticals, software, and engineering, as well as creative services like film, architecture, and advertising, all of which are potentially massive exports. There are good reasons to be hopeful; for example, more than 2,500 of Boeing's 3,350-jet order book is for export, and already Intel's new generation of cheaper, smaller, and more efficient chips offers record profit margins. And American high-tech exports are already rising, especially to the Asian market.

Behind the headlines of falling jobs there is rising wealth, for even with the manufacturing of computer products shifting to Asia, most of the value added and therefore the wealth is created in America. The export value of the iPod was $150 in 2006, but Chinese producers, who simply assemble it, "earned" only around $4. Meanwhile most of the high-value work of producing new designs, software, and marketing techniques has stayed firmly Stateside.

Profits that plummeted in the recession have bounced back, not least thanks to overseas operations, and companies have recovered almost 90 percent of what they lost. But the problem is that they are not investing enough in America's future.[4] The latest evidence is that, far from the much sought-after return to investment, companies are holding back on investment for fear of a further downturn, with some estimates suggesting they are hoarding as much as $1.5 trillion. The five hundred largest nonfinancial firms held almost $1 trillion in the second quarter of 2010, and that money pile will grow larger. So companies are investing less, and hoarding their profits. There is no sign yet that in real-value terms American investment will be higher in 2015 than before the start of the recession.

At the heart of the American dream was the promise of high employment and high living standards for both manufacturing and professional workers. For half a century the real value of American incomes was on a trend to double each generation. For the twenty-five years after 1950, household net worth grew 8 percent a year in cash terms, allowing America to lead the world in car ownership, consumer goods, and home building.

But since the 1970s the gains have not been evenly shared. In the years since the oil crisis of 1973, while the incomes of the top 1 percent have tripled, the incomes of the bottom 90 percent of American families have risen by an average of only 0.2 percent a year.[5] Beginning in the year 2000 income distribution, already sharply unequal, got even more skewed; according to the economists Thomas Piketty and Emmanuel Saez, from 2002 to 2007 two-thirds of all income increases in the U.S. went to the wealthiest 1 percent of all Americans.[6]

It was a sign of American success that by 2009 the number of millionaires had risen to 7.8 million, but as Federal Reserve Chairman Ben Bernanke noted in a speech just before the crisis, "The share of income received by households in the top fifth of the income distribution, after taxes have been paid and government transfers have been received, rose from 42% in 1979 to

50% in 2004, while the share of income received by those in the bottom fifth of the distribution declined from 7% to 5%."[7]

So the middle 60 percent saw their share fall from 51 percent to 45 percent. There are many reasons given for the stalling of middle-class incomes: the loss of skilled manufacturing jobs, the fact that 40 percent of the employed are in low-wage service jobs, low trade union membership, the escalating costs of health care keeping wages low, and so on. We should remember also that for much of this period stagnation in wages could be disguised because lower-priced consumer goods, from cars to computers, made wages go farther. But the fact is that between 1999 and 2010, the real increase in household income was only half a percent on an annual basis.

Looking at this evidence of stagnating wages, one is forced to ask, why was there a consumer boom? One explanation is that what fueled consumer spending was not wages but borrowing. From 1990 to 2007 consumer debt rose from around 80 percent of disposable income to around 130 percent. It's a point that Professor Raghuram Rajan argues in his recent book in a powerful analysis of what he calls "fault lines" in the economy. In the United States the share of the top 1 percent of wealthy Americans reached 23.5 percent of total income by 2007, almost tripling from about 9 percent in 1976.

But as borrowing is cut back, American consumer spending, which was for a whole generation the greatest driver of world growth, has fallen sharply, from 76 percent of a once larger American economy at its peak, to 73 percent of a smaller economy. It is on its way to 70 percent; even after inflation this represents more than $1 trillion less growth.[8]

The hardships arising from such numbers are all too real. In 2006–7 there were 11.7 million families receiving food stamps; today that has risen to 18.9 million households, a rise of some 62 percent. Meanwhile the number of the unemployed has doubled, from 7.5 million to 15.4 million, an official unemployment rate just below 10 percent. Probably nearer 15 percent of Americans are either unemployed or underemployed, with five unemployed workers chasing every job being offered. The October 8, 2010 employment figures state alarmingly that 26 percent of teenagers are without jobs. At issue are not just the individual lives that are wasted, but the cost of unemployment to everybody; if people are unemployed, they can't buy goods, and that puts yet more jobs at risk. A similar argument has been made by Ken Rogoff in what he calls the catch-22 of the recovery; businesses will start hiring when the economy recovers, and the economy will start to recover when businesses start hiring.

But there is something about this recession that makes it also a turning point. Robert Samuelson writes, "[This] has been the most egalitarian of all the 11 recessions since World War II. In various ways, it has touched every social class through job loss, pay cuts, depressed home values, shrunken stock portfolios, eroded retirement savings, grown children returning home—and anxiety about all of the above. The Great Recession (as it is widely called) has changed America psychologically, politically, economically, and socially." With few exceptions, everyone is consuming less, not least wealthier people who have lost more from the fall in shares and home prices.[9]

The economic cycle from 2002, the start of the last expansion, to pre-crisis 2007 was the first when the majority of Americans were financially worse off at the end of a cycle than at the start. If the American dream is that each decade will be better than the one before and each generation's children will do better than the last, then a slowdown in mobility is a heavy blow, and one with consequences far beyond American shores.

For me the key questions, therefore, are as follows: Can the stagnation of ordinary incomes and the growing inequalities in America, which contributed to it, be addressed without another expansion of borrowing? With educated workers and therefore upward social mobility today an essential driver of economic growth, can Americans agree that they need not only an economic policy but a focus on education and an industrial policy, too? Can America recover and resume its economic leadership by making its economic engine not only for domestic consumption but for overseas exports—not least to China—and can part of this be achieved in a new way, by sponsoring the most innovative environmental technologies and products? Is there more America can do to spur economic development first through monetary policy, then through investment, then through measures on employment, then measures for fairness, and then on trade?

To begin, a plan for growth must first take into account Federal Reserve Board anxieties about deflation. One member has warned of "the possibility that the U.S. economy may become enmeshed in a Japanese-style, deflationary outcome within the next several years." Along with Chairman Bernanke, he has emphasized that "the U.S. quantitative easing program offers the best tool to avoid such an outcome. . . . We are not without the weapons that can deal with this challenge."

The second element of a higher growth strategy is what the writer David Brooks calls the "Moon Shot Approach," a 2010 equivalent of the type of world-leading investment America made, amid worries about growth, to put a man on the moon. The modern equivalent would be an infrastructure program to make the overall economy more competitive and a program of incentives focused on key sectors, such as clean energy. "With plenty of slack in the economy and interest rates at historic lows," another brilliant writer, Steven Pearlstein of the *Washington Post*, states, "this is the ideal time to borrow and invest heavily in public infrastructure that has been badly neglected over the past 30 years . . . not only to roads and bridges but also to airports and air traffic control systems, urban transit, high-speed rail, schools and university facilities, national laboratories, national parks, smart electric grids, broadband networks, green generating plants, and health information networks."

This forward-looking approach is best defined not as deficit spending fueling consumption but as investment for the future with fiscal consolidation achieved in a way that supports jobs and growth.

As Joe Stiglitz concludes in his book *Freefall,* "Public investments or joint public-private investments that yielded even moderate real returns (say, of 5 to 6%) would increase activity, cut unemployment, generate more tax returns and mean lower long-term debt."

Of course the key element of recovery we are seeking is private sector revival, but if there is no serious inflationary danger, if governments find it relatively straightforward to fund their debt, if there is no surge in demand for credit that the public sector might crowd out, and if, as I suggest, the crisis in the global economy is structural and not merely cyclical, then the logic is that the U.S. government should invest now, as President Obama has signaled he wishes to do, in technology and education.[10]

I said at the beginning of this chapter that any study of America should begin with America's achievements and the American dream. I believe that any such chapter should also conclude in the same vein. In the past, American social mobility depended on manufacturing success. Today it depends on knowledge and education. To spread the American dream of generation-to-generation prosperity beyond the top 1 to 2 percent, America will want to take measures to widen equality of opportunity and ensure a fair deal for the middle class. Education is the key to meeting that challenge. In particular, America must invest more than the minuscule 0.17 percent of national income spent on active labor-market policies, such as training.

But the advance of the American dream—high employment, high living standards, and good prospects transferred from generation to generation—is also dependent upon a world that continues to grow. We have already seen that America cannot replace the lost growth on its own, at least in the immediate future, so in the following chapter I will turn to the next logical question: Can the greatest new source of industrial power, Asia, become what America has been for decades—the primary driver of the world's growth and the main source of new jobs in Asia, America, and elsewhere?

CHAPTER 7

China's Opportunity

I first understood the scale of China's transformation when I visited a computer factory in Guangdong Province while I was still Chancellor of the Exchequer.

It seemed as though there was no end to the factory: I saw thousands upon thousands of workers producing the computers that in only a dozen years had made China the largest computer manufacturer in the world, producing half the world's total.

In China today there are now more than 100 million men and women employed in a massive manufacturing machine that services the world.

China is number one in the world for its high rate of growth, and it is no longer inward-looking: it is now a leading investor in Africa, Latin America, and the industrialized world. No business anywhere is immune from the impact of China's estimated 1.3 billion people.

The best forecast is that China will be the biggest economy in the world by 2024, with a rate of growth possibly three times that of America between now and then. In the past two years China has been revealed not only as the world's second biggest economy but also its foremost financier. It is the biggest buyer of the world's commodities, responsible for around 40 percent of all copper, nickel, and aluminum purchases, and the holder of the world's biggest reserves. In the past two years alone, China's reserves, built up to avoid the fallout from a potential second Asian crash, have risen by almost $1 trillion. China and Hong Kong now hold 27 percent ($3 trillion) of the world's reserves, compared with 19 percent only a year ago. It is said to be enough to buy most of the NASDAQ-quoted companies on the U.S. stock exchange.

But China is not just a low-cost manufacturer. With its annual overseas investment now around $50 billion, twice the level of 2008–9, China is a big owner of manufacturing plants outside the country and is one of the world's biggest long-term foreign investors.

If China offered no more than low wages, we would already be seeing the next stage of a shift to even cheaper countries.[1] But China is moving forward, not just with cheap labor and cheap products, but with a young and increasingly well-educated workforce, and with their investments in new infrastructure, science education, and research.[2]

All this is making China an integral part of the global supply chain. Company by company, China is making an impact on the world stage.[3] And this is not a one-time event that will pass by as other countries play catch-up. The rest of the world cannot ignore the fact that China's one-sixth share of world manufacturing means that in many of the areas where it competes—most obviously the final assembly of parts or materials from elsewhere—it can lead, with world-beating companies locating innovation and development centers across Asia as well. Likewise, we should expect that it intends to avoid the mistakes of the Asian tigers in moving from booming to uncompetitive within a decade.[4]

It is clear that China will be cautious. But according to the latest work by Jim O'Neill at Goldman Sachs, China's consumer growth in 2010 is surpassing, not disappointing, expectations—adding $300 billion of extra consumption a year. If the ratio of retail sales to industrial production continues to rise (the latest figure for 2010 is 18 percent retail sales growth), the growth in consumer spending will be $500 billion a year—a great sign, O'Neill argues, "for the world and for life without the U.S. consumer." And these retail sales are not all domestically produced consumer goods: according to O'Neill's research, overall imports in 2010 have increased by $400 billion, close to their previous peak rise of $500 billion a year ago. Credit Suisse's 2010 Global Wealth Report sees Chinese household wealth doubling to $35 trillion by 2015, elevating China's new middle class to become the leading driver of world growth.

Former Premier Deng Xiaoping compared China's progress to crossing a river groping for the stones, but China's advance has occurred at a consistently faster pace than Europe's or America's Industrial Revolution. But while China's investment *is* rising fast at home and abroad, can China's consumers really now lead the next stage of global economic development? Can we look for a shift to higher levels of household consumption with a more rapid expansion of the middle class? Or is China's focus on an investment-led economy a barrier to the growth of consumer demand and leading us toward further economic imbalances? The structural issue that underlies these questions is perhaps not so much "How do we boost consumers' willingness to spend?" but rather "How does one redeploy the way capital is allocated in the Chinese economy so that consumption is maximized?"

Whichever way we define the details of the questions, there are two polar-opposite views on China among the analysts: the first that China is on a path where a rising consumer economy will contribute to sustained global growth, the second that China's industrial promotion strategy will derail any attempt to plan sustained global growth in the immediate future. In this debate lies the answer to the more fundamental question—of whether we can build a global system of enhanced economic cooperation or whether, after a boost in international cooperation during the financial crisis, we will descend back into the protectionism of the past.

I have left no doubt as to where I stand. I have seen the rapid expansion of the consumer market, with well-known European and American companies adapting their practices to China. (In China, for example it is not DIY but BIY: buy it yourself and have a low-paid tradesman do the work.) China's growing prosperity—its rising middle class, the millions taken out of poverty, the as yet suppressed consumer demand—means that it has the potential to make possible a faster growing but also more balanced world economy. But my argument is that until China is able to do even more to reduce poverty and expand its middle class, it will not be able, on its own, to replace the lost consumption of America.

Total consumer spending by more than a billion Chinese people is today less than $2 trillion a year, only a fraction—less than 20 percent—of the spending of just 300 million U.S. citizens. China accounts for only 3 percent of world imports of consumer goods, and even now only 4 percent of world import growth.

A rise in the share of consumption by 5 percent of a fast-growing Chinese economy would be worth an additional $300 billion every year of extra consumer spending, making a big contribution to world growth with potential benefits for all continents and helping the world economy return to full employment.[5] But as I said in my summer 2009 letter to President Obama, even if China were to double its consumer spending in one year, it would not be sufficient to replace lost American and European growth.

In the past three decades 400 million Chinese people have escaped extreme poverty and millions have joined the middle classes. But while there is an elite with huge spending power to buy foreign goods, being a middle-income Chinese earner can deliver an income of just $10 a day, and sometimes little more than $2, hardly the immediate platform for a major rise in consumer spending, and in particular in consumer imports.[6]

This comes to the nub of the problem: Chinese workers will

be producing more of the world's goods than anyone else,[7] but they are among the world's poorest consumers. Recently the *Asia Times* reported that China's average per capita monthly income is 2,000 yuan, just $250. Of course China now has many millionaires, and indeed billionaires,[8] but the real contribution to global demand will come when literally millions of the world's new producers become its new consumers too. Chinese labor costs did treble in the decade after 1995, but output per worker rose 500 percent and productivity likewise, so unit labor costs fell, as did the share of wages in national income.[9]

China has struck a unique internal balance between the priorities it places on securing exports and its domestic consumption.[10] By committing huge resources to investment in its industries, China has been unable to substantially expand the income of its citizens. In China exports account for 60 percent of the economy; in the United States domestic consumption accounts for 70 percent of the economy. Even in Russia, India, and Brazil consumer spending is between 50 percent and 60 percent of national income. In fact, *The Economist* has argued that 5 percent, and perhaps even up to 10 percent of China's national output is transferred annually from household savers to banks and net borrowers simply through the interest rate mechanism.

There are, however, some changes that should make us optimistic. For the past twenty years around 150 million migrant workers moving between the country and the factories provided low-wage workers, but there is now no doubt that China's labor policy is entering a new phase. When I first visited China I saw just how dependent industrialization still was on a hostel workforce, especially women and girls: factory workers coming from the country, working long hours, staying in factory accommodation, returning home one month a year, and saving money to then return home for good.

But now more workers are asking to settle where the work is and rightly expect higher wages to cope with food prices and rising property prices.[11] This is much in line anyway with the needs of the Chinese economy for higher skills and the growing requirement to pay for them.

Chinese wages will rise, giving workers more consumer spending power. It is significant too that the Chinese government is now encouraging higher local minimum wages. Today, after wage freezes during the financial crisis, a catch-up in employees' incomes is now under way. By the end of 2010, after a wave of strikes, earnings for many factory employees will double to around $300 a month—not just in Shanghai and Beijing, but in southern Guangdong too, where Honda workers are already paid $280 a month.[12]

Some say that China will inevitably face the Japanese and Korean problem of wages rising too fast, as at the same time labor becomes more scarce and higher skills are needed. However, I believe the sheer scale of China makes China's likely development different. China's vast pool of labor allows China to switch production in its coastal areas to the more sophisticated custom-built goods while moving shoes, clothes, textiles, and mass-manufactured computers inland, where labor costs are much cheaper.

Low Chinese consumer spending is not simply because Chinese wages are a small share of the economy; it is also that Chinese households save far more of what they earn than workers in other countries. A number of factors may have converged to intensify this well-known instinct to save, including poorer safety nets, like the withdrawal of the subsidized "rice bowl," and greater precautionary savings for the rising costs of health care and old age.[13] The instinct to save, and its interaction with what were in any event relatively low wages, has ensured that consumer spending has not kept pace with overall growth.

There is, however, a huge but for the most part unrealized potential for the Chinese consumer to be a massive new driver of global demand. Unleashing this pent-up force will require some brave decisions by Chinese policymakers.

Despite all the history of China's adherence to a strategy for investment-led and export-led growth, we must offer to support China in implementing their own professed policy of "a structural shift" toward domestic consumption and a sustainable end to poverty.

President Hu Jintao came into office in 2002 with the ambitious goal of attacking wealth inequality, equalizing economic growth between the rural interior and coastal cities, and lifting his people out of poverty. We are about to see the implementation of a new medium-term plan targeted on stimulating consumption. Chinese officials stated to the IMF that they are taking other measures that amount to a "structural break" with the past. If they succeed, it could reduce the current account surplus to about 4 percent of GDP and make consumer spending the fastest growing of any country by rising, on average, by more than 8 percent or even more per year.[14] The Chinese government does not usually publish figures that it does not plan to reach.

I believe that in the coming year America and Europe can serve that cause best and achieve the same results not by focusing so much on opposing China for "manipulating" its currency, but on supporting China in its objective of taking millions of its people out of poverty. In doing so we should encourage them to tackle poverty by building up their safety nets for their workers and, in expanding consumer spending, trading more with the rest of the world.

If we continue on the current path, although China will be the biggest contributor to world growth, it will not solve the immediate problem of low global aggregate demand on its own. The benefit of opening up Chinese trade is not simply that it puts more power in the hands of the Chinese consumer. The official IMF view is that if countries like China do not replace lost U.S. and European spending power by boosting domestic demand, "the unwinding of the global imbalances could reverse quite quickly."

Below I offer just three suggestions that could, in my view, make a real and instant difference to the economy of China and therefore of the world. Each of my suggestions draws upon Premier Wen's recent statement that the Chinese economy lacks "balance, coordination, and sustainability."

First, there is more scope for Chinese consumption to rise through redistribution. Today social insurance is costly for the Chinese worker (by some estimates up to 40 percent of base wages) and regressive. A lower level of contributions would boost household disposable income overnight, lessen inequality, and foster job growth. Further increases in transfers to lower-income groups and the unemployed would have the same impact.

Second, at this stage of China's development, its investment should be of such a high level of efficiency and quality that it can afford to release resources for consumption. There is little doubt that measures must be taken to counteract China's lack of willingness to spend, but it is equally important to redeploy the way capital is allocated in the Chinese economy so that consumption can rise: reforming banks' lending practices, reassessing the capacity of state-owned enterprises to retain earnings, addressing other practices that channel support to state-owned enterprises rather than China's more efficient private sector, and thus ensuring better and less risky lending and minimizing the danger of financial instability.

The large budgets for infrastructure spending might also be refocused on housing. A recent survey by the Chinese Academy of Social Sciences found that 85 percent of urban families could not afford an apartment. In the worst case, Beijing, one square meter alone costs more than the typical Beijing annual wage. It is not shortage driving prices (the net new number of housing units provided since 1999 was at least as large as the net increase in the number of households), but land prices, which have risen 800 percent since 2003. A sales tax on speculators and a crackdown on foreign capital coming into the property market have made little difference. But if the government, as planned, built more low-cost housing, Chinese consumer spending would expand.

The expanding investment in infrastructure should now do more to cover health and education as well as housing. Few outside China know that China already has nearly universal coverage of health insurance in urban areas and significantly expanded coverage for rural residents. By implementing decisions already made, health spending will account for an extra $100 billion—2 percent of Chinese GDP. But China could do more: offer universal coverage, free drugs, and free services to patients. According to a recent IMF report, a 1 percent of GDP increase in spending shared equally between education, health, and pension spending, financed by reducing the surpluses earned by government and state enterprises, would increase household consumption by 1.2 percent of national income.[15]

Two-way trade between China and the rest of the world needs to be expanded to the benefit of both.[16] When responding to businesses that openly criticized what they call "Chinese protectionism"—import and inward investment regulation and the lack of protection of intellectual rights—Chinese Commerce Minister Chen Deming promised that China would "open wider in the future." One step is creating a single market in Asia similar to that in Europe and North America. Together China, South Korea, and Japan—70 percent of the Asian economy and just under 20 percent of the global economy—can look ahead to a market that would include 3 billion people.[17]

But China should open up its financial services market to the whole world so that insurance, financial products, and banking services can be sold across China and help Chinese consumers make their money go farther. Giving non-Chinese companies the chance to compete in a fast-expanding area means that imbalances can be unwound through the expansion of a new sector without making larger numbers of Chinese workers unemployed. A report from the consulting company McKinsey claims that China's GDP would be increased by $321 billion annually if it made the right set of reforms in its financial sector.

*   *   *

Of course imbalances are greater because of the value of the renminbi, the Chinese currency.[18] Paul Krugman, the winner of the 2008 Nobel economics prize, argues that victims of what he calls Chinese mercantilism may be right to take protectionist action. He wrote recently in the *New York Times* that by holding down its currency to support exports, China "drains much-needed demand away from a depressed world economy."

However, I think I have shown that there are structural reasons within China for its consumption to be low at this time and for investment to be high. Having said that, I also believe that the Chinese exporting sector is now strong enough to allow a further opening up of its economy.

The reserves China has built up are essentially a response to the mistakes made by the IMF during the Asian crisis. They are both understandable as a policy response and a reaction to a breakdown in trust that is more fundamental still. The international priority is thus a form of global insurance, a global safety net that allows countries to run lower reserves while being protected from capital crises. The long-term and overarching issue is not so much to help China change its policy on its currency as to help China change its policy on investment and consumption.

I am confident that Chinese growth can be a major factor in world economic growth over the next ten years. This will, as I have said, offer the exit from low growth that the world needs. But the repositioning of China as a global consumer, buying more and more goods and services from other countries, is going to take years of gradually raising wages, improving the safety net, expanding the middle class, and raising the value of its currency. China will not, therefore, replace the United States as the "global consumer" in the short run.

However, its growth could do more to encourage the growth of others. I have suggested how China can move the process of raising consumption faster to the benefit of its rising middle class, its antipoverty program, and its contribution to the world economy.

The recommendations I have made will be challenging for the Chinese government. They are not, however, impossible. I believe they represent the best chance to both end poverty in China and contribute to a return to high growth for the world. That is China's opportunity. As we shall explore in the next chapter, it could be Asia's too.

CHAPTER 8

India and the Asian Economies

When I traveled to India as Chancellor and then as Prime Minister I had in the back of my mind the poetry contained in Amitabh Bachchan's descriptions of the New India. He talked of a "new India whose faith in success is far greater than fear of failure," a new India "that no longer boycotts foreign companies' goods but buys up the companies instead," a new India "looking up at the sky and saying it's time to fly."

There is no country in the world that has the potential for growth that India now has over the coming decade. India will see its workforce rise by more than 100 million men and women. There will be a rising number of what some people call the Indian baby boomers: young men and women in their thirties and forties who will comprise half the increase in the working population. A rising number of women will join the workforce (current women's participation in employment is still among the lowest in Asia, at 33 percent, in contrast to China, at 70 percent). And there will be a fast-rising number who leave the land to become city dwellers.

Start in Delhi, with the scale of the University of Delhi and its 400,000 students, and then think of the ambitions for Indian education: a twenty-year plan for one thousand more universities.

Go to Bangalore, as I was fortunate enough to do, and you will see why some are predicting that India, and not China, will become the world's fastest-growing economy. Companies based there looked less like factories than campuses where the engineers and computer scientists of the future are developing their skills. The Infosys campus training center (where fifty thousand young people are trained every year) is itself like a modern American city, with its lecture theaters, café culture, and cinemas. The company states that in 2007, when they took on forty thousand new recruits, over 1.25 million young people applied to join the company; it has increased its workforce from 10,000 in 2000 to over 100,000 today. My abiding memory of India is of highly ambitious young people studying day and night and all weekend to make the most of their talents.

India now has trend growth estimated to be 8.5 percent a year. Five years from now its economy will be half as big again. By 2020 it will have doubled in size.

One measure of the scale of India's fast-developing domestic market is its 600 million mobile phone subscribers. A further measure of the speed of change is car ownership, which will rise fivefold in ten years from today, from 14 million to 62 million. Crucially, as Goldman Sachs suggests, the Indian middle class, 1 percent of the population in 2000 and just 5 percent today, could rise to 50 percent in just thirty years.

But India has more poor people than any country in the world. Indian per capita incomes are half that of China, and on the best recent estimates of poverty, 400 million people live on less than $2 a day.

So if China, with a rapidly rising middle class and falling poverty, cannot on its own yet make the difference in generating the demand to fill the global growth gap, is it really possible that India alone or India and China together can do so? My task is to assess what part India can play in future global growth, and so I will concentrate on what changes in Indian economic policy could benefit the world and what changes in the world's economic policies could benefit India.

The conventional focus is on India's success as a low-cost but high-quality and large-quantity exporter of IT and back-office services (although it has yet to develop its own global consumer brands). I start with a broader perspective on India: that it is a country of huge untapped potential that can become globally competitive and successful in a far wider range of industries and services, become more open to trade, and play an even bigger role in the global supply chain.

Already sixty-three of the top Fortune 500 companies of the world have research and development centers in India. Already Bangalore hosts the GE Healthcare R&D Centre and the headquarters of Cisco East. My view is that an India that embraced reform should be able both to reduce poverty and expand its wealth more quickly at the center of a global growth plan. However, we have to recognize how far India still has to travel; even India's booming IT and finance sectors are still a fraction of the economy.

With 20 percent of the world's population, India still accounts for only 1.5 percent of global trade in services, 1 percent of global trade in goods, and more than half of India's workers are still on the land.

The total consumer spending of India's billion people is just 1 percent of the world economy.[1] Foreign direct investment, which was $100 billion in China last year, was just $20 billion in India.

Unlike the economies of China and Southeast Asia, the Indian economy's growth is already driven less by exports than by domestic demand. So India's future growth does not depend on a big shift of resources from exports to consumption. In contrast to China, India has a large and growing private sector that caters mostly to domestic Indian markets.

Today the faster China and America grow, the more unbalanced the world economy becomes. But today and tomorrow the faster a reforming India grows, the more balanced the world economy can be. So a reforming India should be at the center of a global growth plan. It is not just in India's interests but in all our interests to make sure India is right at the center of global economic decision making.

Reform is important because critical to India's future is the quality of its growth and whether it can reduce its own widespread poverty. This will be best achieved by greater openness to trade and by improving its infrastructure. India has to expand the quality of its education and skills and must be allowed to do so while managing its debt and deficits. So our task, as a global community, is to work with India to open up more areas of trade, to educate more people and to a higher standard, and to tackle the problem its government wants to address most: the low incomes and thus the low consuming power of its citizens.

But if, as I suggest, the Indian challenge is more one of internal adjustment (to be more open, more educated, more pro-poor), the change in India is still best achieved if it takes place in a period of global growth in which India can sell to the rest of the world while importing what it needs to move its society forward. For global growth we need India, and India needs global growth.

For all their current similarities in growth rates, India's path of economic progress, like its path of political progress, has been different from that of the rest of Asia. Its growth model is quite different from the successive waves of industrialization that we have seen in Japan; in the Asian tigers of Korea, Taiwan, Hong Kong, and Singapore; in China; and in the later developers of Malaysia and Thailand. The development of all of these countries was founded on fast growth in manufacturing output and employment. Income from manufactured exports and a rising trade surplus became the source of new wealth. But manufacturing is just 20 percent of India's economy, and exports form little more than 20 percent of its economic activity, in contrast to China's 60 percent.

If the majority of Indians still work in agriculture, most at a subsistence level, it is not manufacturing but services that account for the lion's share—more than 50 percent—of India's GDP. Much of that service trade is in the informal sector and not part of global trade. India is a magnet for high-tech service sector growth, not just because its unit labor costs are among the lowest in the world (that would be a transient advantage), but because it has a commitment to raising its already improving educational and specialist skills. The high growth that India has already achieved in IT services and outsourcing generally can also be attained through its pools of engineering, legal, and research talent across not just banking, insurance, and commercial services but also in mechanical engineering, pharmaceuticals. and biotechnology.[2]

The explosion of these high value added sectors has seen the emergence of an extra million members of India's middle class during the 1980s and 1990s and is part of India's progress as an economy. Of course this growth changes patterns of spending, but it also champions entrepreneurship, challenges endemic corruption, and generally is conducive to even higher consumer-based growth. So if India were able to fully implement the changes it is committed to—in its openness, its infrastructure, and its education—could we look to it to provide the new global consumer demand that is not yet forthcoming from China?

In the long run, yes. Goldman Sachs's projections suggest that over the next decade and a half, India's consumers will spend three and a half times more than they do today as their higher incomes drive consumption upward. But even after including state subsidies and the incomes of a growing middle class, average annual per capita income is less than $1,000 a year. The prospects for those at the lower end of the income scale remain very bleak indeed; one in two Indian children is malnourished, and the World Bank, which defines poverty as survival on less than $1.25 per day, reports that India still accounts for one-third of the world's 1.4 billion poor people. Researchers at Oxford University claim that more poor people live in eight states of India than in the twenty-six poorest African countries *combined.*

No Prime Minister I know cares more about the poor than Manmohan Singh. I have admired him as a writer and economist for years, and it has been one of the greatest privileges of office to have spent an evening discussing with him, his wife, Gursharan Kaur, and Sonia Gandhi and her son, daughter, and son-in-law what they can do together to achieve their life's work and the defining cause of the Congress Party: to end Indian poverty.

It is to their credit that the Indian government is today embarking on a major reassessment of poverty. While China developed a rural safety net and greater equality in access to land in the late 1970s, India has never had a rural safety net for the poor. Today they are doing the opposite of what politicians normally do: they are trying to change the definition so that *more* people are assessed as living in poverty. Poverty in India today is calculated on costing a basket of goods that includes food, fuel, and clothing. Now it will include the costs of education and health care, which often have to be bought privately.[3]

Under the new laws the poorest Indians will have greater rights to food and to the grain they need for subsistence. The review will probably add 100 million people to the welfare rolls and 15 percent, an additional $1.3 billion a year, to the nation's food-subsidy bill. The total support for food, fuel, fertilizer, and other commodity subsidies will rise to $25 billion a year. Families will receive ration cards, and citizens qualify if they earn less than $10 a month in rural areas or $13 a month in urban. By increasing the numbers in official poverty from 300 million to 400 million—from 27 percent to 37 percent of its people—India will increase its social services and development costs to nearly 20 percent of government spending.

So how much more can India now contribute to world growth? Even with high levels of growth, consumer spending will decline as a share of India's national income as investment rises and people save more for retirement. This, for me, is the nub of the argument about global growth today and in the near future: even if we could achieve an annual 10 percent rise in Indian consumer spending this year and each year after (either through antipoverty measures or higher earnings), such a change would inject no more than an extra $100 billion into the world economy. That amounts to only a fraction of the loss of American and European spending power.

So in the short term, India on its own can make only a small difference to bridging the world's growth gap. But as part of a global plan that it signs on to, India can year by year become an ever more important contributor to more balanced and sustainable world growth.

Our commitment to global growth assisting India should be matched by greater Indian openness to benefit from world growth. We know that for millions in India, reform means agricultural reform. So India must do more to ensure that those who are on the land are given the tools by which agriculture can become more profitable and productivity growth can be achieved. It is anxiety about the fate of rural farm workers that has prevented India's support for a trade deal. With the guarantees that the world is prepared to give on farm imports, India should now be part of the campaign for a global trade deal.

Prime Minister Singh knows that the Indian economy will have to create at least 40 million jobs a year to meet the needs of the rising numbers available for work. One of the first ways to speed this up is to open up to trade. If Indian capital is more dynamic than most other countries, its commitment to private enterprise more robust, its corporate governance more transparent, there are—as Prime Minister Singh himself has said—still real limits to the extent of India's integration into the world economy.

Tariff rates in India are still twice those of China. Antidumping measures in India can be more protectionist. Because of its caution about joining the global economy, China has insured itself by preferring to sell to, rather than buy from, the rest of the world and to build up its reserves so that its financial system will never be overwhelmed by a global crisis. India's way of expressing its caution is to stage the opening up of its economy to foreign trade and capital.

Like China, India has drawn hard lessons from the Asian crisis and now the recent global financial collapse. India has concluded that unrestricted movements of capital are dangerous; that there is no simple, risk-free, fast track to sustained growth by opening up too quickly to capital flows; and that, where possible, Indians must finance growth through their savings. So while Indian access to global capital markets is easier now than in the far more restrictive 1970s and 1980s, the country still puts limits on foreign investment, still prevents companies from listing their shares both at home and on a foreign exchange, and still reins in its domestic banks' overseas investments. Because India's banks are prevented from serving the global needs of India's companies, companies as large as Tata Steel have to raise their own finance for overseas operations outside the country.

India worries not only about its exposure to global capital but also, because of its dependence on foreign commodities (it imports 70 percent of its domestic oil consumption), its supply of commodities. As part of a global growth pact, the world could help India by ensuring that it is less vulnerable to the forces of globalization it worries about most: capital shocks and commodity shocks. India too has accumulated significant stocks of international reserves despite its current account deficits, and if we wish those reserves to be better used for growth, then India would benefit from a set of international safety-net policies.

A global growth pact could also support Indian economic reforms. The basis of India's next stage of expansion will be to build successful global companies that will sell in both domestic and international markets. In 2001 India's global acquisitions were only $1 billion; by 2009 they were worth $60 billion a year. Indian companies like Tata work with American and European companies to build high-technology success stories. But as Indian policymakers agree, the country must improve its investment climate. It can take an entrepreneur thirty days to start a business in India, and international surveys complain that it can take 195 days to obtain various licenses and permits and forty-four days to register a property. Even though India is making progress in reducing red tape, firms tend to hire contract labor, which itself is subject to numerous restrictions.

A growth plan would factor in India's need to spend on infrastructure and education. India cannot meet its own high growth projections if vital infrastructure and industrial projects are slowed down or canceled. It needs $500 billion of infrastructure improvements by 2012; the plan is to build twelve miles of roadway daily. (Today they are building less than half that.) For example, the journey from Delhi to the Taj Mahal, which is one hundred miles and takes seven hours, could be reduced to an hour and a half.

Education is at the heart of the Indian future. The economic message India wants to carry to the world is that it has a rising workforce with ever-improving skills. To build that skilled workforce, and to reduce its rising inequality, India must address the pervasive and endemic inequalities that exist in opportunities for boys and girls. As Nobel Prize winner Amartya Sen has suggested, the India that wants to take its place as a global "knowledge superpower" is also the India of poor primary schools and low literacy (35 percent of all Indians are illiterate). "No modern industrial nation," says Sen, "has less than 80 percent literacy. . . . To make India fully literate and to eliminate the gender bias in literacy therefore must be our immediate priority goals."

India's bigger role in the world economy, starting from a very low base, will clearly be founded on the combined strengths of educated people, modern infrastructure, and open trade. In a pro-growth environment in every continent, India can expect to develop its export industries and services. But to employ its new workforce to best effect it has to do what it wants to do: implement its promise of reform. In return the world can ensure that India reforms in a period of high global growth.

I believe that over time, and if the right decisions are made, China and India can replace the lost consumer demand of America and Europe. But they can't do it on their own, they won't be able to do it for many years, and they will not be able to do it without the reforms in the other major and emerging economies which I address below.

THE WIDER ASIAN ECONOMY

When, in July 2010, the Japanese Ministry of Economy, Trade and Industry published its White Paper on the international economy, it spoke of a global economy "at a turning point"—for one very important reason.

Asia, the Japanese government argued, is not only the world's factory, but is about to take over from America and Europe the title of "the world's major consumer market."

The key to future Asian growth, they conclude, is East Asian economic integration, in particular Japan/China/South Korea cooperation. This is the best chance to demonstrate Japan's strengths and to make a historical shift to "create a favourable new balance of domestic and foreign demand."

Two fundamental policy decisions follow. First, Japan would "raise its status as Asia's high value added base," the best location for non-Asia investment in Asia. Second, with a flow of skilled labor into the rest of Asia and of capital goods such as environmental technologies, Japanese manufacturers should focus on selling to the new Asian middle class.

Where once Japan saw China as its factory, now it sees China as a consumer market. Japanese companies have used EXPO 2010, held in China, as a launching pad for selling into China and Asia new environmental technology, health care, and electronic products with an emphasis on quality goods.

In part, of course, Japan is responding to the likely reductions in the growth rate of American and European consumption. Even in the short term, these markets are extremely unlikely to revert to their pre-crisis levels of Japanese imports.

But the redirection of Japanese export is only one part of the new Japanese strategy. The second part, which requires even more activism from Japan and which is essential for our global growth strategy, is to rebalance its economy away from its dependence on exports to domestic consumption.

Japan is still recovering from its lost decade of falling asset prices, toxic assets, and low growth, while at the same time it has been dealing with the demographic shift to a rising elderly population. And we have learned the lesson that Japan did not learn in time: that even as the economy collapsed, the currency strengthened, interest rate cuts were too long delayed, and quantitative easing came too late, with the result that for twenty years consumer spending has been depressed.

Japan's "new growth strategy" of December 2009 sought to balance its plan for export growth to Asia with its commitment, once again, to raising Japanese consumer spending. For the first time the theme of the growth strategy was not manufacturing and export-led growth, but domestic welfare. New sources of domestic demand that would also promote Asian exports were identified, with a focus on safeguarding the environment, boosting tourism, improving health care, and strengthening technology. One idea is that an aging population around the world will need new services and so Japan should focus on advanced technologies in areas such as medical care.

For years Japan's internal problems have made it a smaller player in the G8 than its size and status should permit. But now, as it expands consumer demand, we have to enlist Japan's political and business classes to become leaders of the new global growth plan.

What's more, we have to enlist to a global growth plan Asia as a whole, for it is already a region dependent upon global trade and dominated by exports. Export sales account for 20 percent of most countries' incomes; for the main East Asian economies, export sales are no less than 40 percent of their national income and as much as 70 percent.

While Asia's growth was once confined to East and Southeast Asia, it is now reshaping the whole continent—and we are seeing the transcontinental development of roads, railways, and pipelines. Indonesia and the Philippines have done much better than expected, and Malaysia, South Korea, and Thailand are now middle-income countries. The number of families with incomes above $500 a year will double in the next decade. But take one of the poorest countries, Vietnam. Wage costs are much lower there than elsewhere, especially in textiles, so there are around 1.7 million Vietnamese making footwear, furniture, and clothes on around $80 a month. But GDP per head was below $100 in 1990 and is now well over $1,000.

Indonesia and Korea are invariably mentioned alongside Mexico and Turkey as four countries whose size and growth will, in the future, put them on par with the BRICs. Likewise Hong Kong, South Korea, Taiwan, and Singapore have joined, or are joining, Japan among the ranks of Asia's rich countries.[4] Although it is a country of only five million people, Singapore, with its economic growth of 13 to 15 percent in the first half of 2010, has been not just Asia's but the world's fastest-growing economy.

Can Asian countries make a major contribution to world growth, and in particular world economic demand, by making a smooth transition from the unbalanced pre-crisis economic structure to a more balanced post-crisis structure? The question is really how fast Asia, which cannot expect to maintain its pre-crisis shares of world exports, will improve its domestic demand and be prepared to equip itself for achieving more balanced growth. If China's typical monthly wage is $400, Thailand's under $300, Indonesia and the Philippines $200, and Vietnam $100, we are talking about a region with a huge population but suppressed consumer demand. Again we have to say that over time spending will rise, but not quickly enough.

Regional economic integration is now seen as the way forward across the Asian continent. China has called for an Asian Monetary Fund and made the case for an Asian currency unit. In the immediate future we will see a strengthening of the Chiang Mai Initiative Multilateralization Agreement and an Asian Financial Stability Dialogue to improve economic and financial coordination. This paves the way for discussions on a regional IMF. But so far Chiang Mai has had a link to the IMF, and support to individual countries is conditional on IMF programs. We have to remember that while the regional pool is now in existence, during the banking crisis Korea performed its largest swap arrangement not with Asia, but with the U.S. Federal Reserve.

Japan speaks of Asia confirming its status as the "world's factory" by further economic integration to become top in the world in added value. With specialized production systems and supply chains across the continent, 50 percent of Asian trade is already within the region. This is likely to be sustained as a single market—and more cross-country infrastructure investment—is promoted across Japan, China, and Korea. All this, says the Asian Development Bank, will provide the region with an additional source of resilience against external shocks.

In addition to forty-four free-trade agreements and another eighty-five on the way, three regionwide free-trade agreement proposals are under discussion: an East Asian Free Trade Agreement (FTA), a Comprehensive Economic Partnership Agreement, and a Transpacific Strategic Economic Partnership Agreement (spanning Asia-Pacific Economic Cooperation economies, including the United States). But it is not clear which will emerge, or when.

Will the development of the Asian internal market be at the expense of trade with other continents and make a global growth plan less achievable? Economist Fred Bergsten puts the loss of U.S. exports because of the Association of South East Asian Nations+3 FTA at $25 billion. The EU calculates EU imports to China falling by 1.5 percent, even before any productivity and growth benefits that could accrue from a pan-Asian FTA. Such an agreement would, as the German government has recognized, affect the German car trade with Asia. But this evidence makes it all the more important to recognize the benefits a world trade agreement would bring and to understand that the recent surge in bilateral free-trade agreements is because no global trade agreement is happening. So there is a balance to be struck between the region's making provision for a lower rate of growth in U.S. and European consumption of goods produced in Asia (which is a good thing) and the region's becoming more protectionist (which would be bad). My judgment is that East Asia plays an increasingly important role as a supplier of intermediate goods for the advanced economies. Thus even as the internal Asian market develops, Asia will become more, not less, integrated into the global production network.

We know that global imbalances will remain as long as the Chinese and Japanese consumer is unable or unwilling to spend and the Indian consumer remains too poor to spend. While we have seen consumer spending double outside Japan since 2000, the total consumer spending of these people is, at best, only about 25 percent of the consumption of Europe and America. For while 56 percent of developing Asia's population, or nearly 1.9 billion people, are already considered part of the middle class because they have incomes above $2 a day, 1.5 billion Asians are still living on less than $2 per day.

How likely is Asia to be a willing partner in a global agreement?

The global exposure of Asian financial institutions and their holdings of dollar reserves suggest the need for multilateral engagement. Japan has a large stake in the IMF, and China now has a big role in the G20. While China and India hold 4 percent and 2 percent of the Fund's voting power, with more than 18 percent of world GDP at purchasing power parity exchange rates, giving them more power in the IMF makes it likely they will favor global agreements.

Finally, what do we conclude when we look at Brazil, India, Russia, and China together—what are called the BRIC countries? Can we see them as together capable of bridging the gap in global demand?

Jim O'Neill of Goldman Sachs, who first coined the term BRIC around 2000, said then that they would be as big as the G7 by 2030. BRIC economies have been singled out because they are trillion-dollar-plus economies. They are the fastest growers, and with the exception of Russia have survived the recession well. But perhaps the most important common characteristic is that they have huge domestic markets and large numbers of poor people. Those two facts in combination mean they have the capacity to expand their consumer economies, making millions who are today seen only as producers become also consumers of the world's goods and services.

In the long run the 2 billion consumers of the BRIC countries will create the demand that is essential for the world economy to grow in a more balanced way. The rise of the BRICs suggests the entry into the world economy of one billion more middle-class consumers by the 2020s. But while this offers a long-term exit from lower global growth, it will not offer enough in the short term to offset the very low growth and perhaps even contraction of the demand of American and European consumers.

Russia suffered the deepest recession of the BRIC countries (a fall of 7.9 percent in 2009), but has seen economic growth accelerate out of recession, the return of foreign investment (which in

2009 had collapsed by 40 percent) and the trebling of their stock market index. With its large domestic market, founded upon oil, Russia could make a huge contribution to the growth of the world economy if its hard-pressed consumers were able to spend. In the first decade of this century Russia doubled its national income. But Russia still looks like a two-tier economy. There is the state sector, with government-backed heavy industries like aerospace and armaments becoming world leaders, but outside the state small and medium-size companies that are generally large employers of labor are unable to mobilize funds for investment. Only with diversification out of oil and gas and a program of economic reform can Russia look forward to sustainable levels of higher growth that are not dependent on volatile commodities.

Even with its membership in the G8 and the G20 Russia is not yet a central player in the debate about higher growth. There is of course no certainty about whether Russia's overall direction is toward reform or conservatism. Debates that veer from restoring Russian conservatism, the "bring back yesterday" position, to advancing Russian modernization, the reform position, coalesce in blurred talk of "conservative modernization." But if Russia could resolve questions about the levels of state interference and transparency in its economy and then push forward its economic reforms, its oil wealth could be the foundation of a rising consumer economy and one of the dynamic sources of new growth in the world.

Brazil is growing at 7 percent a year, and although it has been hurt by the revaluation upward of its currency, investment should grow quickly over the coming years. The Olympics and the World Cup alone will drive forward a big increase in public investment, and Brazil's oil assets will yield substantial revenues over the coming decade. With greater investment, a rising labor force, and a growing working-age population, trend growth could rise to as much as 5 percent. But Brazil will contribute to the world economy less by an increase in domestic savings or consumption than by its commitment to higher foreign investment.

*   *   *

A huge transformative change is taking place as emerging countries who had a minority of the pre-crisis share of world growth will soon be responsible for a majority of that growth.

In October 2010 McKinsey estimated that consumer spending in the leading twenty emerging economies will trebel 2010 to reach $120 trillion. So could a wider group of countries in Asia and the fast movers in Africa and Latin America join with China and India in securing a big growth in global demand?

If there is to be sufficient growth, bilateral action will not be enough. Only multilateral action will turn the hopes of development into reality.

The challenge is great, but as we will explore in the next chapter, there is already an example of multilateral cooperation that shows that even former enemies can become firm friends and usher in unprecedented peace and plenty for all their people.

CHAPTER 9

Living with the Euro

No economic project in history has been as bold as that agreed by European countries in the last years of the twentieth century: a commitment to bind together several hundred million people from sixteen different countries in one single economic policy. The creation of the Euro, its recent travails, and its struggle for survival have generated millions of pages of research documents and occupied thousands of hours of attention from every European leader I know.

So unique and preoccupying is the Euro that, even after twenty years of discussion, it still is the dominant issue in debates across Europe. The attempted rescue of Greece is, as I think most people now realize, just the latest chapter in a prolonged economic crisis that is hitting the Euro area. German Chancellor Angela Merkel has even talked of the Euro's "existential" crisis.

I am by nature pro-European in my attitudes to both policy and cooperation.[1] From the esplanade of Kirkcaldy, the town where I grew up and which I now represent in the House of Commons, I can look out over the North Sea toward mainland Europe. Adam Smith was born here, and his belief in the importance of trade grew from seeing dozens of ships a year coming in and out of its port every month. My father and mother, who lived through the Second World War, taught me that there had to be an alternative to war and conflict. Indeed, my father even argued in his youth in the 1930s that to foster unity and avoid war there should be a common European language.

Even as a pro-European, I did not believe Britain should be in the Euro, but I take no comfort in the current fracturing of the European dream. I believe that we must help make the Euro work. Despite its massive structural problems that I and many others have identified, I fear that a breakup of the Euro—and the chaos that would ensue—would be a political as well as an economic tragedy from which Europe itself as well as the very idea of international cooperation would take generations to recover.

The biggest mistake the rest of the world could make is to assume that the Euro crisis is simply a problem for the Euro zone and nothing to do with us. Non-Euro countries such as America and Britain are affected directly. Between them, America and Europe form nearly 50 percent of the world's economy. And if the Euro area does not grow, then the world loses one of its engines of growth. So there is a global interest in policies that will restore growth in Europe. Europe buys a quarter of U.S. exports, and American and European banks are wholly interconnected; in 2009 U.S. bank lending to Europe totaled $1.5 trillion. Although the U.S. Senate voted to limit American participation through the International Monetary Fund in the European rescue, America and Europe are too interdependent for one to walk away from the other. So it is imperative that we have a shared strategy to deal with today's crisis. To achieve it I believe we have to rediscover the common economic interests we share—in Europe and in the wider community of the G20.

Even now the world still thinks of the banking crisis as an American financial collapse, but the impact on Europe has been even harsher. European banks are far more vital to European growth than American banks are to American growth.[2] Even now external finance in mainland Europe is mainly channeled to industry and households through banks.

European guarantees are the foundation of the 2010 rescue of Greece. I believe that George Papandreou, the Greek Prime Minister, has had the courage to take the toughest of decisions and implement the severest of measures. But we also have to make sure he has the best possible advice. For example, in the first months of the year because of delays in the decisions to help Greece the cost to Greece of avoiding default grew from an estimated €30 billion to around €120 billion.[3]

Of course these guarantees do not end the indebtedness itself; they manage only the consequences, not the cause. A loan guarantee cannot itself solve a problem of excessive indebtedness. In other words, you cannot wish away a solvency problem by classifying it as a liquidity problem. While no one yet knows whether Greece will be able to return to growth without a debt restructuring, we must remember that the other side of the coin of Greek borrowing is lending by German, French, Italian, and other European countries' banks. German banks' exposure to Greece is about $50 billion, while the French exposure is $75 billion. And so the worry extends far beyond Greece's ability to repay. German, French, and Italian banks are also weighed down by the debts owed by Spain and Portugal and Ireland.

Stress tests have been necessary and worthwhile, but they have not fully removed the fear that Europe's banking sector as a whole is undercapitalized and that Europe is delaying the further recapitalization it needs. While Euro zone banks have raised $30 billion over two years—but only $4 billion this year—U.S. banks have raised five times as much. Because Europe depends so much on its banks, there is a real risk that they hold back any growth because they haven't raised the capital they need.

Financial markets assumed from the outset the European Central Bank was ready to accept at its discount window the sovereign debt of all member countries on equal terms, thus fostering the impression that all Euro sovereign debt was of equal quality. But while the finance ministers of the European Union were prepared to guarantee that no financial institution of systemic importance in their country would be allowed to default, there was no agreement on a joint Europe-wide guarantee, and the same has happened with the Euro area's mechanism to prevent default; the European Financial Stabilization Fund is guaranteed not jointly but only severally, with the weaker countries themselves guaranteeing a portion of their own debt.

Today of course Greece has also to sort out its fiscal position, and the same is also true for other high-deficit Euro countries. The fiscal tightening in Greece in 2010 will be 7.5 percent of GDP (according to the OECD), and partly as a result the economy will shrink by 4 to 5 percent in 2010 as a whole. Fiscal tightening in Ireland, Spain, and Portugal will be around 1.5 to 2.5 percent of GDP. With so much bank debt guaranteed by its government, Ireland is now in a different league for the scale of its deficit—one-third of GDP—and its indebtedness. The summary of all these numbers is stark; the scale of the fiscal retrenchment is akin to what was asked of Latin America in the 1990s. In return for a European financial backstop, Spain has to reduce its deficit to 6 percent of GDP by 2011—a cut in one year of more than €50 billion. Prime Minister Zapatero's government has had the courage to agree to what the IMF calls a "radical overhaul" of employment law and pensions and an accelerated consolidation of the banks. But even if Spain manages the deep structural reforms the IMF is prescribing, the IMF forecast is of low growth and continuously high unemployment.

Losses in household financial wealth—linked to lower home values—have brought European consumer spending down; it is still well below its real-term pre-recession levels of 2007. Outside Germany and the Netherlands a return to consumer-led growth will be difficult. To Germany's enormous credit, jobs of the equivalent of 1.4 million full-time employees were saved during the recession by short time working. But it is now in the interests of surplus countries to recognize that, while they have to prepare for the costs of a rapidly aging population, every European country will in the end be hurt by a cycle of low growth if surplus countries do not target higher consumer expenditure.

What of investment-led growth? It is important to recognize that a return to the real-term investments of 2007 is unlikely to come before 2015. Investment that had fallen 25 percent in real terms is projected to decline by around 2.25 percent in the EU and 2.5 percent in the Euro area over 2010 and is expected to rise by only 2 percent in real terms a year to 2015—hardly the basis of a strong recovery. It will take years to return to the levels of investment we saw in the past. But restoring growth without losing even more jobs will require new investment and large productivity gains.

So while Europe is in recovery today, still only 73 percent of Europe's capacity is being used, only marginally above the historic low of 70 percent in 2009. While the trend in American growth is around 3 percent a year, now probably reduced to 2.8 percent, the trend in European growth, which has been around 2 percent, has now probably fallen much lower.

Faced with these very real challenges, the issues I want to address are whether and how Europe can make a bigger contribution to world growth and whether there are changes in the world economy that could help Europe grow faster and more sustainably. In particular, does the very structure of the Euro make it difficult to secure the highest level of growth and employment possible and what we can do about it? And what reforms should we consider to avoid what I fear is likely to be a low-growth decade with still high unemployment? I will conclude that the very risks Britain identified when considering joining the Euro remain real and present dangers for Euro countries, risking growth and employment. These are not cyclical problems, nor simply the overhang from a world financial recession but, as George Soros has reminded us in a series of important speeches and articles, structural problems in need of structural solutions. To overcome them, we need substantial reforms in the Euro area and an updated European growth plan that delivers fiscal consolidation that supports rather than undermines growth and employment.

JOINING THE EURO

At the time of my assessment of the U.K.'s membership of the Euro in 1997 I said that the Euro was a risk because interest rates appropriate for one part of the area were not necessarily right for another. It was also a risk because all countries were not growing in harmony and because Europe's countries did not appear to have the flexibility necessary to adjust their economies to crises or even the very tough discipline of a single currency. This risk has been amplified by the growing breadth of the membership, which spreads across Europe from Ireland in the West to (beginning in January 2011) Estonia in the East. Indeed, one remarkable illustration of the tensions that have arisen across the Euro area is how little the debate in national capitals has been about a common European economy or interest, and how quickly we reverted to talking of the problems of Europe's south and north; of the German position, the French position, the Greek or Spanish position.

And so as deficits rise, growth diverges, and some countries are perceived to be at risk of default, the question we asked in Britain in the 1990s has reappeared in a new guise: What are the circumstances in which a European single currency can work and deliver sustainable high levels of growth and employment across Europe?

When in 1997 I first set out the U.K. government's position on the Euro I listed the potential benefits for Britain of a successful single currency in terms of transparency of costs, currency stability, trade, and long-term interest rates.[4]

This and my later assessment made clear that, with the advent of the single currency, trade within the Euro area had already expanded, and that, with Britain in the Euro, British trade with the Euro area could increase substantially. Our assessment on trade and output was that, inside the Euro, British national income could rise over a thirty-year period by between 5 percent and 9 percent.

So I was not blind to the potential benefits of British membership, but I was deeply concerned that without the flexibility to enact fail-safe measures that would counter the inflexibility of the locking of our exchange rates forever, the Euro could not work for the Britain of 2005 or 2010.[5]

Ours was more than an economic stress test—it had big social and political implications for all aspects of government policy, including what would happen not just to inflation and interest rates but to investment, home ownership, and public services. Ed Balls led a brilliant team of Treasury officials in conducting the most comprehensive set of studies any government has carried out on the Euro. As we absorbed the results I met every Cabinet minister of the day and listened to their views. When I first expressed my doubts about Britain's entry, I stood virtually alone in the Cabinet. Indeed I was ready to resign as Chancellor if I was unable to persuade my colleagues of the grave risks of taking us immediately into Euro membership. But having considered all the arguments, we concluded unanimously that although the Euro was right in principle, it could not work for Britain at that time.

Of course the more flexible the economy, the easier it is to tackle problems that arise from the divergence of business cycles. But we had to have—and this issue has yet to be addressed across the Euro area today—sufficient flexibility to be able to adjust our economy quickly to any shocks that arose, and thus to prevent low growth and high unemployment. So we had to be sure that Britain could gain all the potential benefits in high levels of investment, strong financial services, and employment, growth, and trade. Without sustainable convergence and sufficient flexibility, I could see clearly that we would not be able to realize the potential benefits for stability, jobs, and investment.

Of course convergence did not mean market structures identical with those of other countries; all countries have unique market features. But British house prices and market volatility had required interest rates higher than in other countries (only 7 percent of mortgages in Britain were long-term fixed-rate agreements). But if, inside the Euro, Britain's inflation rose faster than that of the Euro area, Britain would suffer a loss of competitiveness. What I feared was that to restore lost British competitiveness following a period of higher inflation than that prevailing in the Euro area required a period of British deflation.

Inside the monetary union, Britain's economy would be one-sixth of the entire Euro area economy. I remember saying to others that if we faced a British inflationary spiral that was not matched in other Euro countries, the Euro could at best offer us one-sixth of the interest rate response that was necessary. And if there was a British deflationary spiral, we would have an even bigger problem. The European Central Bank does not view deflation as seriously as it does inflation. But even if it did, we could, within the Euro area, achieve at best a fraction of the response we needed.

When the Euro project was planned in the late 1980s and 1990s the test applied to all countries seeking membership from Italy to Portugal and Spain to Greece became arithmetical: ceilings for inflation and interest rates and debt ratios and deficit limits. But I have asked myself whether the U.S. single currency area would have worked if what it focused on was the convergence of inflation rates and similar debt and deficits levels in the fifty states. For the U.S. single currency to work there had to be other, greater

forces at work: labor mobility, wage flexibility assisting high productivity, and central government support to ease things when
states diverged. In the United States, when there was unemployment and low growth in one area, people would simply migrate
from less prosperous areas. Europe is different; fewer than one
in forty (less than 2.5 percent) of one country's national citizens
now live in another part of the European Union—with the proportion moving each year between European countries as low as
one-third of that moving between the states of the U.S. And, ten
years into the single currency, productivity per hour worked by
German, Dutch, and Belgian workers is at least 50 percent higher
than in Slovenia, the Czech Republic, Portugal, and Greece, and
30 percent higher than in Italy and Spain. And far from the convergence that was envisaged, there are still within Europe widely
varying income levels (there is a 50 percent variation across the
Euro zone) as well as these widely varying productivity growth
(again a 50 percent divergence), and very different labor, product
and capital markets, many of which are not so open or so flexible that they can now cope easily without an adjustable currency
when things get difficult.

The other force at work that encouraged convergence between
the states in America is a very large federal budget, which helps
cushion and even reduce economic disparities between the
states. In marked contrast, the entire European budget is 1 percent of Europe's output. The muscle of the U.S. federal spending is, as a proportion of GDP, twenty times that of Europe's
central spending.

The studies Ed Balls did convinced me that we had not achieved
anything approaching convergence with the rest of Europe (nor
had many Euro members); that we had few weapons at our dis-
posal if a crisis threatened; and that the Euro was not for us an
optimal currency zone. The distinguished former European com-
missioner for trade, Mario Monti, who has recently examined the
state of Europe's single market, concluded: "The bold decision

to share the same currency . . . requires, at the very least, a high degree of sharing effectively a single, integrated, flexible market: a prerequisite for an optimum currency area and a vector for improvements in productivity and competitiveness." As things stand, these conditions are not met.[6] So there was no mechanism for convergence of members' competitive positions, no mechanism to prevent major imbalances within the Union and no mechanism or indeed plan to resolve crises.

In the early years of the Euro, the slower growing part of Europe—Germany in particular—needed interest rates at a level far lower than those of the South and indeed Britain, which maintained higher rates throughout. From 2000 to 2008, while exports generated 66 percent of the growth in a recovering Germany, Euro-area competitiveness as a whole deteriorated by around 10 percent, and with the appreciation of the Euro until October 2009, the Euro zone as a whole continued to lose export market share.

Over these ten years, with European interest rates low and with wages rising outside Germany, unit labor costs rose in Spain, Italy, Ireland, and Greece to at least 25 percent above those of Germany, and according to a recent Goldman Sachs study, those Southern European countries lost an astonishing 25 percent of their global market share. Borrowing by public and private sectors at low interest rates on the back of the Euro's credibility, some countries ran up debt even as their competitiveness declined. No one country had the power to adjust their currency to deal with their competitiveness problems, so while Germany's huge sacrifice—in containing wage rates—paid off, Greece, Spain, Ireland, and Portugal headed for a low-growth decade. So just as I found when studying the Euro's impact on Britain, the Southern European countries have found that there is a potential contradiction between the goal of higher growth and the workings of the Euro. In the past, currencies could adjust to higher prices and less competitiveness in one country or lower productivity growth and employment levels in another. And each country could continue to trade even as they had different growth rates or prices or levels of productivity growth. But I learned from the Treasury study of the Euro that when countries give up the means to adjust through devaluation or revaluation, there can occur what economists call the "mispricing of wages, products, and financial risk" that has to be confronted. And without a plan to deal with potential crises, deep recession can result.

The first days of the Euro in 1999 did not expose these problems (although the Exchange Rate Mechanism crisis had to a degree before), and fears that the adoption of the Euro could have been a technical disaster as people switched currencies proved groundless. The smooth transition to the Euro as a usable currency was a technical success for which the designers of the Euro deserve credit. Deutsche marks, drachmas, liras, and francs disappeared almost overnight with little disruption. To the credit of the Central Bank, which is now led by the very able Jean-Claude Trichet, a far more transparent interest rate decision-making process was agreed on than had prevailed in the old Bundesbank. This played a large part in convincing people that Europe could achieve both low inflation and high levels of sustainable employment and growth.

But despite these initial successes, the Euro, tested in its first crisis, has found it difficult to overcome the challenge it has faced. And today, with forecasts for annual European growth now much less than 2 percent for the years to come, Europe is finding it difficult to agree on how to cope with the challenge of rebuilding European growth without a prolonged crisis. The standard view of the missing elements in the Euro system is that there is no fiscal integration—although the U.S. doesn't have fiscal harmonization—and inadequate incentives or sticks for fiscal discipline. And I am certain that new measures for enhanced discipline within the Euro area will not be sufficient if it is merely the naming and shaming of individual countries. But I am also of the view that the European challenge is far broader and the problem more deep-seated than that. To maintain high levels of growth and employment living with one single currency, the Euro area will have to agree to greater flexibilities in other areas of policy. Fiscal consolidation, while critically important, must support rather than derail the high levels of growth and employment we need or we face a decade of low growth and high unemployment as Europe loses more of its global market share.

At the same time the European Central Bank—already more than a central bank, the lender of last resort in the Euro area—will have to deliver additional monetary stimulus. If emerging Asia does not change its exchange rate policy to offset the reduction in aggregate demand in the U.S., a marked appreciation of the Euro will ensure that the adjustment burden will fall mostly on the Euro area, reducing growth in both the Euro area and the world economy.

This is the time for European innovation in policy to make the most of global markets and the ever-accelerating pace of technological advance that can give Europe new products to sell. There is a case too for European-wide investments—for example, in super-fast broadband digitalization of Europe—as measures to improve productivity across the whole of Europe and raise employment. And just as Japan is considering itself a hub for environmental technologies, addressing in a systematic way the problems of climate change, so Europe should pool its efforts to effect a low-carbon economy. Proposed by the European Climate Foundation's "Roadmap 2050" to supply 40 percent more carbon-free electricity by 2050, a low-carbon European super-grid—an enhanced transmission network connecting European renewable and nuclear sources to European demand—could complement the pan-European digital initiative I propose and make Europe a leader for new low-carbon technologies, jobs, and exports.

*   *   *

If I understand their position correctly, Professor Niall Ferguson and others suggest that there is no difference between a "consolidation strategy based on growth" and a "credible fiscal adjustment plan." The assumption is that a credible fiscal adjustment plan will by itself create the conditions for growth. Yet the evidence is that real-term investment will not be rising fast at all between now and 2014. So with public investment cut and private investment stalled, there is no evidence that investment is, as assumed, going to be the driver of growth. Yet Asian competition and large imbalances inside and outside the Euro area have to be addressed.

Far wider structural reforms with labor, product, and capital markets—backed by encouragement for investment to build better technologies, from digital to low-carbon products[7]—and the skills to make that infrastructure more efficient are the way forward. Of course no European worker is going to be so inspired or motivated by the cause of the extension of the "single market" that it will bring millions to call for these reforms, but these are essential for a return to higher levels of competitiveness, growth, and especially jobs. It is about Europe finally creating the millions of jobs we need, and doing so in an enterprise-friendly way. A new study by McKinsey—soon to be backed up by a major cross-national study by Timmer, Inklaar, O'Mahony, and Van Ark already summarized in *The Economist*—suggests wide cross-country variations in service sector productivity. But it also suggest that for the decade after 1995 two-thirds of Europe's lower productivity growth, compared with America, has been due to services from retail to wholesale that were not sufficiently open to wider competition. Medium, small, and micro enterprises are at the heart of Europe's future job creation, yet today only 8 percent of the 20 million EU small businesses engage in cross-border trade. Only 5 percent have subsidiaries in other countries. Nineteen million of our 20 million businesses do not yet look outward. If they did, thousands of jobs would follow. There are huge potential gains here. At the moment, only 20 percent of the service sector trades across borders, with the result that there are few economies of scale, too many protected sectors, and a 30 percent productivity gap with the U.S. By opening up the services we become more competitive and win service jobs for Europe. There is also a gain—worth an additional 4 percent of European output and perhaps two million jobs—from stimulating the rapid development of an as-yet-fragmented digital single market. While nearly 40 percent of EU families—up from 20 percent in 2004—are linked up to digital communications, cross-national services and infrastructures need better coordination. And opening up public purchasing—the acquisition by public entities of goods, works, and services through competition in the European marketplace—could itself raise European GDP by around 1 percent a year.[8] In all these areas there are investment opportunities that the European Investment Bank ought to be able to support and jobs that can be created.

Let us remember that in a situation where growth is slowing across the continent, where banks are deleveraging (hitting small companies), and where large companies are hoarding money, no precedent demonstrates that public sector retrenchment will stimulate an early private sector expansion and then jobs. So my conclusion on Europe, in particular the Euro area, is twofold. First, Europe and the Euro zone will have to reform fast in the search for competitiveness, productivity, and jobs. Speeding up the jobs recovery from recession is the justification for renewing the momentum of the single-market program, and this can be Europe's contribution to the global growth plan.

Indeed, and this is my second point, higher European growth is best achieved—indeed, probably can only be secured—as part of a new global compact. Only in the context of a faster-growing world economy will the difficult decisions Europe has to make seem possible.

In these discussions Germany's fear—that even as its working population falls and the costs of pensions and health care rise, it may be asked to underwrite many of the costs of repairing the Euro—can be best addressed not by excessive retrenchment all around but by Europe playing its part in pushing for and achieving higher global growth.

I remain optimistic about a strong global role for Europe because a long period of low growth for—or worse, a disruption of—the Euro zone would be very bad for everyone and everything: bad for a very large number of people who will become and remain unemployed in southern Europe; bad for German manufacturing; bad for deficit countries and surplus countries alike; bad for Britain; bad for Europe and for the Western world; and bad for global growth. Reform for jobs is worth fighting for. It is one great challenge for which it really is in everyone's interests to find and agree on solutions—and to do so as urgently as possible, before any more damage is done.

CHAPTER 10

Post-crisis Africa

It was July 2009, and a total of forty-five world leaders sat around a large rectangular table in the heat of a northern Italian afternoon. Prime Minister Silvio Berlusconi was chair of the meeting. Because of the earthquake that had devastated Aquila earlier that year we were, on his initiative, meeting not in a luxury resort in Sardinia as planned, but in a simple college only a few miles from where people were living in tents and prefabricated homes.

Inside the college the gathering of leaders seemed to be expanding with every session. We had started as the G8: the U.S., Britain, France, Germany, Italy, Canada, Japan, and Russia. Then, by adding India, China, South Africa, Brazil, Mexico, and Egypt, we had become the G8 plus 6. Then the G20 met, and then the Major Emitters' Climate Change Group. Now there was only one more meeting to go: on Africa and its economic development.

The current president of the African Union, Col. Muammar al-Gaddafi of Libya, opened the discussion and spoke at considerable length. His speech seemed to be addressed to only one man, the president of the United States, and blamed America for all the problems of Africa, and much else besides. When I had met him at the official British-Libyan meeting he was soft-spoken, but given a wider audience, the tone of his rhetoric and its decibel level had risen markedly. Then President Obama spoke, courteously and patiently taking Colonel Gaddafi through all the commitments we were making on African economic development.

A few minutes later it was my turn to speak. Time was passing and I knew I had to be brief. I said that the real question we had to address in a financial crisis was how Africa could be assured of our support, that on too many occasions Africa had waited for us to honor our promises of help, and we had failed to deliver.

To this international gathering I told the story of David, a ten-year-old boy who had been murdered in the Rwandan genocide. His picture hangs in the final hall of the Kigali memorial to victims of the genocide. Accompanying his picture is a short biography that reads:

> David Mugiraneza
> Age: 10
> Favorite sport: Football
> Enjoyed: Making people laugh
> Dream: To be a doctor
> Cause of death: Tortured to death
> Last words: The United Nations will come for us.

The meeting fell silent.

I told them that his story had shocked me the most because David was a boy who had believed the best of an international community which had failed him. At this meeting, as we discussed the response to the crisis, we couldn't ignore the economic plight of Africa.

With tears in his eyes, Prime Minister Berlusconi said he would never forget the story of that young boy's tragedy, and at his press conference afterward President Obama cited this one single horror of the genocide as powerful evidence of why we must not stall or falter in delivering justice for the poor and vulnerable of Africa.

My own relationship with Africa had begun decades ago, in my father's small church in Kirkcaldy, where he was the minister. In our congregation, solidarity with those who have stumbled in the struggle of life was considered the most fundamental duty, and we held regular collections for Christian Aid and other charities that worked in Africa. When I was ten my brother and I printed a local news sheet which we sold to raise money for an Oxfam campaign called Freedom from Hunger; on entering university, I made the transition from fund-raiser to activist when I joined the anti-apartheid movement and fought a successful campaign to get Edinburgh University to disinvest from South Africa.

As I noted in the introduction, my first chance to campaign for justice for Africa on a bigger stage was on entering the Treasury in 1997. I immediately set about promoting the cause of debt cancellation.

The campaign progressed in fits and starts, but I believe that one of the most significant moments in its history was when Nelson Mandela came, at my invitation, to address the G7 finance ministers' meeting in London in 2005. He told us, "In this new century, millions of people in the world's poorest countries remain imprisoned, enslaved, and in chains. They are trapped in the prison of poverty. It is time to set them free."

That summer, as the Gleneagles G8 Summit agreed to 100 percent multilateral debt cancellation for Africa, I hoped that we had done enough to answer Mandela's call. Freed from debt slavery, countries were able to put resources into health and education, and have already achieved some stunning successes. I cherish all my meetings with Nelson Mandela, but above all else I feel privileged that I persuaded him to launch Britain's Education for All plan in Mozambique in 2006. This arose from my decision to spend $15 billion over ten years to ensure that four million children, previously denied any education, would go to school.

The following year, only a month after I became Prime Minister, I went to the United Nations to argue the case that "for too long we have talked the language of development without defining its starting point in wealth creation—the dignity of individuals empowered to trade and be economically self-sufficient."[1] That idea—that we should focus not just on aid but on growth—was a theme I was to return to again and again, alongside the idea that the peoples of Africa should be empowered to shape their own destiny, including by sending their representatives to global meetings at the highest political levels.

Throughout my entire eight-year service as chairman of the IMF Leaders Committee, then subsequently in my involvement with the G8, I was determined that Africa should be at the center of our discussions. The impact of the banking crisis on the continent that had had the least responsibility for creating it seemed to me to make that need even more acute when it came to the London G20.

I insisted that Prime Minister Meles of Ethiopia, a friend of mine who had championed the reform program of the Africa Commission, and Jean Ping, the secretary of the African Union, who has been a constant voice for a stronger African role in the world, had to be there as equal partners. The G20 could not itself represent all 190 countries, but if it did not have members from Africa and the developing countries, it would represent only a favored fraction of the world. I was determined that African representation at the meeting would be a right, not an act of charity.

On the day before the G20 meeting in London, Australian Prime Minister Kevin Rudd and I spoke in St. Paul's Cathedral about the need for ethics in our world economy. There was loud applause when I said, "We must never, ever forget our obligations to the poor. . . . I can confirm today that, even while others may use this financial crisis as an excuse to retreat from their promises to the poorest, nothing will divert the United Kingdom from keeping to our commitments to the Millennium Development Goals and to our promises of development and aid."

In the following days I shared with leaders evidence I had compiled which showed that in Africa alone, 100 million people were being pushed into poverty as a result of the recession. I showed how up to 50 million more children were now in poverty and five million more would die avoidable deaths.

Demand for African exports was falling, as were export prices. Investment flows, including those into Africa's nascent IT industry, were collapsing. Ambitions that Africa had worked toward for decades, aims that Africans had suffered to achieve by accepting painful economic reforms, were being destroyed in weeks. Over a period of just a month of the crisis, all the successes of the past decade—which had turned real per capita GDP growth from a negative number to 7 percent—were wiped out. Behind these numbers were real families and real countries, with tales of hopes dashed, ambitions crushed, and lives lost.

The setback was greatest for those countries that had begun to move from reliance on aid to attracting significant investment. They had been gaining access to capital markets and thereby reducing steadily their aid dependence. Much of the proceeds from the bond issues in capital markets had been going into the infrastructure so critical to the continent's future growth. Within weeks of the crisis starting, funding had become difficult, indeed almost impossible, to acquire.

Further risks lay ahead: the twin dangers of fiscal and trade deficits made it difficult for African governments to deliver services, let alone pursue their ambitious development programs. So, despite all we said and tried to do, there was an inevitable loss of momentum for the educational, health, and antipoverty objectives of the Millennium Development Goals.[2]

We were still failing in our moral duty to come to help children like David who expected the international community to care about their lives. But beyond the moral imperative to help, I had another reason for promoting Africa's involvement. Africa, I argued, was part of the solution to our problem. A recovering world would need new sources of economic growth, and just to the south of Europe was, as I would later say in a speech in Uganda, a "magnificent continent full of more untapped potential and unrealized talent than any other."

Everything I saw during that G20 and since has convinced me that African leaders are committed to meeting not simply the challenges of that continent, but the challenges of the world.

In this chapter I want to argue that Africa—just like the United States, Europe, China, and India—can play a part in delivering the world's return to growth. But only a radically different approach to development can make this possible.

Ngozi Okonjo-Iweala, vice president of the World Bank, surprised an audience by asking, "What trillion-dollar economy has grown faster than Brazil and India between 2000 and 2010 . . . and is projected by the IMF to grow faster than Brazil between 2010 and 2015?"

Even avid readers of economic news were surprised by the reply: sub-Saharan Africa.

Sub-Saharan Africa is on the verge of joining the ranks of the BRICs (the rising powers of Brazil, Russia, India, and China), whose wealth and clout have increased dramatically in the past decade.[3] Moreover many of the continent's countries are now regarded as frontier emerging markets,[4] including Botswana, Cape Verde, Ghana, Kenya, Mauritius, Mozambique, Namibia, Nigeria, Seychelles, South Africa, Tanzania, Uganda, and Zambia.

Two-thirds of African economies implemented reforms during the global financial crisis to make it easier for investors. In 2008–9 alone, Rwanda completed seven Doing Business–related reforms, Mauritius six, and Burkina Faso and Sierra Leone five each. Indeed Rwanda's and Liberia's measures were so significant that they both received "top reformer" status: Rwanda was the number-one reformer worldwide in Doing Business 2010, and Liberia was number ten.

Today the African continent is perhaps at about the same point as India was twenty years ago, and China thirty years ago: about to embark on higher levels of economic growth. International companies are increasingly focusing on emerging economies as a source of future growth; a report just published by the McKinsey Global Institute is also bullish about Africa's prospects, expecting Africa's consumer spending to reach $1.4 trillion in 2020—a 60 percent increase from 2008. In other words, in ten years African consumer spending will be as big as the whole African economy is today. As Ngozi says, people should now talk not just of East Asian tigers, but of African lionesses.

The World Bank estimates that Africa's middle class, now small, will grow to reach 43 million by 2030. Other experts say that if we put the qualifying income limit at $5 a day, the middle class is much larger, as much as 300 million, representing the population that is between the masses of Africa's poorest and the continent's elite few.

Africa has already shown it can grow at the same rate as the rest of the developing world. I believe we should now talk of the "new Africa," and we should speak the truth: that there is no third world, no second world, no first world now—only one world, one highly interconnected world of massive inequalities but shared interests.

While the growth trajectory, like the potential of Africa, can be huge, harnessing it to benefit from global and not simply pan-continental forces will require the creation of an open-trading Africa with a strong internal market; new investment in telecommunications, transport, and education; and better public-private partnerships to ensure that aid is a spur to private sector growth and not a substitute for it.

Behind the rhetoric of optimism, we have to recognize that dealing with Africa's slow productivity growth—the lowest in the world—is now an urgent necessity. Liberalization and privatization did not of themselves deliver the productivity improvements originally claimed for them. In any case, the real drivers of growth and improved productivity we identified for Europe and other advanced industrial areas are not dissimilar to those for developing countries: competition, supporting enterprise through better regulation and access to finance, science and innovation, skills, and investment in physical capital. If this happened we would have the supply-side response that has often been lacking—and that explains much of the failure of many structural adjustment programs of the past.

To succeed, Africa's countries need to formulate growth strategies. Growth taking off in a few countries could serve as an engine for the rest of the continent. But for this to happen, Africa will need common infrastructure to achieve economies of scale; a major expansion in skills, coupled with the ability to absorb global knowledge on an Africa-wide basis; and aid increasingly benefiting from vigorous investment partnerships between business and government across the whole continent.

Africa is the only continent yet to converge economically with the rest of the world, and no country has moved its people out of poverty without trade. First, then, Africa must be both regionally and globally integrated. A world trade deal is in Africa's interest. Indeed to grow out of poverty, Africa, today a net importer of agricultural goods, will have to claim a greater share of world trade. And with world food production due to rise over 700 percent by 2050, Africa's extensive unexploited cropland offers a huge export opportunity.

A fourfold increase in exports drove Africa's last decade of growth. But 80 percent of its exports were in oil, minerals, and agriculture. The continent must commit to diversifying its trade and exports. Regional integration—and trade between different parts of Africa—is essential for this, and for the ability to withstand external shocks. Indeed during the financial crisis there was a strong correlation between regional integration and the ability to withstand external shocks.

The crisis proved that the faster the pace of economic integration with Africa, the deeper and more diverse the markets, the greater was the continent's resilience to global shocks. The view of the African Development Bank—now the leading source of funding for regional integration in Africa, with $9 billion invested over nine years—is that unleashing the dynamism of trade among African countries could make Africa the fastest-growing economy after Asia. But Africa can trade successfully with itself and indeed with the world only if its principal means of transport, roads, offers cheap and efficient ways of getting goods to people. Today Africa has fewer miles of road than it did thirty years ago: half the road density of Latin America and about a third of Asia.

Not surprisingly, the Africa Competitiveness Report 2009 identified infrastructure as one of the top constraints to business. It notes that as much as 25 percent of sales in companies in some African countries are lost because of unreliable infrastructure, contract enforcement difficulties, crime, corruption, and poor regulation.[5]

A big push in infrastructure is the obvious first step. Cross-regional investments in infrastructure (energy, water, power, IT) take up 60 percent of African Development Bank commitments. Infrastructure spending needs for sub-Saharan Africa alone are estimated at $93 billion per year. In 2009 bilateral donors gave $27 billion in net disbursements of aid to sub-Saharan Africa. I agree with Ngozi's proposal that, instead of aid, they should issue African development bonds in New York, with a market yield akin to the thirty-year U.S. Treasury bond rate, now around 4.5 percent per year. If donors agreed on paying out just $6 billion a year in cash toward interest rate payments on African Development bonds African countries could invest $100 billion in infrastructure immediately.

Second, the exponential growth of information and communications technology provides an opportunity for leapfrogging stages of development. UN data show that mobile phone subscriptions have grown faster in Africa than in any other region of the world since 2003; between 2003 and 2008, the continent saw the number of mobile subscriptions surge from 54 million to almost 350 million, an increase of almost 550 percent. There are now more than ten times as many mobile subscriptions as fixed lines in Africa, and more than twenty times as many in sub-Saharan Africa. Investment in telecoms with private participation virtually tripled, from $4 billion in 2001 to close to $12 billion in 2008. In Kenya skilled agricultural workers can receive information on crop patterns, weather, and prices through cell phones. In Somalia farmers are using computers at Internet cafés to sell livestock. Mobile banking is bringing finance to millions of people. Text-messaging technologies empower farmers with real-time pricing information. Broadband networks—and the deployment of the national backbone, including the cross-border links—are buttressed by two new submarine cable systems and by satellite facilities.

But broadband use in Africa is highly concentrated, covering only 1 percent of the population. The World Wide Web Foundation, which started work in November 2009, aims to create and maintain web-based platforms that will help local farmers and others in the agricultural ecosystem in the African Sahara to share local innovations for growing vegetation in very harsh environments.

Third, there has to be a push on quality education and skills, just as Korea and other East Asian countries did in their time. For while rapid progress has been made in primary and secondary school enrollment, gross tertiary school enrollment has barely crept up, from 4 percent in 1999 to 6 percent in 2007. We know it is not years of schooling that makes the difference to long-term growth, but cognitive skills and learning, often measured by reading, mathematics, and science tests. New research shows that in Mali, 94 percent of students in second grade cannot read a single word; and in Uganda, that is still true for half of students in third grade. So the new mantra needs to move from "Education for all" to "Quality education to advanced levels for all."

Fourth, social protection is important not just because it is right morally, but also because it can provide a platform for growth. A good example is Ethiopia's productive safety net program (supported by the U.K. Department for International Development), which provides people with jobs. The program reaches some three million people, enabling vulnerable households to protect and build their productive assets.

Fifth, financial exclusion will need to be tackled if people are to save to invest in their future. About 80 percent of the population in the poorest countries still lack access to a bank account of some form, yet cross-country regressions have shown that economies with better-developed financial systems experience faster drops in income inequality and faster rates of growth.

Finally, health is a human right, at the core of any human progress. Good health determines that parents can work, children can attend school, mothers can survive childbirth and bring up their children, and infants can grow into healthy adults who work. Today Africa has 25 percent of the global disease burden,[6] but only 3 percent of health care resources and 1 percent of health workers. North America, in contrast, has 3 percent of the disease burden but 25 percent of health care resources and 30 percent of health workers. Where health services are strong, families and communities flourish. Where health services are weak or nonexistent—where the spread of diseases is unchecked, illnesses are untreated, and women give birth alone—families suffer, breadwinners die prematurely, and communities unravel.

So the agenda for Africa becomes clear. Instead of just 10 percent of African trade being trade within Africa, we should aim for a majority of African trade within Africa—by promoting an internal market. We should aim to strengthen the investment climate, including through increased investment in infrastructure, information and communications technology, and education and skills, and we should ensure that all citizens have access to financial services, social protection, and health care. But perhaps more than any other single issue, we should focus on ensuring that the policy response to Africa's challenges is driven from within Africa itself.

The lesson I draw from the past three years is that globalization can work for Africa if managed properly. The new paradigm is one of markets working in the public interest in a strategy for regional economic integration and supportive investment in educating a new generation. This has meant a reassessment of the partnerships between the public and private sector and of the importance of infrastructure in IT and regional economic integration. But it has put Africa on a better course for the future: pro-trade, pro-openness, pro–market globalization. If it continues on this path, Africa will soon be a genuine and much-needed dynamo for the largest prize: the return to global growth.

When I spoke to leaders at the African Union summit in Kampala earlier this year I gave them a simple message, which is as true today: "It is time to rise. Rise, because just as Africa needs the world, the world needs Africa."

CHAPTER 11

A Plan for Global Growth

I have shown earlier that in this decade a new but unsustainable balance in world economic activity is being struck between the two industrialized centers of the last two centuries—Europe (the European Union 27) and the United States of America—and the rest of the world. In 2010, for the first time in 200 years, America and Europe no longer produce a majority of the world's goods, nor do they trade a majority of the world's exports, nor do they account for a majority of the world's investment. They are pre-eminent only in consumption. It is hardly surprising that the 800 million population of America and Europe would at some point be out-produced, out-manufactured, out-exported, and even out-invested by the billions of people in Asia and the rest of the world. This new phase of globalization in the world, which has grown more and more interdependent and is awash with opportunities and full of promise, has also been characterized by an unevenness in the way the world economy has developed—so much so that in the financial crisis it looked as if the economy has moved beyond any individual nation's ability to manage or even navigate on its own. The latest figures from the IMF suggest that now, in 2010, America and Europe have less than half of world economic activity. Perhaps more worryingly, Goldman Sachs suggests that America and Europe will account for much less than 40 percent of the total investment the economies of the world make in their future.[1]

But even amid the uncertainties of a fast-changing world, there is a huge opportunity for America and Europe that must be seized. By around 2020, Chinese, Indian, and overall Asian consumer spending is likely to have risen to the point at which it becomes a new engine of the world economy, making higher overall levels of world growth possible. As many as 1 billion new Asian middle-class men and women—Asian producers today who by then will be consumers also—will, potentially, buy their goods and services not just from Asia but from the rest of the world. This new period of high growth is clearly the best and most sustainable exit strategy from the current crisis.

But what of the immediate future? Now that the first decade of the twenty-first century has seen a shift in economic activity from America and Europe to the rest of the world, the defining feature of the years immediately ahead threatens to be the slower rate of growth of the old engine of growth, American and European consumer spending, with slower rises in investment in America and Europe themselves a real possibility also. How can these lost years with lower American and European growth be avoided? Clearly America and Europe are unlikely to regain their lost two-century-long advantage in mass manufacturing. For the rest of the world can continue to compete on low wages with America and Europe. If Chinese wages at $400 a month become too uncompetitive, then we have already seen how Thailand today offers manufacturing wages of $300, Indonesia and the Philippines $200, and Vietnam $100 a month. So a strategy for America and Europe that is based simply on our ability to compete in low-paid manufacturing jobs is not credible. Still, as Asian consumption prepares to rise substantially, America and Europe should be equipping themselves to produce the high value added, technologically driven, custom-built products and services that depend on an educated workforce. These are the goods that global consumers will buy. Underinvestment in American and European education, skills, and technology will be a short-term saving but at a long-term cost.

It is clear to me, as I will show, that America's and Europe's future lies not in competing on low pay or cutting off trade in imported goods, but balancing out levels of consumption by higher levels of exports in high value added goods and services sold to the rest of the world. The answer is not an economy founded on low pay or on restricted and thus lower levels of trade, but on high skills. The uneven development of the global economy cannot be blamed on one country or one continent and, not surprisingly, this global problem does not offer simple national solutions. While each country has its own challenges and choices, its own priorities and plans to address, globalization has thrust upon us shared problems we have to face in common together—and which, in my view, cannot be resolved without coordinated action. The retreat from globalization—taking the easy option of banning imports, restricting capital flows, or introducing trade tariffs or restrictions—in other words, walking away from the global sourcing of goods and from global capital flows—offers no long-term answer. An already uncompetitive product will become less—not more—competitive by shutting out competition from the rest of the world The way forward is not to stop globalization in its tracks but to manage it better. And in a world economy that is growing more and more interdependent, this requires specific measures that add up to concerted international action of mutual benefit to all.

In the preceding chapters I discussed the regional economies on which I feel best placed to make some observations. I have found that on current policies:[2]

- America cannot yet grow fast enough on its own to substantially reduce unemployment and meet the aspirations of the American dream.
- Europe cannot put its underutilized capacity to work, and therefore unemployment will remain far higher than is economically necessary and socially acceptable.
- Chinese consumer spending, today just 3 percent of world economic activity, cannot at this stage replace that lost growth overnight.
- India, China, Brazil, and Russia—the BRIC countries—cannot bridge the growth gap. All their consumer spending added together amounts to no more than 7 percent of world economic activity. And the main developing countries—the so-called N11—cannot yet fill the gap either. Together with the BRICs, their spending power is one-quarter of that of Europe and America.
- Africa's entrenched poverty means that millions of potential consumers are simply missing from the global economy.

I have also discovered that if each country continues to pursue its national policies in isolation, we cannot achieve sufficient and balanced high levels of global growth. Instead high unemployment will remain without remedy—probably above the 200 million level—over the next few years, and we will not see the fast reductions in poverty in the poorer countries of the world that we want to see.

In his optimistic five-year projections Jim O'Neill of Goldman Sachs forecasts that the world economy will have grown by 25 percent between 2010 and 2015 as a result of continuing high levels of growth in Asia, Latin America, and Africa.

But this enormous change in the world economy has little impact on investment in America and Europe, his prediction for which is very bleak. Investment in Europe and America together will be below its 2007 level for the whole of that period, representing a cumulative deficit of $5 trillion by 2015. This deficit in aggregate demand represents, in human terms, large-scale, persistent unemployment.

So while, taken together, the advanced countries have insufficient demand to replace lost global growth, rising investment levels in the emerging markets will not be enough to push global demand upward at the level we need.

Trend growth in America, which was once above 4 percent, is now 2.8 percent. Trend growth in Europe, once above 2 percent, is now well below 2 percent. To get employment in these continents back to where it was in 2007, we need persistent above-trend growth. Instead, even the optimistic O'Neill forecasts leave the regional growth at 0.5 percent to 1 percent below its trend. This subtrend growth will make the demand gap greater and more challenging to reverse, with unemployment becoming more difficult to reduce with each year that passes.

These forecasts are thus a warning that America and Europe are about to miss out on the enormous opportunity that lies in the social change in Asia, just as Japan missed out on the acceleration in trend growth thanks to the dot-com revolution in America.

By 2020 an exit from low growth may be possible because of the continuing high rates of growth in Asia and the development of a strong middle class willing to buy consumer goods made in Europe and America. It may even be possible to make producers in Africa and the poorest parts of Asia and Latin America consumers in this growing economy.

But the conclusion I draw about the first years of this new decade is that at current trends, high levels of employment and prosperity will elude us and big reductions of poverty in the emerging world will not happen quickly enough.

It is important to base our conclusion on where people are and what they are thinking about the economies in which they live: how they see the problem, how they see their future, and whether the ambitions of different countries' citizens can be advanced by stronger, more coordinated action around the world.

If you were to ask Americans what America has to do now to sort out its economy, some would say "Cut deficits"; many would say "Cut taxes"; but most would also say "Cut the foreign imports that are stealing our jobs."

If you were to ask Europeans what their answer is, they would probably say "Cut the debt"; and some might even complain about the very viability of the Euro.

If you asked the Chinese what their solution was for their best future, they would probably answer that they are a developing country, so other countries should stop threatening them with protectionism and complaining about their currency.

If you asked the developing world, they would call for an end to unfair trading practices that ruin their basic ability to export and say that aid is unfairly being cut or withheld.

But let me put the question a different way. If we asked the same group of citizens "What do you really want to achieve as a country?," I am sure that we would get different answers.

In America people would say that the main issues for them are jobs and rising living standards for the working middle class.

In the countries of the European Union people would tell you that Europe needs to get its young people into work and cut its high levels of unemployment.

If you were to ask the Chinese people directly about their priorities, they would almost certainly say that they want to see more personal prosperity—and that means cutting the numbers of poor people and giving the rising middle class the opportunity to buy homes and access opportunities.

In many developing counties, people would tell you the problem was poverty.

Yet in the absence of a bigger vision of what can be achieved, the politics of each country inevitably pulls toward the narrow tasks and not the broad objectives.

But what have I found so far in my reviews of each regional economy?

First, I have discovered that America must reduce its consumption as a share of national income; that the best way to achieve this lies in a growing world economy; and that to succeed in their strategy to double their exports, Americans have to invest quickly to equip themselves with new and better skills and technology. This is the only long-term way to address middle-class living standards in America: improving Americans' ability to earn by upgrading their skills. But a strategy to double American exports, which assumes high levels of world trade, does not sit easily with a position that by cutting imports threatens world trade.

Second, I have discovered that the Euro area will always under-perform—operating far below its capacity, with high unemployment—unless it is more flexible; and that the way forward is combining labor market, product market, and capital market reform with an outward-looking strategy for exports to the rest of the world.

Third, I have discovered that China's real objective is to reduce poverty and increase the size of its middle class; that the over-reliance on export-led growth has now reached the point where it may be in conflict with building domestic prosperity; that we should help China increase consumer demand in its own country; and that as part of the growth pact China should consider opening up its closed service sector to imports.

Fourth, in my assessment I have discovered that Japan's real objective is to return to 2 percent growth; that we should actively support their policy of raising consumer demand; and that part of that must include Japan's opening up their services sector to the rest of the world.

Fifth, I have discovered that India's real objective is to reduce poverty; that to be able to do so it must be a more competitive economy, trading more with the world; and that to achieve this we must support India in investing in its infrastructure and education and opening up more of its economy. If India needs the pressure of global competition to become a more prosperous country, it is also in India's interests to join a global growth pact, so that as it reforms it does so in a supportive global environment, giving it the best chance of alleviating poverty, building a middle class, and growing in size to become, over time, the world's third largest economy.

Sixth, I have discovered that Africa can become one of the future poles of growth, but that to do this it has to be willing to make the economic reforms necessary and pursue a vigorous regional economic integration. Africa is a $1.5 trillion economy that needs to be factored into our thinking. To cut aid to Africa now would be a huge mistake politically, economically, and morally. But we should also think of Africa as a continent where new investment now will pay rich dividends later. Infrastructure and educational investment can rise dramatically in African terms without being large in world terms; financing a 20 percent increase in the coming year in investment in Africa would mean just a 1 percent increase in overall levels of world investment.

It is hard to resist one conclusion: China, India, Asia, and Africa generally have too much poverty, Europe too much unemployment, and America too much inequality. And part of the way back to growth is sharing our resources more fairly.

But have I any evidence that by each country cooperating more closely they can achieve these national objectives more effectively? Can I demonstrate that entering a global growth pact is more likely to advance different countries' objectives than to hold them back? Is it possible to reconcile the desired objectives of different parts of the world—which would require there to be more sustained and balanced growth in the world economy—with the need for low inflation and a stable economy?

Since the days of industrialization we have been looking for national solutions to national problems.

In recent years, as globalization has gathered pace, we have continued to look for national solutions to global problems.

My argument is that we need global solutions to global problems.

Indeed, because each country's problems are so interconnected, global solutions are perhaps the only way to fully answer each country's national problem. It is the absence of a unifying global vision of what we can achieve together that is impeding every country's progress—and making people feel that there is no alternative to the old protectionism which in the end protects no one at all.

As they look at the world from their own national perspectives, the countries I have examined are concluding that, for them, there is no alternative but to retreat into their own domestic policy shells.

America needs to export to the world, which requires less protectionism. But fearing jobs lost to Asia it is at risk of becoming more hostile to imports and more protectionist.

All countries of Europe need to raise employment by trading more with the rest of the world. But fearing both inflation and a sovereign debt crisis, they believe it is safer to retrench and allow the economy to grow well below its capacity.

China wants incomes to rise. But fearing the loss of export earnings and worried that at some time protectionism will cut off its wealth, it continues to divert resources from its antipoverty program to its export-promotion program.

India wants to raise its citizens' living standards, which requires them, among other measures, to cut the cost of services and thus requires them to favor more open trade. But its fears that opening to the world in a low-growth environment will overwhelm its economy demands that we show India we have a plan that they can benefit from: higher global growth.

The developing countries fail to seek the inward investment they need because they do not believe that the world will genuinely assist in their economic growth out of poverty.

Thus nowhere in the world do the economic remedies we are adopting in 2010 really match the real ambitions of the peoples of the world or the long-term interest of the countries themselves.

National-only solutions are thus not just a barrier to achieving general global objectives, but a barrier to achieving specific national objectives. And the most likely next step is more protectionism, and indeed mercantilism in trade, in industrial policy, in finance, and in banking.

But at the same time no one seems to believe that there is an alternative to the reductions in economic activity we are seeing in Europe and America, or an alternative to the imbalances in China and across Asia, which means that they continue to consume only a fraction of what they produce.

I have said that instead of a global solution to a global problem, we have today national solutions to a global problem. But it is also true that instead of structural solutions to what we now know are structural problems, we have inadequate attempts to muddle through, retreating to the old tired orthodoxies that failed in the past.

I believe that we need instead a properly coordinated plan for global growth, a plan that offers both jobs and justice.[3] And all G20 governments should agree to work within a medium-term budget framework of fiscal consolidation that supports a long-term strategy on economic transformation to promote growth.

I accept that in a world skeptical of political leaders and cynical about the benefits of globalization, we have to give people reasons why global cooperation is essential to achieve our economic objectives.

First, we have seen in parts 1 and 2 of this book that global cooperation works in practice. When countries acted in 2008 and then in April 2009 to prevent a depression, we agreed on a series of coordinated policy measures that amounted to the biggest monetary relaxation in history and the biggest fiscal boost we have ever seen, injecting into the world economy $1.5 trillion of funds each year: 2 percent of world GDP each year for two years. We also saw the biggest guarantees and support for the banking system the world has ever witnessed: $2 trillion of support, $7 trillion of guarantees. When world trade collapsed by 30 percent, we had to act together, and it is estimated that the combined impact of acting together made the stimulus substantially more effective.

Our task now should be to do together what no one continent can do on its own: raise world output much more than is forecast. If the G20 worked when we faced banking collapse, can it now work together again as we face an even greater challenge?[4] I believe it can, and that doing so could magnify and multiply the impact of its actions by the leaders of each regional economy making the decisions I have outlined in the preceding chapters.

Second, as I have said, no one country or continent—not even—the United States—can deliver the necessary growth, employment, and prosperity on its own and without international cooperation. In the next year the world will lose $1 trillion of fiscal stimulus, about 1.5 percent of global GDP, and America will continue to have high levels of unemployment because of higher savings and lower consumption. Current projections for investment suggest that real-value investment in 2015 will be $2.6 trillion (at 2007 prices), still lower than the $2.7 trillion of 2007. China and Asia will grow fast, but China's future remains dependent on export-driven growth—and therefore a healthy Europe and America—and on maintaining the value of the dollar. With the exception of major Chinese investment, which itself is not substantial enough to drive the world economy, there will be inadequate global drivers for growth in underdeveloped countries and emerging markets. The risk of not acting together is greater than any risk associated with attempting it.

And that is perhaps not surprising, because the scale of this crisis is comparable only to the 1930s. But it not only is global in its repercussions but is the first crisis to have its roots in the very process of globalization itself.

That leads to the third reason global cooperation is essential. We talk rightly of the problems we have had to deal with in American subprime, in Greek debt, in the Chinese currency, in Spanish property, in the Euro's flexibility—but as I have said, we are not dealing just with a set of national-only problems that have national-only solutions. For most of the two centuries of industrialization, national answers to the economic problems of inflation and infrastructure were sufficient. Today with global capital markets and global sourcing of goods, global problems arise that cannot be solved in the old ways. Unless we address fundamental problems inherent in the transition from the old world of sheltered national economics to the new world of the global economy, we cannot deliver the level of growth—and thereby jobs and justice—that people have a right to expect.

Fourth, I am convinced that the greater the coordination, the more the impact of each action is magnified. When the U.S. government examined the impact of stimulus measures, they discovered that if action was coordinated, the impact in saved jobs was multiplied 50 percent. We need more academic work on a new global growth economics, but it seems logical that if the right actions are taken in a coordinated way, there is a multiplier effect.

There is a fifth and perhaps overriding reason to promote global coordination: the evidence we now have today of what a coordinated global strategy could achieve, raising global growth, employment, and prosperity.

What gives me confidence is the compelling results of recent work that the staff of the IMF did for the G20, which was published in June 2010. I do not agree with every one of the IMF assumptions, but the IMF shows that cooperative policies could bring about $1.5 trillion more of economic activity by 2014, 2.5 percent higher global GDP, and, crucially, more than 30 million[5] more people with jobs and tens of millions of men and women taken out of poverty.[6]

Their conclusion, in what they call their upside scenario, projects an American unemployment rate down 2 percent from the baseline. As the IMF concludes, such a plan for global growth would also make growth more balanced and thus more sustainable. It is clear to me that fiscal consolidation, which I favor—in Britain's case cutting the budget deficit in half over four years—can best be done in an environment that does not destroy the prospects for growth and jobs but supports them. The impact on confidence of rebalancing global growth by a credible global growth plan is impressive.

The process of delivering a growth pact could start either in Europe, the United States, or in Asia. Understandably, the Germans do not want to be burdened with the liabilities of other European countries, so without global coordination the most obvious solution appears to them to be the largest program of deficit reduction Europe has seen. But that will also mean higher unemployment in the Euro area and slower growth, which will affect German exports (60 percent of the German surplus is with the rest of Europe). German growth comes from an export advantage that it has built up with the rest of Europe and with China, but to continue to enjoy that advantage the rest of the world must be growing fast enough to continue to import. So higher growth inside and outside the Euro area is in Germany's interest. Instead of focusing mainly on deficit reduction, it is in Germany's interest for it and the whole of Europe to focus attention on measures for growth.

Bringing Europe to the discussion on global growth is crucial, because it will be difficult to achieve purely bilateral agreements on imbalances between America and China. I believe a global agreement is not just better than a stalemate; I believe it is positively in the interests of Europe and America. The Chinese would benefit not only from growth in Europe and America but also from an international insurance scheme, so that they can redirect their priorities from having to self-insure against crises by holding high foreign reserves. And it is not in Europe's or

America's interest to see Asia looking in on itself. Indeed, the moves afoot within Southeast Asia to start forming a trade bloc affect us all. For Japan, it is clearly a way out of its twenty-year recession, and for China it is about creating an Asia-wide supply chain. An America excluded from this new common market would lose exports; an America included would be able to access the fastest-growing economic bloc in the world. This would of course bring trade back onto the negotiating agenda. I have been very frustrated about the lack of progress on the Doha Development Round of Trade talks; we have a very clear idea of what the problem areas are and where the negotiations have fallen down. But a trade deal, as part of a growth plan, would be attractive to the remaining BRICs, N11, and sub-Saharan Africa.

I remain cautious on a world trade deal because we have been disappointed a number of times in the Doha rounds. But if we take to heart the lessons of 1933—only meet when there is an agreement and keep the draft announcement under wraps— there are enough potential benefits for each region to participate.

What, then, is the framework for such a global growth pact? I began part 3 by pointing out that I am a politician and not an economist. So let me explain my own experience as a politician and how it has informed my iron conviction that the world can return to higher growth if we make the right decisions now.

The crises of economic policy in the past century teach us that the conventional wisdom of the day can easily become the misjudgment of history. In the 1920s all conventional opinion sought a return to the "gold standard" on the grounds that there was no credible alternative. In the early 1930s all conventional opinion said that there was no alternative to retrenchment as the route to recovery. "There is no alternative" was also the theme of the 1980s, giving us the orthodoxy that condemned us to the worst and longest long-term unemployment since the Second World War.

But any framework that is not founded on the objective of stable and low inflation, the task of central banks, will prove inadequate. In the contemporary academic version of a Keynesian model, low and stable inflation delivered by an interest rate policy is indeed the optimal policy, delivering a zero gap between the economy's potential and its actual rate of growth. In my Mais lecture of 1999 I set out why I believed we should adapt to our own British circumstances such a Keynesian model.[7] The low inflation delivered by our granting independence to the Bank of England allowed us to focus on supply-side improvements in the productivity of the economy and the investments necessary in education, IT, science, and infrastructure to bring these about. Supply-side economics and fiscal policy were therefore able to combine, playing a stronger role in helping to deliver Labour's most important goal: full employment. Of course the particular conditions of the British economy are not replicated in every country, and there was more to the high levels of growth and employment we achieved in the first ten years of the New Labour government than simply a shift in macroeconomic policy.

I believe we must not forget our twin objectives of growth and employment when we deal with the related questions of debt and inflation risks. By around 2020 a more balanced, faster-growing global economy will offer the most comprehensive exit strategy from current problems. The large addition to the global middle classes and the additional reduction in poverty will create an enormous market for the global private sector, which will allow revenues to rise and government borrowing to decrease and stabilize. Of course the global growth plan will make us more cautious about inflation, but I personally am more sanguine about the short-term path of inflation because of the low level of capacity utilization. However, I also note the enormous hoarding of cash on the balance sheets of corporations globally. While explaining this as another example of self-insurance in our global economy, I'm also conscious about its potential to energize growth if the global growth plan engineered the same recovery in long-term confidence that the $1 trillion plan did to short-term confidence.[8]

That we need to monitor global growth to coordinate the easing of the fiscal stimulus should now be clear. By doing so we can avoid an uncoordinated inflationary spiral, because if global confidence is high, it's my view that we will be able to reduce levels of borrowing faster in a coordinated fashion.

I do not doubt that policies have to be implemented in a way that seeks to prevent future asset bubbles and keeps debt low. But based on my assessment of the longer term, I believe that debate is missing the point. In the past the idea that deficits would lead to inflation was the single most pressing reason people supported immediate public spending cuts. But today the picture is not one like that of previous postwar recessions: inflation may of course reemerge, but no one is predicting that will happen immediately. In the past, especially in the 1980s, the case was made that public spending would crowd out private investment. But that simply does not fit with the underinvestment we are now seeing; indeed there is a financial surplus in the private sector of $3 trillion for the developed world in the balance sheets of private companies. Moreover just as there is no immediate danger of inflation and no danger of a huge surge in demand for credit, there is little immediate danger as I write for most countries, a few excepted, of failing to sell their debt.

The rationale for instant and severe deficit cuts cannot now employ the crowding-out argument or the inflationary-risk argument or for most countries the unwillingness-to-buy-debt argument. What's left is the argument that higher premiums have to be paid for the risks associated with "going for growth." This is what the European Central Bank means when it talks obscurely of government indebtedness as having "opened up a number of hazardous contagion channels and adverse feed-back loops between financial systems and public finances." The logic of this is that even when there is no inflation threat, even when there is no crowding-out of private investment, and even when there is little difficulty in selling government debt, we should do nothing for fear of the risk that the markets may think going for growth is itself a risk. We could equally well say that the same markets that marked economies down because they had not cut enough are now marking economies down because they have cut too much—and that today the bigger risk is in refusing to act when unemployment is on the rise. OECD analysis shows that a 1 percent reduction in structural employment would not only enhance prospects for growth but on average improve fiscal position by .25 to .50 of a percentage point of national income. But as the IMF also argues, collective action is even more important if we are to mitigate the risk of a further downturn. Indeed the IMF also provides evidence that the sum of upside gains and the avoidance of downside losses would yield nearly $4 trillion, or 5.75 percent higher global GDP. The number of jobs that would be created (or saved) globally would total more than 50 million. These gains would lift more than 90 million people out of poverty across the two scenarios.

Since Keynes we have understood that insufficient aggregate demand means unemployment; that countries can produce more than they consume; and that some countries will build up reserves that keep demand lower. So while some will continue to say that governments around the world should focus only on monetary policy and keeping deficits low, we know that this will not be sufficient to keep unemployment down. We must never forget that, even with the fiscal and monetary stimulus, private investment in the advanced economies will remain weak. So I am clear that monetary support must remain on the agenda in Europe and America and that the fiscal consolidation we are all committed to should be designed to support growth and jobs now—and not undermine them. We could express this another way by saying that, in general, deficit reduction will be linked to the speed of economic recovery.

But let us not underestimate the difficulties of agreeing on a global pact and the barriers that have to be overcome. Of course increased Chinese wages might lead to production moving to the rest of Asia—such as Vietnam, where wages are much lower per month as in China—and fail to stimulate Chinese consumer demand. Increased Chinese imports might not lead to increased American exports, leaving the world economy still unbalanced. Rising Chinese consumption will not, of course, remove the German surplus, most of which is with the rest of the Euro area. Even if Germany were to bring its overall trade surplus to zero, the U.S. trade deficit would be reduced by a mere 0.2 percentage points. Japanese consumer demand, like that of the rest of Asia, is low: one-third of that of the U.S. Like Asia's, Japan's consumer demand will take time to expand. And if imbalances were the central issue and not just one of the issues, imbalances could be reduced by lower growth all around, especially in the United States.

My conclusion is that even with these caveats, which are obstacles to a growth pact, we can make the case for countries to synchronize their policies.

We know that Europe and America need measures to promote private sector investment, even as they restrain spending.

We know that if external investment in Asian service industries is encouraged—with greater market access in the region to U.S. and European goods, capital, and services—then U.S. and European balance of exports will improve and Asian current account surpluses will be reduced. Removing import restrictions on service sector products in Asia would open up trade, reduce imbalances, make for lower consumer costs in these countries, expand their middle classes, and reduce poverty. And we know that this can be done without forcing mass unemployment in these economies.

We know also that shifts in policy—moving Asia away from exports to consumption, moving Europe and America away from consumption to exports—are best achieved in an environment that spurs growth. The IMF finds that, on average, countries that in the past fifty years have enacted policies to end their current account surpluses have not lost any growth or exports and have gained in employment, capital, and imports. But we know that there is a greater chance of persuading surplus countries to act if there are greater guarantees that there will be a growing world economy. And we know that the spur to the much-needed correction of imbalances within the European Union—structural reform in labor and other markets, which is itself the European growth solution—is best achieved within the context of a Europe more able to export to the rest of the world.

Stronger export performances will help deficit countries maintain employment while rebuilding savings. This is made possible by reducing poverty and unemployment through higher domestic demand in surplus countries. At the same time, reductions in poverty in emerging economies are made possible by structural reforms boosting internal demand. Higher levels of world growth make it easier to achieve fiscal consolidation in advanced economies. It is also the case that structural reforms in the advanced economies tackle high unemployment. Under the IMF model, Asia raises its domestic demand, both its safety net provisions for the poor and its infrastructure spending on education, by $1 trillion by 2014 (half by higher deficits).

I favor something beyond a set of bilateral agreements that can by their nature deal with only some of the challenges. I favor a global agreement. And so the question for policymakers is whether countries can be persuaded to see their long-term interest in adjusting policies at a domestic level to meet the global growth plan. Or, putting it more directly, whether national economic policies can be brought together in multilateral agreements that advance the global good. This is the challenge addressed in *Fault Lines* by Professor Raghuram Rajan, who rightly states that there is no mediator of last resort, and no sanctions that can ever be imposed. He writes, "The IMF cannot overrule countries and countries would be unwilling to give up any sovereignty." The

World Trade Organization can impose sanctions, and national governments use executive orders, which even then have not been enough despite the valiant efforts of the WTO director Pascal Lamy to move trade forward.

But there are no clear rules for the wider economy on what is permissible and what is not. We could, of course, examine a set of incentives that might make country-by-country participation easier—such as IMF and World Bank funding for participating countries or what have been called "rebalancing triggers" that induce agreed-upon action (for example, if imbalances rise beyond a certain amount). Now in October 2010 we must support the leadership of both the G20 and the IMF, who have rightly advocated deeper surveillance of individual economies and of the world economy as a whole and have proposed that they assume a responsibility to promote exchange rate cooperation. When asked whether the IMF aspired to the status of arbiter, judge, or just analyst, Dominique Strauss-Kahn said, "You perfectly described it. It is all of that."

Could a global growth pact be successful without better exchange-rate cooperation? This cooperation was achieved by the Plaza Agreement in 1985, when Japan agreed to boost private demand through tax reform, Germany agreed to cut taxes to stimulate its economy, and all countries present agreed to intervene in foreign exchange markets to bring down the value of the dollar. In the next few months, the dollar fell 30 percent. But when the IMF under Rodrigo Rato sought to achieve a plan for dealing with global imbalances in 2005–6, Rajan tells us, he was left "dejected," believing that it is almost impossible to get the big countries to agree internationally on action they should take within their own countries. "No one we spoke to could commit to the actions that were needed." Today, says Martin Wolf, we are witnessing something far worse: "a form of monetary warfare: in effect the United States is seeking to inflate China and China to deflate the U.S." The problem is that when you ask each country what its strategy is for the immediate future, they all say "to export." But because under current circumstances not every country trying to export can do so successfully, the risk is competitive devaluations, a currency war, and the rise of a new protectionism: everyone trying to export and wanting to cut their prices to win export orders, and more and more countries engaged in competitive interventions—not just China but Japan intervening in the foreign exchange markets for the first time in six years; Brazil's sovereign wealth fund authorized to sell the real; South Korea intervening intermittently to hold down the won— what the American economist Ted Truman has called a policy of competitive nonappreciation. These attempts at devaluations could of course end up as a form of semi-coordinated monetary easing, but they are not as good as each country making a clear-cut decision to ease monetary policy or, better still, global coop-eration. Global cooperation is the most effective way forward in avoiding a race to the bottom in global currency competition. But global cooperation can also prevent the inefficient buildup of currency reserves by providing an international safety net and "insurance" against capital crises that will spur rather than detract from economic growth.

So any pact would have to deal with imbalances and also with one of their consequences: the accumulation of international reserves and self-insurance against capital flight. The long-term role of the IMF Special Drawing Right is one issue (for there are proposals to expand the pool of SDRs available for external financing). But the availability of new instruments that permit policymakers to counteract shocks—and a better safety net and better insurance system—could release reserves for investment. Proposals for such an international insurance agreement should be pursued alongside revisiting Keynes's original proposals for dealing with imbalances. In the meantime, weapons to antici-pate crises must be improved. The creation last year of the IMF's new Flexible Credit Line, financed by the New Arrangement to Borrow for countries who would prequalify for contingent credit, is a necessary but not sufficient measure of crisis prevention. The creation of a Precautionary Credit Line for countries with sound policies that do not qualify is a useful next step. An additional short-term precautionary IMF facility may be necessary as a standing facility offering liquidity available under preannounced rules. We also need the proposed systemic crisis prevention mechanism, a type of financial safety net, to channel support when there is a systemic crisis.

These measures are necessary because no one can be sure that support will be available in a financial crisis and because there is no global cushion or safety net or even insurance that reserves are being built up and held beyond and above day-to-day needs. Since 2000 reserves have doubled, yet half the total is now held by only six countries: Japan ($1 trillion in reserves), Taiwan, Hong Kong, and Singapore ($500 billion), Korea ($200 billion), and China ($2.5 trillion). Emerging market countries' reserves are now a third of their national income since the crisis reserves have risen again to $8.3 trillion, five times what they were ten years ago. Growing oil wealth has amassed $3 trillion in sovereign wealth funds. There is at least a fear that as protectionist sentiment rises, these reserves may become investment instruments used by governments for political purposes rather than commercial vehicles for high returns on assets.

So how can this wider debate contribute to global growth? "History teaches us," writes Bradford DeLong, "that when none of the three clear and present dangers that justify retrenchment and austerity—interest-rate crowding out, rising inflationary pressures on consumer prices, national overleverage via borrowing in foreign currencies—are present, you should not retrench." Yet in the absence of seeing a different (and global) route to greater prosperity, each country is trying, post-crisis, to return to its old ways. But the security people crave will come not from countries clinging to an old world, but from reinventing themselves for our new interdependent world: Asia reducing poverty and building their new middle class; America and Europe exporting high-value-added goods by building a more skilled middle class; all undertaking structural reforms but in a growing economy. This is the answer to those who travel today not with optimism but in fear. But there is no Old World to return to: it has gone. The transition between epochs is always the moment of maximum danger. It is also the moment of maximum opportunity.

I spoke in chapter 3 about one of the opportunities which is now open to us: the chance to create a global banking constitution. I can now propose that we have another, far greater opportunity that we must seize: the chance of a global growth plan.

As I have shown in this chapter, such a global growth plan is not an impossible dream, something for idealists and internationalists to argue about, knowing that hard-headed policymakers will always choose another path. What we now know is that the self-interest of each country is best pursued by advancing the common interests of all countries.

In 2011 Nicolas Sarkozy, whose dynamism and foresight were so critical to the success of the G20 in 2009, will be the first world leader to combine the presidency of the G8 and G20. President Obama has already led the way to that summit with his commitment at Pittsburgh to a G20 global growth agreement. With these two leaders working during the early months of 2011 alongside our Chinese, Indian, and other European colleagues and our international institutions, the ambitious plan that is now essential to secure growth and jobs and end the poverty of millions can be delivered. We can forge a new consensus that reflects the very same insight the founders of the IMF and the World Bank had when they themselves were creating a new dawn: "Prosperity is indivisible. To be sustained, it has to be shared."

PART FOUR

CONCLUSION

Markets Need Morals

The crisis is not over.

With more than 200 million people worldwide registered as unemployed and one billion people in extreme poverty, nobody who believes in a people-centered globalization can be satisfied. For far too many of our fellow men and women the first crisis of globalization has meant the loss of their income or identity—and in some cases their lives.

This goes to the heart of what politics is about: not the contest between competing parties, but the battle for jobs and justice. That's why the protestor I talked about in the introduction needs to dig out her "You are G8. We are six billion" banner again.

Throughout this book I have warned of what will happen if the world does not coordinate our economic recovery. The conclusion is terrifyingly clear: whereas for the past twenty years we have had uninterrupted growth, we now face ten years of low growth in Europe and America.[1] It will be a lost decade of mass unemployment in the developed world and mass poverty in the developing world.

But it doesn't have to be like this.

Under the dome of St. Paul's in the City of London, on the eve of the London G20, I said that the argument that the economy operates according to iron laws and the only role of men and women is to live by what these laws dictate demeans our humanity, because there are always options, always choices, always solutions that human ingenuity can summon.

A few years ago when economists were pressing the most dogmatic of free market policies on some of the poorest countries in the world, they argued for it by saying "Tina"—there is no alternative. But African people came up with shorthand of their own, not Tina, but "Themba"—short for "there must be an alternative." In that cry, Themba, we hear everything that must guide us today, because while it was an acronym, it was also the Zulu word for the most important thing that humans can have: hope.

Themba—the confidence, conviction and certainty that where there are problems there are always solutions, that we do not need to accept the defeatism of doing nothing. It is the conviction that through pursuing cooperation and internationalism, we need never return to the isolationism and protectionism of the past. It is the certainty that there is always an alternative to fear of the future, and what conquers fear of the future is our faith in the future: faith in who we are and what we believe, in what we are today and what we can become; faith, most of all, in what together we can achieve.

That is the also the spirit in which I have written this book. When millions of jobs and livelihoods are at stake and the security and serenity of millions of families are at issue, the outcome of this risk-laden and rocky journey the world economy is now on should not be left to the vagaries of chance or the failed ideologies of the 1930s: our journey must be shaped by our own beliefs, priorities, and judgments, and by concerting our global efforts to realize the values we hold in common. This book is my attempt to sketch out the alternative I believe in and to show that there is a way forward to jobs and justice—that there is a plan waiting to be implemented that would create more than 50 million jobs worldwide and lift 90 million people out of poverty.

I have written about my upbringing in the Scottish industrial town of Kirkcaldy. I will never forget what happened to my community when the linoleum factory closed and hundreds of people faced not just the deprivation but the shame of unemployment, knowing that their children would leave the house in the morning before they did. I have never forgotten it, and I never will.

That is why as Chancellor and Prime Minister I sought at all points to make Labour once again the party of full employment. Under that Labour government more people were in jobs than at any time in our history, and I am proud of what Labour members and MPs achieved together—first domestically and then through global processes like the G20. But in reality the battle for the right to work was not yet won when I left office earlier this year. So this book is a progressive promissory note, showing what I believe can be achieved if we take up that fight anew.

The challenge—at once structural and global—of creating higher growth and more jobs can be met and mastered only with a global compact among the major economic powers. Some argue that global economic cooperation in this decade will be as illusory as global cooperation was in the 1930s, because countries are by nature more protectionist in a crisis. Others suggest that the breakdown is occurring in the existing world economic order and that we risk replacing a U.S.-dominated unipolar global system not by a multipolar order, but by what Nouriel Roubini and Ian Bremmer describe as a "nonpolar order," in which America's chief competitors remain much too busy with problems at home and along their borders to bear heavy international burdens. Getting these varied groups to agree on anything beyond declarations of vaguely worded principle will be profoundly difficult.

But I believe it is possible. And it is in the space between the possible and the perfect that campaigners for justice must always be.

The stronger, more sustainable growth I want to see will not happen just by hoping for Asian consumer spending to rise. Nor will it come from simply hoping for private investment to recover swiftly and strongly. It will require an agreement among the economic powers of the world, something bigger, more imaginative, and more lasting than even the Marshall Plan for Europe: a constantly updated plan for economic growth. The way to a global growth compact is to move forward on two fronts: persuading individual countries, continents, and leaders that future prosperity is now indeed indivisible; and appealing to global citizens to support the case that global cooperation can create jobs.

Such a plan will have to be accompanied by a constitution for the supervision of global finance, for otherwise we will find ourselves in the same race to the bottom in financial standards that characterized the past decade. It will also require a new academic discipline of global growth economics, which will have to do more to focus on the interconnectedness of policy action across continents.

We need to give countries enough reasons to be part of a global pact. Every country in the world suffered a loss of trade as a result of the economic crisis, and half the countries of the world suffered a cut in growth. And there was no automatic mechanism by which growth could recover. The global economy is now too interconnected for one country's policy not to affect another's and for challenges we share in common to be subject to national solutions rather than global cooperation. We are also learning that cooperation can not only avoid harm but can lead to greater benefits. Global growth—regularly 5 percent a year for two decades—went into reverse in 2008. And in 2009 trade fell by 12 percent.

We have already seen from the G20 coordinated fiscal injection that when the world does do things together it can multiply the impact: each continent doing what it can to stimulate our economies, each recognizing that global problems need global solutions, each combining to introduce new global financial supervision, each believing that international institutions can contribute to growth—and therefore giving not just national governments but international institutions like the IMF, World Bank, and regional banks the resources to recapitalize banks and create new demand in the world economy.

My idea of the global New Deal is that every continent not only signs up to global financial regulation but signs up to an agreed plan to improve global supply and demand. I believe that in the absence of a global growth pact now, the world will be pushed toward protectionism later. Americans and Europeans will not see their living standards improve by continuing to buy the illusion that if you stem the tide of imports from abroad you will be better off. Only with carefully prepared agreements on growth will our living standards—and those of the rest of the world—rise.

There is no comfort in the status quo. If, as I believe, the world's problems are structural, then we have to deal with them by major surgery, not by waiting for something to change.

But as the crisis revealed, market disciplines—particularly self-regulation and regulatory approaches based on greed—were completely inadequate to deal with the problem. The evidence shows that the market is a necessary but not sufficient mechanism for a continuously successful economy and society. And because we are agreed that markets depend on trust, which has to be underpinned by self-discipline (which failed) or imposed discipline, we have a duty to act in the public interest.

In their set of essays on "animal spirits," George Akerlof and Robert Shiller have, as I have written earlier, brought forward compelling evidence that our economy can be understood only by looking at the "real motivations of real people"—the tides of optimism and pessimism, the sense of fairness that is not just self-interest, and the mood swings between willingness to take risks and aversion to risk. This is the basis of their contention that a stable and enduring financial system will not happen by chance; it must be underpinned by values that try to harness people's animal spirits for the public good. As I look at clear evidence of reckless risk-taking, the role of animal spirits, and the weaknesses of rational "efficient market" models, I am persuaded of a more important underlying truth: that markets need what they cannot generate themselves. Markets need morals.

Morals are not made and cannot be made by markets. They are made in families, schools, and communities. They are founded on custom, tradition, and ethical norms. They are passed on by religious leaders, role models, and parents, and they rest ultimately on the existence and potential enlargement of our moral sense. So the battle is now on for the soul of the twenty-first century. We must affirm that markets are in the public interest but not to be automatically equated with it, be honest that the fault is not with markets but with the dogma that markets alone are all we need, and then act on the truth that markets cannot flourish or even survive by market forces alone and demonstrate by the standards we insist upon that markets are free but never again values-free.

Yet the assumption that grew was that our global economy existed in some space completely separate from the ethics we apply in the rest of our lives. The theory was that the more global the markets, the more that these markets would harness self-interest and produce results; that individual gain would somehow always lead to collective gain; that selfish motives would invariably produce better results than selflessness. But as we discovered to our considerable cost, this unsupervised globalization has not only crossed national boundaries—it has crossed moral boundaries too. The problem, as Britain's chief rabbi Jonathan Sacks has put it, is that unfettered markets can reduce all relationships to transactions, all motivations to self-interest, all sense of value to consumer choices, all sense of worth to a price tag.

Interestingly, Adam Smith did not argue that self-interest was the most admirable quality, but that prudence, humanity, justice, generosity, and public spirit were "the qualities most useful to others." So to state that markets need morals is not an anti-market statement but simply a reaffirmation of what that great economic thinker from my hometown argued so long ago: that the market economy must live within certain rules.

For today's world that means that the operation of markets must balance the necessary encouragement of risk-taking with proper standards of responsibility. I want competition to be underpinned by morals not because I am against competition, but because I want competition to work in the public interest.

Smith thought that sympathy—the ability to put ourselves in other people's shoes and appreciate their predicament—might exercise some control over our animal spirits and that our basic sociability was the best way of restraining human selfishness. And of course the best way to deal with Keynes's animal spirits is self-control, backed up an ethos of corporate social responsibility and by moral education: individuals taking responsibility for behavior worthy of trust.

In the absence of a consistently high code of standards set by bankers for themselves, we need a shared set of moral rules that can be the basis of a constitution for our banking system. The reentry of the moral claim into economic policy—the revival of political economy—is what makes me confident that the argument for a global growth and employment plan can be won within nations and then between them.

As I said in my speech to the American Congress, the crisis was provoked by the use of cutting-edge technical and financial innovations that seemed very new, but the lessons of the crisis were very, very old—enduring lessons I had first learned in my father's church long ago.

Those timeless values were the ones I tried to live up to in office and which have, I hope, informed the writing of this book: that a good economy is one where prosperity endows more than the prosperous and a good society is one where fortune favors more than the fortunate few. I speak as a believer in wealth creation when I say that wealth has to serve more than the short-term needs of the wealthy and that riches are of lasting value only when they enrich not just some of us, but all.

These are the values of the peoples of the world. If we fight, we can make them the values of globalization, too.

APPENDIX

There can be no more appropriate country to discuss the challenges facing the new global economy than the United States of America: the preeminent architect of the postwar global system.

There can be no forum more appropriate than the Kennedy School, named after the President, who on July 4th more than a third of a century ago, matched the Declaration of Independence of 1776 with a new declaration of economic interdependence for our time.

And there can be no more appropriate institution than Harvard where fifty years ago, the Marshall Plan, the most ambitious multinational effort for economic reconstruction the world has seen, was first launched.

More than half a century ago, leaders who were still engaged in war took the time to prepare for peace. In a breathtaking leap into a new era, the world created not just new international institutions—the IMF, the World Bank, the GATT as well as the UN— and a whole set of new rules for a new international economy, but gave expression to a new public purpose based on high ideals.

A generation of leaders who had known the greatest of depres-

243

sions and the greatest of wars knew also that just as peace could not be preserved in isolation, prosperity could not be maximized in isolation.

What they did for their day and generation was so dramatic that Dean Acheson spoke of that period as akin to being present at the creation.

One of the signal events was the Bretton Woods conference—and I ask myself why it was held not in Washington, or New York, or Boston, but in the White Mountains of New Hampshire. In fact the location was the price the Roosevelt administration had to pay to persuade a New Hampshire senator to abandon isolationism. As Tip O'Neill used to say, "All politics is local" . . . even global politics. If Massachusetts and not New Hampshire had threatened to be isolationist we might be talking today of the Cambridge Agreement. Nothing could more vividly show the practical nature of the visionaries who created the new world than their choice of Bretton Woods.

But as practical as it was, Bretton Woods also defined a new public purpose characterized by high ideals. The conference was about more than exchange rates, the mechanics of financial arrangements, or even new institutions. As the American secretary of the treasury said at the very start of the opening session:

> Prosperity has no fixed limits. It is not a finite substance to be diminished by division. On the contrary, the more of it that other nations enjoy, the more each nation will have for itself.
>
> Prosperity, like peace, is indivisible. We cannot afford to have it scattered here or there amongst the fortunate or enjoy it at the expense of others.

In short, prosperity to be sustained had to be shared. Practicality and morality went hand in hand.

George Marshall reaffirmed this in his own historic speech here at Harvard. We must fight against "hunger, poverty, desperation, and chaos," he insisted, to secure "the revival of a working economy in the world [that would] permit the emergence of political and social conditions in which free institutions can exist."

So the postwar arrangements were founded on the belief that public action on a new and wider stage could advance a new and worldwide public purpose of high ideals rooted in social justice:

- To achieve prosperity for all by each cooperating with every other.
- New international rules of the game that involved a commitment to high levels of growth and employment.

In short, the job of every economy was to create jobs for all.

The founders of Bretton Woods resolved that the failed policies of laissez-faire which resulted in vast inequities and recurring depression from the 1870s to the 1930s would not be repeated. Untrammeled, unregulated market forces had brought great instability and even greater injustice. In the postwar era governments had to work collectively if they were to achieve either justice or stability.

The initiatives and institutions of that era were shaped to the conditions of the time—a world economy of protected national markets, limited capital flows, and fixed exchange rates. And for nearly thirty years the system worked; for hundreds of millions who enjoyed unparalleled prosperity, Bretton Woods took us a long way. Yet even in the '70s with hundreds of millions still in poverty we had still a long way to go.

In the first historic phase of international economic management, nation states spoke unto nation states, with an unprecedented degree of cooperation between separated and still largely insulated economies. The international rules of the game then largely consisted of open current accounts, fixed exchange rates, and closed capital accounts and of collective support when countries ran into balance of payments problems.

But over the next generation, that new world, too, became old, as the existing order of nation-states and collective international action was increasingly bypassed by the growth and eventually the sheer force of international financial flows, successively ending dollar convertibility into gold, the fixed exchange rate system, and postwar Keynesian certainties, bringing in its wake an outbreak of inflation and then stagflation that spread across the western world.

The 1980s saw a new consensus emerge, essentially an attempt to return to laissez-faire. It focused not on what governments should do, but on what governments should not do, emphasizing private pursuits almost to the exclusion of public purpose. Enlightened self-interest gave way to sheer self-interest. Instead of rising to the challenge of applying the high ideals of the post-war world to a new world, instead of aiming for high levels of employment and prosperity for all, sights were lowered, the vision was narrowed. The new right consensus focused almost entirely on inflation and minimal government.

Of course it was and is right to say that inflation is costly, and once out of control, it is even more costly to reverse. Macroeconomic stability, based on low inflation and sound public finances, is an absolute precondition of economic success. Indeed there is a new premium on economic stability in the global economy. A nation state relying on investment flows from round the world—and also vulnerable to them—now knows that retribution for getting things wrong is swift and terrible.

The 1980s consensus did understand the importance of liberalizing economies from excessive regulation and bad government. But they confused means with ends and said in effect that inflation alone, not jobs and growth also, were exclusive concerns. And they said that all government was bad: that government can't make a difference, at least a positive one, in jobs and growth, and that global markets have to be left entirely to market dogmas, which have no place for the public pursuit of high ideals. But this

1980s consensus failed even in its own stated purpose—bringing the largest fiscal deficit in American history and reducing Britain to inflationary boom-and-bust.

And by 1997, an increasingly turbulent and inadequately supervised international financial system threatened to create boom-and-bust on a global scale. Now both of the Bretton Woods objectives—not only prosperity for all but stability for all—were at risk. The postwar hope for an indivisible prosperity was replaced by the sudden fear of indivisible instability. The 1980s consensus could not endure.

As the downturn in Asia reverberated around the globe, President Clinton said that "the world faces perhaps its most serious crisis in half a century."

In recent months as interest rates have come down, and the G7 group of leading industrialized nations have set a timetable for reform, financial markets have become less unstable.

But this is no time for complacency. We must recognize how far we have come—in purpose as well as time—from 1945 and how, without public purpose in this new global economy, one set of events in one continent could inflict so much damage on so many people.

This year we have experienced events that were unthinkable just two or three years ago:

- Free enterprise Hong Kong taking publicly owned stakes in all its private companies.
- Japan nationalizing its banks.
- Russia going into default.
- In America the mounting of one of the biggest ever emergency refinancings not for a bank, but for a hedge fund.
- Most damaging of all, the biggest growth economies of the last decade in East Asia suffering larger contractions in output even than experienced in the Great Depression of the 1930s.

The political dimension, as George Marshall foresaw, is equally far-reaching: in only one year, revolution in Indonesia; civil strife in Malaysia; the loss of authority in Russia; and as unemployment rises, unrest in South America, typified by the outcome of last week's Venezuelan election. It is a sign of the times that only one of the Asian finance ministers I met with in Bangkok last September is still in office today.

The ultimate price of all this is profound human suffering. In Korea unemployment has trebled in one year. In Indonesia ten years of growth have been wiped out; and in the Asian crisis countries as a whole the number of people in poverty is set to double by 2000. We can't simply declare whenever the stock market bounces back that the crisis is over and we can return to the status quo. We must act—both because it is in our self-interest—to safeguard our own prospects and prosperity—and because it is right.

So now the responsibility falls on this generation to be present at a new creation—of new rules that break with the past and both effectively and fairly meet the demands of the new global economy. We must reject the false choice between clinging to laissez faire and retreating to 1930s protectionism or the tightly controlled, restricted capital markets of the 1940s. We must meet the new challenge but we must remember that while times and circumstances change, ideals endure.

Our aim must be an international financial system for the twenty-first century that recognizes the new realities—open not sheltered economies, international not national capital markets, global not local competition. It must be one that captures the full benefits of global markets and capital flows, minimizes the risk of disruption, maximizes opportunity for all, and lifts up the most vulnerable, in short, the restoration in the international economy of public purpose and high ideals.

Our predecessors did this for the postwar world of distinct national economies drawing closer together. Now we must do it for the post-national economy—where economically no nation is an island.

The consensus of the 1980s with its narrow focus on inflation, privatization and deregulation must evolve into a new 1990s consensus with a new and broader emphasis on competition, supervision, and the right conditions for growth and employment.

Before I describe the specific reforms we need, let me be clear that this new public purpose will require public endeavor.

In the international economy the era of absentee government is over.

We need that middle way between government doing everything and government doing nothing.

It was here in your country that Franklin Roosevelt in the '30s found a third way for a national economy—securing the benefits of the market while taming its excesses.

And I believe that the third way initiated and developed by Tony Blair has profound relevance for the challenge we now confront on the global stage. The issue is not one of either markets or government, but how markets and government can best work together. And the way forward for the new global economy is not to retreat from globalization—into either protectionism or old national controls—or to retreat into a failed laissez-faire. It is to ensure global markets can work in the public interest. And transparency in policymaking is one way to develop the informed and educated markets we need.

In a world where the new frontier is no frontiers, we must rediscover the public purpose and high ideals of 1945 with four major reforms that add up to a transformation of the international financial system—a new economic constitution for the new global economy.

NEW RULES OF THE GAME
FOR THE GLOBAL ECONOMY

First, internationally agreed codes of conduct for transparency and proper procedures that ensure educated markets. These would cover monetary, financial and fiscal policy and corporate governance and would be applied by all countries, rich and poor, as a condition for participation in the international financial system.

Recall that the first constitutional settlement of the world economy in 1945 was not simply about institutions but about rules of the game. And we must now return the international financial system to this idea of rules of the game. While the founders of Bretton Woods devised rules for a world of limited capital flows, we must devise new rules for a world of global capital flows. But our guiding principle remains the same—the promotion of global economic stability and international cooperation to promote growth and employment.

The codes will require accurate reporting to the international community, by each national economy, of all relevant information—for example, the size of a budget deficit, the state of bank reserves, and the level of currency liabilities.

And the codes will require not only this flow of information but the adherence to specific timetables and proper standards for transparency and disclosure.

The new disciplines involve both the private and the public sector. We need new standards of corporate governance—including an international standard of best practice for financial institutions and their regulators.

We used to think that all that industrializing countries required was raw materials, good communications, a supply of labor and the funds and ability to tap commercial inventions. But we now know that all nations also require a sound robust financial system: no nation can afford—and the international community cannot condone—national financial systems that are reckless, disordered, and dishonest. Lack of transparency anywhere can create lack of credibility everywhere.

By requiring exposure of deteriorating conditions, the codes would prevent the temptation for countries to deliberately mask problems, which is what happened in Thailand and South Korea with consequences felt across Asia and then the world.

And we should not be so complacent as to assume that codes of conduct are needed only in other countries and not our own. Given that the most recent threat to global stability came from lack of transparency in hedge funds in both the United States and Britain, we need tougher standards and requirements for disclosure all round.

The codes I propose will mean radical changes in the way governments and financial markets operate.

These new rules of the game are not incidental to the financial architecture for the new global economy: they are the financial architecture for the new global economy. They require countries to pursue self-discipline with the prospect, if they do not, of imposed discipline. So the right to participate fully in the system should thus be conditional on meeting explicit responsibilities. In this way the codes will reduce the risk of future failures. And if failures do occur, a stronger financial system will be better able to deal with them.

The codes are as relevant for underdeveloped Africa as they are for industrializing Asia and Latin America and industrialized America and Europe. They help us to lay down a route map for sequencing capital account liberalization. By making sure that economic facts can't be manipulated and underlying problems can't be hidden, citizens will know their country's real problems and prospects; the codes will deter corruption, restore public confidence, and build public support for the sometimes painful reforms that are essential to long-term economic growth and prosperity. And this is critical for investor confidence in the wake of the Asian crisis. Without transparency and the proper procedures that the codes of conduct will require, investors may not reinvest on the long-term scale that is necessary for jobs, growth, and social progress.

National governments should not pick and mix which standards they choose to meet and which standards they choose to ignore. So proper implementation of the codes should be a condition of any IMF and World Bank support. In the global economy national governments have rights but they also have responsibilities they must meet.

GLOBAL FINANCIAL REGULATION

And because today's financial markets are global, we need not only proper national supervision but also a second fundamental reform—global financial regulation. That is why Britain has proposed bringing together the IMF, the World Bank, and key regulatory authorities: a new permanent standing committee for global financial regulation charged with delivering the global objective of a stable financial system.

The G7 have now agreed on the urgent need for this kind of coordination, and we are grateful to the president of the Bundesbank, Hans Tietmeyer, who has undertaken the critical task of preparing detailed recommendations.

I see the standing committee not as an additional institution but as process of monitoring developments in global finance, ensuring that necessary worldwide standards are put in place, and providing timely surveillance of financial conditions and international capital flows.

The standing committee's work would make cooperation between international institutions and national regulators a fact of international economic life. In short, the standing committee would be the world's early warning system for regional and global economic risk.

GLOBAL CRISIS PREVENTION
AND RESOLUTION

Our aim must be crisis prevention where possible, crisis resolution where necessary.

So in place of the old approach whereby crisis triggered intervention, we need, thirdly, a modern mechanism, rooted in transparency and reliable surveillance, and built on public and private sectors both accepting their responsibilities, which can identify potential problems at a stage where preventative action can be effective.

The mechanism they agreed in 1945 for crisis prevention dealt with imbalances in current account flows in a world of restricted capital flows and fixed exchange rates: to tackle public sector deficits and balance of payments crises, it offered temporary financial support or permanent exchange rate adjustment.

The new mechanism for crisis prevention must deal with imbalances as a result of global capital flows.

We need a process of active and transparent surveillance that is a matter of course for all countries, operating in normal times, all the time: not one triggered only by the warning signs or onset of crisis in a particular region or country.

And all main participants, public and private, must accept their responsibilities.

So emerging market economies in particular must not only be transparent in their activities; they must now also forge regular contacts and lasting relationships with their private investors. An open and honest dialogue, in which investors can ask hard questions and then advise, will make it more difficult to cover up bad news, and make it easier to assess what policies will increase or reduce market confidence, thus making it more likely that we can prevent today's problems from deepening into tomorrow's crisis.

The shorthand phrase for these creditor-to-country arrangements is country clubs, but these are not exclusive clubs, old boy networks, an informal means of defending privilege. These are modern investor networks that can bring real benefits in return for real responsibilities: networks that every country should form and every creditor should join.

To make these work there should be a new presumption across the board, in favor of the release of information wherever possible.

The G7 have proposed greater openness from the World Bank, the IMF, and other international financial institutions. Their monitoring tells them much of what is happening in every national economy. Clearly in exceptional cases some policy discussions will have to be kept confidential, but I strongly support the publication of the IMF's country surveillance reports under Article IV. The case for an exception must be made and justified, while openness should be the norm.

Put simply, we should establish an international right to know that is not occasional or voluntary but ongoing and mandatory.

This will work best if the IMF and other international institutions are more open about themselves. They should do more to explain their practices and procedures to the public. And they too should join in a new partnership with the private sector—ongoing discussions about broader and more systemic issues facing the world economy.

With a right to a greater flow of information comes greater private sector responsibility. We need a system of debtor-creditor agreements—crisis resolution procedures signed up to in normal times with private sector responsibility clauses, such as agreement on collective representation and majority voting when creditor decisions are being made. When trouble hits an economy, the private sector must be prepared to do more than simply pull money out and accelerate the panic. On an ad hoc basis investors did the opposite in South Korea and Brazil and their decisions were essential in halting the flight of capital.

With these three changes—transparency, enhanced surveillance and investor networks—we can establish a markedly lower threshold for effective response than the old ad hoc crisis-triggered system.

Detailed discussion should now take place on the right mechanisms for private sector involvement in crisis resolution. Of course more information and more participation must not become a licence for reckless investment or insider dealing. Instead, by universalizing reliable information and creating orderly consultation procedures open to all, we can minimise the risks arising from insider information on the one hand and moral hazard on the other.

In the new framework it should be the duty of the public sector to inform, the duty of the international financial institutions to monitor, and the duty of the private sector to engage.

And because of the new disciplines we propose the public sector can now justify a system of mutual financial support, assistance to countries pursuing sound policies, and to contain the spread of financial contagion.

In the last few weeks the international community has proposed a temporary preventative facility, with short-term lines of credit for sound economies that are the victims of contagion. Once transparency, surveillance, and agreed private sector responsibility clauses are embedded in the new system of crisis prevention, this facility should be made permanent, and be properly funded.

Of course countries that do not follow these procedures or act on advice cannot expect that they and their private sectors will secure crisis support. The moral hazard would be to guarantee such support independent of whether they do the right things.

With the reforms we propose, we have a real opportunity to

move the emphasis of international financial governance from one of crisis resolution to one of crisis prevention and crisis containment.

A GLOBAL SOCIAL CODE

There is a fourth reform: we propose a code of global best practice in social policy which will apply for every country, will set minimum standards, and will ensure that when the IMF and World Bank help a country in trouble the agreed program of reform will preserve investment in the social, education and employment programs which are essential for growth. This should be an indispensable goal for government in the new global economy: not guaranteeing that nothing will change, but equipping people to turn change into new opportunity.

International economics is not just about numbers in a ledger, but about the lives of people. For too long it has been assumed that the cost of crises will inevitably be paid by putting more burdens on the poor—by cutting health, education, and basic social services.

This is wrong in the short term and it will not work in the long term because it erodes both the economic and the political foundations of a society. For reasons of self-interest as well as conscience, we cannot accept a worldwide regime of the well-off in the castle, and the vast majority at the gate. Creating national support for needed reform depends on sharing gains, and helping those who are hurt by economic crises. As Jim Wolfensohn, President of the World Bank, has so vividly put it, "Social and economic issues are inseparable, they are like breathing in and out."

In their October statement the G7 recognized the urgent need for a code for good social practice and asked the World Bank to work with countries and with the United Nations and others to develop the principles and provisions of such a code.

This is an historic opportunity to realize the enduring public purpose, the high ideals of 1945. And we should not see this code in narrow terms as merely creating social safety nets. We should see it as creating opportunities for all by investing more not less in education, employment, and vital public services.

The way forward is not leaving people defenseless—and tolerating a culture of poverty; not repeating past mistakes, which have created a culture of dependency; it is equipping people to cope with change, through a new culture of opportunity.

The first building block is, of course, minimum social provision such as safe water supplies; universally available vaccinations and basic health care; and in every society universal access to schooling for girls as well as boys.

The second building block is the chance to work and the assurance that work will pay, a commitment that we must, stage by stage, year by year, fulfill in developing countries as well as developed ones. The code would set out best practice that can help people find and remain in paid employment: programs to move them from poverty or welfare to work; lifetime learning so that people can move themselves up a ladder of opportunity; and pension systems that mean a lifetime of work will be followed by a decent retirement.

We should forge new partnerships between the public and private sectors—and the NGOs. But of course the existence of a program today should never be the excuse for its perpetuation tomorrow. And the reforms the IMF and other international authorities require must be consistent with the social principles and make a virtue of preserving necessary social investment.

For the poorest highly indebted countries of the world we must create a virtuous circle of debt relief, poverty reduction, and economic development. We should never leave countries with an impossible choice between paying or defaulting on unsustainable levels of debt. Immovable mountains of debt run up in the 1980s have become impassable barriers to progress for poor countries in the 1990s. It should now be our ambition that every highly indebted poor country will be in the process of debt relief by the millennium.

And for countries like hurricane-hit Nicaragua and Honduras, weighed down by the burden of debt and devastation, it is right to create a new World Bank trust fund—now with over 130 million dollars pledged—to alleviate their debt payments. It is also right to devise the new post-disaster facility that will give faster relief from debt, to all countries in this position. I believe 1999 must bring a new urgency to relieving third world debt.

CONCLUSION

So what we must together create is a new economic constitution for a global economy, born out of new realities, grounded in new rights and responsibilities, enshrined in codes of conduct that are agreed nationally and applied internationally, rediscovering public purpose in the international economy and bringing to life again the high ideals of 1945.

We need to build quickly, not debate indefinitely.

Agreement on the codes of conduct should be reached at the IMF meetings in April.

A new system of global financial regulation should be in place by the summer.

The new mechanism for crisis prevention and crisis resolution should be agreed in principle this summer and the detail should be the subject of intensive discussions between the private sector and national and international institutions to reach agreement by the end of 1999, and the code for best practice in social policy should be agreed at the next World Bank meetings in the spring.

This is a program of reform for our generation. It is more than simply a collection of proposals. It rests on a modern vision of government, doing the right thing, but not everything; of markets working, but not always perfectly; of principles of economic and social justice that reflect our best values and ultimately determine world stability and growth.

This project is indivisible; each element is essential to the success of the whole. And all of it is built on the understanding that increasingly we are part of both one global economy and one moral universe. Now more than ever, in the phrase of the Scottish author, William McIlvanney, we must understand that "the economy should be there to serve the people, not the people to serve the economy."

Ours is an age of great challenges but also great possibilities. What Franklin Roosevelt said to the citizens of his nation in 1933 is now powerfully relevant to the citizens and governments of all nations.

If I read the temper of our people correctly, we now realize—as we have never realized before—our interdependence on each other, that we must be willing to sacrifice for the good of a common discipline—because without such discipline no progress is made.

Today I believe that we in our generation have the vision, the values, and the will—as had the generation which preceded us—to make the world economy anew; the public purpose and high ideals to make a better world economy in every sense of that word.

GLOSSARY

Capital gap: The gap between what a bank would need to weather some losses on its assets and its reported capital.

CDO: Collateralized debt obligation, a structured investment created by investment banks. The investment banks buy a diversified portfolio of loans and bonds which are medium to high risk. Because the portfolio is diversified, the rating agencies see the risk of losses from the whole portfolio as being lower than the constituents, and give the portfolio a higher credit rating. The second part of the CDO is that the investment banks find investors who want to take and are prepared to take the first or second loss on the portfolio for a higher return. That then lowers the risk of the remaining part of the CDO, which can be sold to an investor who can only hold highly rated "low-risk" investments. Each type of investor—the first loss investor (equity piece), the second loss investor (mezzanine), and the highly rated investor—has different investment targets. Investment banks would often create CDOs to satisfy the demand of one type of investor and warehouse the remaining risks until the other investors returned.

CDS spreads: A credit default swap is a contract that references the performance of a loan or bond of a particular corporate-, bank-, sovereign-, or mortgage-backed security. The seller of the contract undertakes to compensate the buyer of the contract for any impairment to the credit if there is an event of default, and in return receives an interest payment from the buyer. The CDS spread is normally quoted in hundredths of a percent.

Demutualized mortgage banks: Ten of the largest mutual banks in the U.K. demutualized and have mostly disappeared during the crisis: Abbey National and Alliance & Leicester, now owned by Santander; Cheltenham & Gloucester, Halifax, and Birmingham Midshires, all owned by Lloyds; and two went bust: Bradford and Bingley and Northern Rock.

Fed discount rate: The interest rate at which the U.S. Federal Reserve will lend money to banks in return for collateral. During the crisis, the acceptable collateral has expanded greatly, keeping the system going.

FSA: Financial Services Authority, created in 2000 as a statutory regulator for the U.K., replacing self-regulation.

HBOS: HBOS PLC was the holding company for two brands, Halifax and Bank of Scotland.

Jubilee 2000 campaign: An international campaign that called for the cancellation of the debts of the world's poorest countries, afterward renamed Drop the Debt, then the Jubilee Debt Campaign.

Leverage: The total assets a bank holds as shareholders equity. An institution with high leverage is at risk from a small fall in the value of its assets wiping out its equity.

Liquidity: Broadly, liquidity is a measure of the ability of an company to repay its debtors. It is particularly important for banks, because they borrow and lend for very short time periods, so a bank can quickly go bust if it runs out of liquidity, for example, if there is a run on the bank.

Lloyds: Lloyds TSB PLC.

London Summit 1933: The London Economic Conference, held June 12–July 27, 1933, where sixty-six nations met to agree on measures to bring the world out of economic depression. It failed.

Make Poverty History: A broad-based campaign that targeted the 2005 G8 meeting to demand the G8 pursue policies that would promote reduction of global poverty.

Mortgage-backed bonds: Tradable bonds that paid an interest and repaid principal in accordance with the pool of mortgages that backed each bond. They were constructed by an investment bank buying a portfolio of mortgages from an originator. A servicer would also be hired to handle the contact with the individual mortgagees, and the costs would be deducted from the interest paid to the bondholders. All other economic proceeds were paid through to the bondholders, who were in essence providing the mortgages. This structure created a new asset class and allowed investors to lend mortgages without having to set up a bank, hire staff, create a brand, and build branches. It greatly lowered the cost of mortgages and made them more available, but was very vulnerable to agency problems.

Mortgage-backed securities: See *Mortgage-backed bonds.*

Quantitative easing: When interest rates are low, the central bank engages in quantitative easing to increase the stock of money in the economy. The central bank does this by buying assets, sometimes just government bonds, but also other assets, and in return the central bank credits the bank with money.

Recapitalization: An injection of equity into the balance sheets of banks.

RBS: The Royal Bank of Scotland Group PLC was one of the five largest stocks on the FTSE 100. It owned Citizens Bank in the U.S. and RBS and National Westminster in the U.K. and bought ABN Amro's investment bank operations in 2007.

Shadow banking system: This is the name given to the large system of investors that looked very much like a bank, but were unregulated. By and large they bought mortgage-backed bonds and borrowed money in the money markets on the basis that the assets they owned were very high quality, for which they paid a little more than other Triple A borrowers. Economically they were borrowing short-term and lending long-term mortgages, hence they looked very like a bank.

Special Liquidity Scheme: This was introduced in April 2008 by the Bank of England to expand the collateral to high-quality mortgage-backed securities that banks could use to give to the Bank of England in return for sterling. Previously the banks could use government bonds only as collateral.

Subprime mortgages: Higher risk mortgage lending. In the U.S., they were loans to individuals with FICO scores below 620.

TARP: Troubled Asset Relief Program.

Taylor rule: A rule for setting central bank interest rates that combines an inflation target with a concern to ensure that unemployment is not too high.

The Crosby Report: Sir James Crosby's report to the British Treasury looked at how mortgage lending could be reopened. It suggested providing government guarantees on some mortgage-backed bonds to create greater investor demand, and thereby assuring long-term financing for the banks. It was this idea that became the guarantee for term funding in the U.K.'s recapitalization plan.

Tier 1 capital: A regulatory measure of the leverage of banks, with a trigger for intervention by the regulator. It tried to take into account the need for a proper return on capital by allowing banks to hold only a small amount of capital against assets that were regarded as low risk (i.e., Triple A assets). However, it exposed the banks because some of those Triple A assets were wrongly rated. Core Tier 1 refers to Equity + Preference Shares / Risk-weighted assets.

Treasury Select Committee: The oversight committee in the House of Commons dealing with the Treasury, the FSA, and the Bank of England.

Triple A: The highest rating given by a rating agency, implying the lowest probability of default. Aaa in Moody's, AAA in Fitch and S&P.

Triple B: A credit rating that most nonfinancial corporations now hold, and so relevant to investors who were looking to invest in alternative mezzanine tranches of CDOs. Baa1—Baa3 in Moody's terminology, BBB+ to BBB- in Fitch and S&P.

Undercapitalized: A bank that has less than 4 percent of Tier 1 is defined as undercapitalized from a regulatory perspective. However, the market might take a different view of the adequate level of capitalization of banks in periods of stress, when there are concerns about the quality of the bank's lending and assets.

NOTES

PROLOGUE

1. For example, on January 18, 2008, Citigroup had raised $12.5 billion, and on the same day Merrill Lynch raised $6.6 billion.
2. Throughout 2008 the price of oil hit a number of record highs, peaking at $147 a barrel on July 11. During 2008 the threat to the real economy was not just from the financial crisis but also from the commodity price crisis, and we spent as much time and energy dealing with the latter as with the former.

INTRODUCTION:
THE FIRST CRISIS OF GLOBALIZATION

1. To put the crisis in its context, from September 2008 to June 2009, the U.S. economy alone lost 6 million jobs. Output, exports, and jobs fell farther and faster in the autumn and winter of 2008 than at any time in the history of the world, faster than even in the first stage of the Great Depression.
2. In America, the richest country in the world, there are now 8.5 million fewer people in jobs than in 2008. In the poorest countries, 100 million more of our citizens are in poverty. From its peak to its trough, from April 2008 to May 2009, the fall in world trade was 20 percent; world output declined by some $1.5 trillion.
3. Globalization has a number of eloquent critics, and antiglobalization rhetoric is a mainstay of populist politics, particularly on the European center-left. I am proud that whatever my faults, I have maintained a reso-

lutely antiprotectionist, pro–free trade, pro-market, and pro-globalization stance throughout my time as Chancellor, as Prime Minister, and since. My speeches to the European Parliament and the U.S. Congress were elucidations of my views in this regard, deliberately given in environments I did not anticipate being 100 percent receptive.

4. The commodity crisis was not, therefore, as commonly understood, simply a contemporaneous event with the financial crisis, but a huge driver of the need for global action in its own right.

5. In 2007 and 2008 around two hundred banks went under. These were failures on a huge scale, accompanied by revelations of around $2 trillion in rotten assets. Even today, in 2010, $7 trillion of government guarantees protecting the banks from collapse are still in place.

CHAPTER 1:
"ALL I NEED IS OVERNIGHT FINANCE"

1. But the first real sign of the banking collapse to come was the closure in spring 2007 of two hedge funds owned by the Bear Stearns bank. Bear Stearns High-Grade Structured Credit Strategies Master Fund and Bear Stearns High-Grade Structured Credit Strategies Enhanced Leverage Master Fund were hardly household names. Nor, reflecting the new shadow banking system that had developed and which I discuss in chapter 4, were they even based in America; both sought bankruptcy protection in the Cayman Islands Grand Court. They had been exposed to— and brought down by—subprime loans, having bought up packages of mortgages originated by lenders in the U.S. and now sold throughout the world. What mattered was that their total value was not negligible: the write-offs alone from subprime lending have exceeded $2 trillion. To put that in context, writing it off was like writing off the annual output of the U.K. economy.

2. On December 17 the Fed announced twenty-eight days of over-year-end funding, amounting to $20 billion, and the European Central Bank made €500 billion available on December 18.

3. The first commodity to peak was wheat, at $13 a bushel, on February 25, having been $9 at the beginning of January and only $4.80 a year earlier. The numbers for the other commodities were as follows: gold ($1,017 / oz., March 17, 2008; $900; $637); corn ($7.60 / bshl, June 23, 2008; $4.90; $3.80); oil ($147 / brl, July 7, 2008; $92.60; $61.50).

4. Throughout this year commodity prices were hugely volatile; for example, gold reached its 2008 peak that month at $1,017 per ounce, up from $637 in January 2007.

5. At the meeting were John Thain (Merrill Lynch), Jamie Dimon (JP Morgan Chase), Bill Rhodes (Citi), Dick Fuld (Lehman Brothers), Kenneth deRegt (Morgan Stanley), Brian Moynihan (Bank of America), and Bob Kelly (Bank of New York).

6. In fact when the Special Liquidity Scheme closed on January 31, 2009, £185 billion had been lent.

7. Because the share price was now trading below the rights price.

8. And I think the U.K. government will be in the end.

9. Then the world's biggest insurance company, AIG, came under pressure and was nationalized to prevent it from collapsing. This was, as Federal Reserve Chair Ben Bernanke explained, because of its entanglement, its interlocking connections with so many other important and systemically significant institutions. AIG, as he explained, had insured many billions of dollars of loans and securities held by banks around the world, and its failure would have rendered those insurance contracts worthless, imposing large losses on the global banking system. It was the official recognition that in addition to the problems caused by a shadow banking system and a race to the bottom, we also had severe risks posed by the dependence of each financial institution on the other.

10. Mutual banking has a long history in Britain, and I'm pleased to say that the many building societies that didn't demutualize continue to thrive today.

11. This then happened on October 9.

12. By the time we arrived home from Paris, news was also coming out about the multibillion-Euro German rescue of Hypo real estate.

13. Simultaneously the Fed went to 1.5 percent and the European Central Bank to 3.75 percent. Other countries followed suit.

14. In the end, the reaction was that the leak had derailed the plan, but that its impact was still enormous. The *Financial Times* concluded:

> "Calm and orderly" decision-making? Hardly. Now that we finally have details of the government's leaked plan, how does it look? The good news is that it is comprehensive, dealing with the banks' liquidity, capital and funding crises. In that sense, it is bolder than the U.S. bail-out. . . . The most significant element of the plan, though, is the bold attempt to unjam banks' wholesale funding markets through a £250bn guarantee. The novelty is that, instead of a blanket deposit guarantee, the U.K. government is taking more careful aim. What banks have desperately needed in the past few weeks is term funding. So far they have staggered along with overnight funding and central bank liquidity. That is obviously not sustainable. Will it be enough? Barclays, HBOS, Royal Bank

of Scotland and HSBC between them have about £110bn of debt securities maturing in 2008 and 2009. But the U.K. banks do not operate in a vacuum. The U.K. government has done its bit. If funding markets are to unfreeze, other governments need to join in.

15. Despite working so hard, they still had the sense of humor to refer to our bank plan as "the balti bailout," after the take-out curry dish that had been so regularly delivered to officials trapped in meeting rooms hammering out the deal and unable to leave for meals.

CHAPTER 2:
THE PROBLEM FORESEEN: LESSONS
FROM THE ASIAN CRISIS

1. At the point they were bought, shares had been falling for so long they were cheap. The reason nobody was buying privately was because people thought they'd fall further. But as soon as there was a public capital injection there was a floor put under the price.
2. It was that decision—the commitment to low inflation as the means to high investment and high employment—that, in my view, paved the way for a further step forward: what most people now recognize as the major improvements in Britain's public services between 1997 and 2010.
3. I believe that when the G20 met in London eleven years later I was the only surviving member from that original meeting.
4. The old and now obsolete idea was that the IMF visited a country and merely gave private advice to the government of the day. But the system was the wrong one for markets that needed to be informed of the results of independent surveillance. For example, Japan went through the years of its financial crisis with the IMF giving strong private advice but little public information.
5. I managed the transition by assuring everyone that their speeches would be published, but for the purposes of the meeting they should speak to the issue at hand. But when countries represented constituencies—so that prior agreement had to be reached on the text of their submissions—it was impossible to prevent leaders from simply reading out their scripts.
6. Consider, for example, the following extract from my Harvard speech. If you replace the names of the countries, the process is almost exactly the same as the one we lived through ten years later: "This year we have experienced events that were unthinkable just two or three years ago: free

enterprise Hong Kong taking publicly owned stakes in all its private companies; Japan nationalizing its banks; Russia going into default; in America the mounting of one of the biggest ever emergency refinancings not for a bank, but for a hedge fund; most damaging of all, the biggest growth economies of the last decade in East Asia suffering larger contractions in output even than experienced in the Great Depression of the 1930s."

CHAPTER 3:
THE PROBLEM REVEALED: CAPITALISM
WITHOUT CAPITAL

1. The traditional justification for those flows, despite their inherent instability, is that finance serves industry (i.e., the financiers provide the backing for the businesspeople who make and do things in the real economy). But consider this: by some estimates only $2 billion or $3 billion a day, only 2 percent of the eventual total, was necessary to maintain international trade and productive investment. According to the McKinsey Global Institute, the ratio of global financial assets to annual world output has soared from just over 109 percent in 1980 to more than 300 percent. At the time of the crisis the global stock of core financial assets reached $140 trillion, twice the size of the world economy.

2. We know that by early 2007 assets held in hedge funds grew to roughly $1.8 trillion and that asset-backed commercial paper conduits in the form of structured investment vehicles, in auction-rate preferred securities, tender option bonds, and variable rate demand notes had grown in size to $2 trillion. To put these figures in context: the combined balance sheets of the five major investment banks at the time totaled $4 trillion, and the total assets of the entire banking system about $10 trillion. On the eve of the financial crisis, as the report of the New York Fed shows, the volume of cash under management by regulated investors was $2.5 trillion, by unregulated money market intermediaries $1.5 trillion, and by direct money market investors over $3.7 trillion. That figure is greater than all checkable deposits, savings deposits, and time deposits of $6 trillion, but was expected to be repayable on demand, though not supported by any amount of capital.

3. If anything, the problem had been too little government interference in the market, not too much.

4. More than surprised, I was furious—because in a last-gasp attempt to save itself in New York, Lehman had transferred huge amounts of money from London overnight, leaving British employees bereft of any retirement payments, or even their last month's salaries. A similar tale can be told of Mer-

rill Lynch. The latest account, *All the Devils Are Here,* by Bethany McLean and Joe Nocera, as previewed in *Vanity Fair* (October 2010), states that while a board meeting in July 2008 was told that the risk on the firm's books amounted to no more than $83 million, Merrill Lynch's subprime exposure was $55 billion—with Merrill Lynch later recording $8 billion in subprime writeoffs. Yet Merrill paid its traders and executives over $3 billion in bonuses just before its merger with Bank of America.

5. In fact Lehman was acquiring potentially illiquid assets that made it more difficult to raise cash quickly, more difficult to hedge risks, and more difficult to sell in a downturn.

6. Repo, or repurchase, is an agreement on the sale of an asset and a future repurchase. It is a way of funding an asset in the short, or sometimes medium, term.

7. Its total capital ratio went from 18.2 percent in early 2006 to 10.5 percent in the summer of 2007. At the same time the industry high was 18.7 percent.

8. "Tier 1" capital is core capital as a percentage of risk-adjusted assets. Of course being risk-adjusted meant that assets such as subprime synthetic CDOs, because they were Triple A rated, required little capital to be held against them.

9. In evidence to the Valukas Report, Lehman's global financial controller confirmed that "the only purpose or motive for [Repo 105] transactions was reduction in the balance sheet" and that "there was no substance to the transactions."

10. British and American banks were not alone in their bad behavior. Of course we still know too little about what's been happening in the greater part of the world—in China, Russia, India, and Brazil—where state-controlled banks hold the majority of assets in the financial system. But we now know that in Germany too the Landesbanken, which are banks owned by the regional states and make up one-fifth of the country's banking assets, lost nearly €10 billion in 2008 alone, the consequence of years of cheap financing unwisely invested in a range of securities—including U.S. subprime mortgages—that then went wrong. In 2009 four regional banks alone—HSHNordbank, WestLB, Landesbank Baden-Württemberg, and BayernLB—made a combined €5.3 billion net loss. We will come later to what is a widespread belief, that the scale of write-downs, in Germany and other parts of Europe, that have still to be made has been underestimated.

11. Even as the financial crisis built up and controversy raged around him, RBS Chief Executive Fred Goodwin signed up a £1 million sports deal with the Indian cricketer Sachin Tendulkar in September 2008.

12. One irony was that even as he did the biggest banking deal of all time, the

prize that Fred Goodwin had really wanted—another prestigious entry into the American market with LaSalle—was denied him. As part of the deal it was sold off to Bank of America.

13. This is cited, for example, in Ian Fraser's blog, July 13, 2009, "The Recklessness of Cummings."

14. The deals HBOS was involved in included some of the best-known companies in Britain. In 1998 they were bankers to the City Inn chain of hotels, but made it a 50-50 joint venture, worth £110 million. In 1999 they were themselves part of Scotland's largest management buyout, buying into a £100 million takeover of the property firm CALA. They then financed Sir Rocco Forte's RF hotels (buying £70 million in equity and offering £200 million in loans). Then came Sir Philip Green's well-publicized purchase of Topshop owner Arcadia in 2002. Here HBOS provided the entire working capital of £950 million and took an 8 percent equity stake. When Green went on to take a tilt at Marks & Spencer in 2004, he again turned to HBOS. HBOS deals also involved the retail tycoon Sir Tom Hunter, Prince Al-Waleed of Saudi Arabia, and the Icelandic entrepreneurs behind Baugur, co-owning with them large parts of British main street properties. To this were added shares they took in David Lloyd Leisure, House of Fraser, and the cinema group Vue.

15. In other words, the gap between rich and poor has increased because the very top have pulled ahead quickly, not because the living standards of those toward the bottom have fallen or stagnated. In fact, through the national minimum wage, the Child Tax Credit, the Child Trust Fund, and other initiatives, the living standards of those in middle- and modest-income Britain rose substantially during the thirteen years of Labour government.

16. Countries have also introduced unilateral policies in this area. In January 2010 the U.S. government announced that it would seek to impose a 0.15 percent tax on the uninsured liabilities—defined as total assets net of Tier 1 capital and insured deposits—of large financial institution, to raise $90 billion during 2011–20. The French government has implemented a temporary tax on bonuses granted in 2009 by banks and other financial institutions (excluding insurance and portfolio management companies). And in March 2010 the German government announced plans to introduce a systemic risk-adjusted bank levy to mitigate the negative externalities associated with systemic risks. The Swedish Financial Stability Fund (SFSF) was introduced as the financing vehicle of four instruments available to the Swedish government to protect financial stability: bank guarantees, capital injections, emergency support, and deposit insurance. The SFSF covers deposit-taking institutions incorporated in Sweden, with a target size of 2.5 percent of GDP in fifteen years.

CHAPTER 4:
THE PROBLEM ASSAILED:
THE ONE-TRILLION-DOLLAR PLAN

1. Previous G20 meetings had taken place only at the finance ministers' level.
2. Transparency, supervision of hedge funds, new requirements for bank capital and liquidity, and a new college of supervisors to deal with multinational institutions.
3. The figure of $1 trillion was planned well in advance but revealed to only a trusted few outside this circle. Having worked through that we needed $1 trillion to provide a backstop, we approached the IMF, the World Bank, and governments one by one to agree to the detailed paragraphs in question.
4. It was on this trip to Chile that Jens Stoltenberg made his quip about my rhetorical consistency.
5. As we finished our meal in the rather grand setting of the state dining room of No. 10, we enjoyed a lighter moment. As our partners joined us from a dinner they had enjoyed with some of Britain's most successful women, our chef for the evening, Jamie Oliver, came through with his apprentice chefs to be introduced and thanked. But for him it was no routine catering evening: his wife was expecting a baby that night. The next day, when we heard the good news (a healthy baby daughter), the G20 sent him and his wife and new baby our congratulations.
6. The degree of secrecy about the figure was important not because we wanted an "announceable" for the day, but because unveiling something far in excess of expectations was an important part of jump-starting the market.
7. The press seemed fixated on the precise language around fiscal stimulus and supposed splits between the U.S.-U.K. and France-Germany. The reality was that there was enormous common ground, and this was not for me the main objective. The most important battle for me was always going to be about the precise figures we put to the tangible support the global economy was being given.
8. I am particularly proud to have campaigned while at Edinburgh for a pay increase for campus cleaners and for the university's disinvestment from apartheid South Africa. I felt my life had come full circle when I was later able to introduce the minimum wage as Chancellor and to campaign with Nelson Mandela for increases in aid, for debt cancellation, and for trade justice.
9. Needless to say, making mobile phone calls from the chair of international meetings is not normal protocol.
10. Back in 2008 we could never have contemplated the scale of the individ-

ual rescues that international authorities would have to support, but by the summer of 2009 the IMF had already authorized $5 billion in stand-by payments and $78 billion in flexible credit lines. Ukraine was bailed out, with the European Union and the IMF together contributing a total of $16 billion in support. Since then Hungary, Latvia, and Greece have drawn on the facility.

11. But to accompany national monetary stimulus there had to be national fiscal stimulus too. We now know that a total of $3 trillion was injected into the budgets of national economies to take us out of recession.

12. A commitment that has disappeared in Europe following the Greece crisis.

13. Indeed, so important to Europe was that outcome that Chancellor Merkel broke off from the last days of her election campaign in Germany to attend the summit.

14. As I left the first night of the summit I talked with President Sarkozy. We agreed that the G20 had to work not just as a short-term emergency summit, but as a long-term pact between the major economic powers. And we had to make sure the G8 aligned with the G20 in ways that did not alienate the non-G8 members, but still ensured that the G8 retained its role in foreign affairs. Since Sarkozy had been such a brilliantly innovative president of the European Council, I thought the best way forward was to nominate him as chair of the G20 for the year in which he was also president of the G8. The next day there was agreement at the summit that the G20 chair nation in 2011 would be France.

CHAPTER 5:
GOING FOR GLOBAL GROWTH AND JOBS

1. Uncertainty about the future has meant that while much of Europe and America have had only what might be called an "inventory recovery," companies are undergoing a "balance sheet recession," what economists tell us when the private sector does not take up low interest rates to invest but pays down debt to hold up their balance sheets.

2. If the story of the past twenty years, the rise of China and India, is well understood, the sheer scale of it—and what it means—has never been fully absorbed. Together, India and China, more than a third of the world's total population, are growing their economies at between 8 percent and 10 percent a year. Jim O'Neill and his team at Goldman Sachs have christened the cluster of huge growth countries the BRICs (Brazil, Russia, India, and China) and report that in the years up to 2020 the BRIC countries will be growing twice as fast as the rest of the world—and three times as fast as America and Europe.

3. The latest report from Goldman Sachs is that U.S. unemployment will remain at around 10 percent even if there is no fiscal tightening until 2013 and no monetary tightening until 2015. Even with a massive fiscal world stimulus worth $3 trillion and the widespread injection of money on an unparalleled scale into the world economy, the overall decline in global demand for goods (of around $2 trillion) is not being fully replaced, putting employment and prosperity at risk.
4. Imports of high-income countries are still 20 percent below that earlier pre-crisis peak, but the rise in their exports is still far short of 20 percent.
5. Under good policy coordination, fiscal consolidation, structural reforms, and growing domestic demand in surplus countries combine to deliver 2.5 percent higher growth after five years, 30 million more jobs, world output growing by over $1.5 trillion (in a $70 trillion world economy), and an estimated 33 million people brought out of poverty. But a scenario in which the worst risks materialize would cut global output by more than 3 percent (about $2.25 trillion) over the medium term relative to the refined baseline, with 23 million jobs at risk and 60 million people falling into poverty.
6. Half a century ago America was responsible for nearly one-fifth of all exports, but has seen its share of exports halved. In 1970 China accounted for just 1 percent of world exports. That share only reached 2 percent in 1990, and it was around 3 percent at the turn of the century. But in an astonishing leap forward, from 2000 to the start of the great recession, China's share of world exports has soared to almost 10 percent, overtaking Japan and then Germany, and looks likely to hit 12 percent by 2014.
7. Take the computer industry. As Andy Grove, formerly of Intel, has explained, the computer industry now employs 1.5 million workers in Asia but just 165,000 in America. In fact there are fewer computer workers now in America than there were in 1975, when the first PC was invented.
8. This trend shows no sign of decelerating. As Alan Blinder, formerly of the Federal Reserve, has argued, as services become global the cost over twenty years to America alone will be the export of at least 30 million service jobs, in addition to those already lost in other areas of the economy.
9. On the eve of the recession the spending of just 600 million consumers in Europe and the U.S.—just 10 percent of the world's population— amounted to 36 percent of the world's economic activity. In contrast, the consumer spending of China, with 20 percent of the world's population, was worth only 2 percent.
10. The case for global rebalancing is strong. More credible fiscal adjustment would mitigate but would be unlikely to reverse the decline in domestic demand in those economies undergoing consolidation. Current account deficits would narrow in advanced deficit countries and be matched by

lower external surpluses in emerging and advanced surplus countries. The Euro area current account would be broadly unchanged, but imbalances within the area would narrow. While global imbalances would narrow, global growth would be lower. This reflects insufficient rebalancing of global demand; accordingly, monetary policy in advanced economies could afford to stay accommodative for a more extended period, since inflation pressures remain contained and inflation expectations are well anchored.

11. Some would even go as far as was said in Grover Cleveland's presidency: "It is the job of the people to support the government, but not the job of the government to support the people."

12. There is another reason for pursuing an aggressive growth strategy in industrialized Europe. Our societies are ageing, so we have to work harder at achieving high growth to ensure that, even as the working-age population falls, the growth rate ahead is not lower than in the second half of the twentieth century.

CHAPTER 6:
THE AMERICAN CHALLENGE

1. Almost all the great inventions of recent years have come out of America—from the revolutions in distribution with the car and airplane, the revolutions in energy, the revolutions in production itself with glass, paper, metal, and plastic to biotech, to new products from the computer onward.

2. Long-term unemployment, permanent employment losses, young people waiting for their first job.

3. With the workforce growing by 1 percent per year and productivity around 3 percent, growth needs to exceed 4 percent. The end of the fiscal stimulus will take 1.5 percent growth out of the economy in 2011, and the deficit will start to fall from 10 to 3 percent of national income by 2015, a degree of fiscal tightening that has been achieved only once over a ten-year period. At least $1 trillion is yet to be taken out of the economy, making the achievement of 4 percent levels of growth more difficult.

4. GM now sells more cars in China than it does in the U.S., and makes most of them there too. The company now employs 32,000 hourly workers in China. But only 52,000 GM hourly workers remain in the United States, down from 468,000 in 1970. And GM isn't just hiring low-tech assembly workers in China. In the summer of 2010 the firm broke ground there on a $250 million advanced technology center to develop batteries and other alternative energy sources.

5. In this period the earnings of chief executives have risen from, on average, twenty-six times median incomes to three hundred times.

6. Today, as the Congressional Budget Office found from their analysis of tax data, the top 1 percent of households own twice as much of the corporate wealth in the United States as they did even in the early 1990s.

7. He went on to say, "The share of after-tax income garnered by the households in the top 1% of the income distribution increased from 8% in 1979 to 14% in 2004."

8. This reflects the 20 percent shock Americans have felt since the recession hit; a 20 percent fall in the wealth of American households, a 20 percent cut in wealth in shares, and a 20 percent fall in credit cards. Despite strong sales of new goods like the iPad and the iPhone 4, Americans' discretionary spending is now at its lowest share of national income since the post-1945 austerity years. As I write, months into the recovery, U.S. banks have repossessed nearly 258,000 homes in one three-month period; mortgage applications are at their lowest level since the mid-1990s, and housing starts and sales of new homes have fallen to an all-time low. Where once U.S. homeownership ran at 69.2 percent, it has now fallen to 66.9 percent.

9. The value of American homes, $13 trillion at its peak, is now below $9 trillion. Pensions and overall retirement assets, American households' second-largest source of wealth, have fallen from $10 trillion to $8 trillion, and on top of that savings and investment assets have lost at least a trillion. According to the American editor of the *Financial Times,* "To invert the classic Horatio Alger stories, in today's America if you are born in rags, you are likelier to stay in rags than in almost any corner of old Europe." He goes on to cite the distinguished American economist Larry Katz, author of a seminal work on education and the economy: "Think of the American economy as a large apartment block. A century ago— even 30 years ago—it was the object of envy. But in the last generation its character has changed. The penthouses at the top keep getting larger and larger. The apartments in the middle are feeling more and more squeezed and the basement has flooded. To round it off, the elevator is no longer working. That broken elevator is what gets people down the most."

10. Standard estimates suggest that a dollar of public spending raises GDP by around $1.50. Republican thinking in the U.S. is essentially that a deficit through tax cuts leads to incentives, which generate new activities and higher revenue. They have been using the research of Roemer, which suggests that every dollar spent on tax cuts boosts GDP by three dollars. But whether by spending or tax cuts, "an increase of 40% in ratio of public debt to GDP," says Martin Wolf, "would cost the taxpayer 0.4 per cent of GDP and is a small price to pay for low unemployment."

CHAPTER 7:
CHINA'S OPPORTUNITY

1. But we must remember Guangdong-based manufacturers also have the option of moving to cheaper locations in China's interior. Today's urban population is less than 50 percent, lower than the average figure for other nations at the same stage of economic growth, and with a large number of mainland cities yet to be developed. Today most enterprises are in China's towns and villages. When the American Chamber of Commerce in China surveyed U.S. companies last year they found that already half of them had a presence outside the country's established hubs. At the Delta Electronics plant in Wujiang, Jiangsu Province, the minimum wage is 50 percent lower than in the cities, at just $200 a month; in Wuhu, Anhui Province, it is 60 percent lower. So some factories have shifted inland, closer to the provinces from where migration to the cities originated.

2. China, of course, has a long way to go in improving its infrastructure and its investment in its workforce. Fixed investment per person is still only about 5 percent of what the American or Japanese worker has. But in 2009 total fixed investment, which goes wider than public infrastructure to include all business investment, amounted to about half of all Chinese economic activity, whereas in most developed countries it accounts for, at best, around 20 percent of GDP. Investment in Chinese domestic infrastructure projects, including the speeding up of construction of one hundred new airports, has risen to become 15 percent of China's gross domestic product, something no other country has been able to do and in sharp contrast to America and Europe, where such spending is 2 or 3 percent of national output.

3. For example, with half a billion customers, China Mobile is the largest Chinese company listed overseas by market value, and has overtaken Nokia Siemens as the second largest creator of telecom hardware behind Ericsson. Today it has a global market share of 20 percent. Haier is the world's fourth largest maker of appliances, with a growth figure of 10,000 percent since 2000. Geely has licensed the Volvo brand; Tsingtao Lager is ready to challenge Bud Light and become the top Chinese consumer product exported. And the speed and scale of the rise of Palm Baidu—China's version of Google—has given it over 70 percent of the Chinese search engine market in partnership with China Mobile.

4. In the 1980s Japan became exporter to the world; then the Asian tigers took over. But the difference between the 10 percent share of China now and the 10 percent share Japan won in the 1980s but then lost is that when Japan moved into the higher value-added technology-driven

products, wages rose and traditional export industries, like their textiles, became too expensive.

5. One study suggests that a 20 percent rise in Chinese consumption might well lead to an extra $25 billion of American exports; that could create over 200,000 American jobs.

6. It is important to put China's phenomenal rise in perspective. It is the major beneficiary of the huge trend toward the global sourcing of goods and services and as such is part of—but not all of—the global supply chain that has developed. Much of the value of the Chinese goods consumed in America and Europe is created outside China in a global production chain, as is the case for the iPod, as discussed in the preceding chapter.

7. For example, China is not only the world's leading exporter, but the biggest exporter by far to the U.S. Recently China's market share of American imports rose to a record 19 percent, so one manufacturing product in every five America buys is from China. Eighty percent of toys sold in the U.S. are now made in China, but also 50 percent or more of computers, of mobile phones, and even of iPods and iPads.

8. There is of course in China an elite of luxury goods spenders. The French Hermès Group has just unveiled a brand, Shang Xia, designed specifically for Chinese millionaires. But the gap between rich and poor is such that even if China could match the U.S. in total output as early as 2020, as a World Bank forecast suggested in June 2010, average Chinese per capita income would still be one-quarter the U.S. level.

9. Although average incomes have risen very rapidly in recent decades, they still stand at between one-seventh and one-eighth the levels in the United States, lower than in Turkey or Colombia and not much higher than in El Salvador or Egypt. China is ranked 124th in the world for income per person.

10. There is another reason for China's unique economic decision making, one that is intensely political, but with ramifications that are profoundly economic. The one-child policy has ensured that Chinese society is ageing quickly. Many people fear that, unlike India, which will have a growing population of thirty- and forty-year-old workers, China will run out of labor. But China's labor supply is still growing. While it is true that the number of younger people entering the labor force will fall by almost 30 percent over the next ten years, and it is also true too that older workers are less willing to move to the coastal factories that depend on migrant labor, China still has 40 percent of its labor force in agriculture (with productivity at about one-sixth of the level in the rest of the economy), and that percentage will drop only slowly. Britain has only 1 percent of its population still working on the land, America 2 percent, but even in 2020 China will still have 25 percent on the land. Moreover, the coun-

try's rural villages still contain perhaps 70 million potential industrial migrants, who might be expected to leave in search of work. And there are others who might work in the growing number of factories moving inland close to their homes. In addition there remains the "floating population" of 130 million migrants who work where the boom is, earning around $200 a month.

11. China is now building one thousand towns and one hundred airports for the new industrial population. In the next ten years, China will build ten new cities the size of New York. Over the next twenty years, by 2030, China will add 350 million more new city dwellers, more than the entire population of the United States today. For the month of January 2010, the hostels were virtually empty, showing how few workers had decided to make the new industrial towns their home.

12. A new study by Dennis Tao Yang of the Chinese University of Hong Kong, Vivian Chen of the Conference Board, and Ryan Monarch of the University of Michigan suggests that Chinese workers, in the cities at least, are now as expensive as their Thai or Filipino peers. But the fact is that while labor costs in China's bigger firms tripled between 1995 and 2004, as stated by Chen, Bart van Ark, also of the Conference Board, and Harry Wu of Hitotsubashi University, labor productivity more than quintupled.

13. China's public spending, which recently doubled, is still only 6 percent of the Chinese economy, compared with the West's 25 percent.

14. In 2009 China's exports slumped by 17 percent. But other countries' fell even more, and China overtook Germany as second only to America for exports. China's share of world exports is set to rise dramatically again, to an astonishing 12 percent by 2014, according to the IMF economic outlook, overtaking America as its share falls back to 8 percent.

15. Allocating a larger proportion of the expenditure increase to health and pensions would generate an even bigger rise in consumption. Allocating all of the 1 percent expenditure increase to health would raise consumption by 1.3 percent. If allocated just to pensions, consumption would rise 1.6 percent.

16. Chinese trade with Germany is one example on which we can all build. German trade with China has risen 60 percent since 2007. In fact German exports to China will soon exceed exports to France. This $100 billion trade between the two countries already is more than twice that of Britain or the nearest European competitor. While less than the U.S., Hong Kong, or South Korea, Germany is by far the biggest European investor in the country.

17. The Economic Cooperation Framework Agreement between Taiwan and China has already removed a thousand tariffs.

18. In the three years before the crisis, China's currency revalued upward

by around 20 percent or so, but with the crisis the domestic priority became saving Chinese jobs. Applying a purchasing-power parity (PPP) approach, Menzie Chinn of the University of Wisconsin at Madison and his collaborators estimated an undervaluation of about 40 percent. But after the World Bank's 40 percent downward revision of Chinese GDP in PPP terms, that undervaluation disappeared completely. Nick Lardy and Morris Goldstein of the Peterson Institute of International Economics suggested that the renminbi was probably undervalued only by 12 to 16 percent at the end of 2008. Yang Yao at Peking University found even less misalignment. The expert view of Fred Bergsten of the Peterson Institute remains that the renminbi may be 40 percent undervalued against the dollar. Bergsten claims that China now has to intervene in currency markets to the tune of $350 billion a year to stop the renminbi rising against the dollar. He says the trade deficit can be expressed as an effective 40 percent tariff on imported American goods and a 40 percent subsidy to Chinese exports to the United States—an effective loss of one million U.S. jobs, and many more if we include the other Asian economies, such as Singapore, Malaysia, Taiwan, and Hong Kong, all linked to the dollar.

CHAPTER 8:
INDIA AND THE ASIAN ECONOMIES

1. We know that India's manufacturing sector is expanding and that its service sector exports are growing, but China produces 13 percent of the world's manufactured goods and has nearly 10 percent of world exports. India's manufacturing is 2 percent of world output, and it has only 3 percent of world exports. In services China's share of world trade is 3.1 percent, higher than India's 2.2 percent.
2. Of course if India is to truly expand the rate of education it needs to deal with the problem of child labor. Nearly 15 percent of India's ten- to fourteen-year-olds are in the workforce. The figure is less than the shocking rates of Mali, Niger, and Uganda, which are over 45 percent, but worse than China and Egypt.
3. For the Indians, "inclusive growth" now rightly has to mean more than that the income of the bottom 20 percent should rise with the average, by up to 10 percent a year, but that their share of the proceeds of growth should be 20 percent. If this were to happen, the distribution of subsidies, two-thirds of which go to those who are not poor, would have to be reviewed.
4. In Taiwan income per capita is almost seven times that of China.

CHAPTER 9:
LIVING WITH THE EURO

1. In my speech to the European Parliament on March 24, 2009, I put it this way: "I stand here proud to be British and proud to be European, representing a country that does not see itself as an island adrift from Europe but as a country at the centre of Europe, not in Europe's slipstream but in Europe's mainstream."

2. The European Central Bank and the newly created European Financial Stability Facility—a €440 billion ($545 billion) special purpose vehicle to stabilize the European bond markets—have, together, still to absorb all the low-grade debt that came with the integration of European banking. In the absence of the ECB's generous liquidity provisions, many more banks would have gone under. "We now know the European Central Bank will refinance sovereign debt for a long time," writes Simon Johnson, author of *13 Bankers,* "but there are 22 trillion Euros of credits (more than twice Eurozone annual GDP) provided by the Eurozone banking system largely to the private sector. . . . If the banking system decides it needs to tighten up on risk-taking, some of this credit will be cut off—thus further slowing growth in the region."

3. Without this program Greece would be unable to pay debt interest and default. But as a result of it Greece does not have to go back to the markets for two years. In return, Greece has to cut spending over three years by 5 percent of GDP. Average pension benefits will be cut 11 percent, wages for government workers will be cut 14 percent, and the basic rate for the value-added tax will rise from 21 percent to 23 percent. Tax yield in a country not known for getting its taxes in has to rise by an additional 4 percent of GDP, which will also require a crackdown on tax evasion. According to the London School of Economics, tax evasion has consistently reduced Greece's tax yield by as much as one-quarter. Deficits will fall below 3 percent of GDP not in 2012, as once promised, but only by 2014. But no other European country has ever managed to raise revenue equal to one dollar in every fifteen of its national income to pay for its debts and run a primary surplus of 4.5 percent of GDP. Greek unemployment—today at 10 percent—is forecast by many economists to rise, and to peak nearer 20 percent. With a fall in unit labor costs, and wages, Greece is likely to find itself in a prolonged slump. But even with wage cuts, public debt will rise to 150 percent of GDP. The deal is that as Greece cuts its deficit, the European Central Bank will underpin Greek banks, suspending the minimum credit rating required for the Greek government-backed assets used to secure its liquidity.

4. The first benefit would be lower transaction costs for business and consumers. We estimated these as worth around 0.1 to 0.2 percent of GDP, £1 billion a year, with the gains greater for smaller companies and permanent for all. The second would be diminished exchange rate volatility, with gains for both large and small companies, especially in the manufacturing sector—again with potentially the greatest gains for smaller companies. The third benefit would be greater cross-border trade, and thus the potential for increased commerce and growth.

5. I had to ask whether we had achieved, or could achieve, sustainable and durable convergence between Britain and the rest of Europe. Convergence would mean that the British economy could live permanently with Euro area interest rates and still be able to advance our objectives of high and stable levels of growth and employment, and of sustained and stable funding of our schools, hospitals, and other public services. I discovered that over the past thirty years interest rates in Britain have had to be, on average, 3 percent higher than those in Germany. The short-term interest rate divergence between Britain and the Euro area had fallen from 4 percent in 1997, when we came to power, to 1.75 percent by 2004. But we still had to be sure that there was not just a cyclical convergence in inflation and interest rates at a particular point in history, but a structural convergence that was sustainable for the long term. Moreover, we had to be sure that, if real interest rates or business cycles did diverge, Britain had the necessary flexibility to deal with the resulting stresses and strains and still sustain what I consider to be the overarching moral goals of economic policy: stability, growth, and employment.

6. President Barroso said, "Europe 2020 is about what we need to do today and tomorrow to get the EU economy back on track. The crisis has exposed fundamental issues and unsustainable trends that we cannot ignore any longer. Europe has a growth deficit which is putting our future at risk. We must decisively tackle our weaknesses and exploit our many strengths. We need to build a new economic model based on knowledge, low-carbon economy and high employment levels. This battle requires mobilization of all actors across Europe."

7. Enhanced cross-border cooperation in public-private partnerships to address climate change, a potential €50 billion of additional public and private investment, will also create the low-carbon jobs of the future.

8. Today less than 20 percent is contracted across the Union.

CHAPTER 10:
POST-CRISIS AFRICA

1. Shriti Vadera and Justin Forsyth accompanied me on this visit to the UN. Justin was then my Downing Street senior adviser on development, and later became the Director of Strategic Communications. As with many of my senior staff, his background was in the campaigning movement to make poverty history. I reflect on that with some pride. I don't believe there has been any administration anywhere in the G8 with so many of the strategic roles occupied by people whose life work has been global justice concerns.

2. The year 2009 saw the numbers in absolute poverty in Africa increase to 388 million. As the Africa Progress Panel (chaired by former UN Secretary General Kofi Annan) reported in June 2010, desperately needed improvements in growth and living standards and the strengthening of democracy had shuddered to a halt at the decade's end. Countries on the verge of graduating from aid to global capital markets found their growth stalled. The hopeful trend in governance was interrupted by a series of coups d'état. The number of conflict-ridden African states, which had fallen to seven in 2006, was eleven in 2008 and 2009. Battle-related deaths, which fell from around 60,000 in 1999 to 1,400 in 2005, increased again to 6,000 in 2008. The only good economic news of 2010 was that in twenty-seven countries, real per capita income was at least not contracting. In contrast, economic growth in twenty-six countries has fallen back to below the rate of increase in population.

3. Even though together they account for four-fifths of the population of developing countries, the BRICs plus Africa generate just a third of all their imports. For decades the imports of developing countries have never been more than half the imports to developed countries, but in the world recovery developing countries now account for more than half of the increase in world import demand since 2000.

4. By 2050 Nigeria is expected to be bigger than Canada, Italy, and Korea. Egypt will be bigger than Spain, Pakistan, and Bangladesh.

5. Kenya's factory-floor productivity is close to China's, but Kenyan firms face a 40 percent cost disadvantage because of so-called indirect costs.

6. According to the charity WaterAid, only four in ten Africans have access to a basic toilet, and 570 million lack adequate sanitation. This situation results in two thousand deaths a day from diarrhea, which is now the biggest killer of children under five in Africa. We need the next stages of scientific medical advance in Africa, the development of new drugs, vaccines, and procedures, to be accompanied by progressive

building up of permanent health capacity, especially with the training of health workers.

CHAPTER 11:
A PLAN FOR GLOBAL GROWTH

1. These figures are from private conversations with the author. The best estimate Goldman Sachs could give me was that the US and EU share of investment in world investment might fall from 40 percent now to around 35 percent by 2015 and 30 percent by 2020.
2. South America and Australasia are therefore excluded not because they should not be part of a global growth compact, but because my exposure to the particularities of those economies has been far less than to those analyzed in part 3.
3. This is something we touched on in the 2009 G20s, but we have been pushed off track by the focus on debt crises. The time in between, however, has reinforced my point, because the recoveries have been anemic and reveal more concrete data that give a greater measure of the challenge.
4. The fragility of global growth prospects is emphasized by the World Bank, which has said that a 1 percent increase in bond yields would slow world growth from 3.3 percent to 2 percent in 2010, and from 3 percent to 0.7 percent in 2011, with the developed world experiencing growth at only 0.9 percent in 2010 and 0.6 percent in 2011.
5. The jobs figure includes eight million more men and women employed in America and Europe.
6. Of course they also present the downside to their baseline case: 30 million unemployed worldwide. And it is all too easy for the leading world economies to fall into this downside case by following national solutions to this global problem.
7. The Mais lectures are an annual event in the City of London.
8. It is for that reason that I advocate measures to deal with the moral hazards that have grown and for action to be coordinated. Of course one country striking out on its own could face an adverse market reaction.

CONCLUSION: MARKETS NEED MORALS

1. There is no reason to believe that the world will automatically shake itself from that. For example, we have watched Japan lose twenty years' worth of growth and their tight-knit society slowly fray at the edges.

BIBLIOGRAPHY

As we, as a British Government, addressed the global crisis, I read widely starting with Ben Bernanke's work on the 1930s.

And in the last three months since leaving government I've read in even greater detail a large number of articles, documents and treatises on the causes and consequences of what I call "the first crisis of globalization."

Below I cite the books I have consulted. I want to acknowledge the depth and width of the scholarship already in print that analyzes the crisis from its deep roots to its wide repercussions. And I have benefited from the work that was started in Number 10; James Bowler Matthew Style and a team of civil servants produced and published their examination of how the crisis happened and the actions that had to be taken.

The books below highlight my starting point: what has been happening to the world economy as a whole. And as I have examined each continent and the contribution it can make to global economic growth, I have been grateful for the chance to consult highly impressive research work done by Goldman Sachs, McKinsey, the IMF, the World Bank, the African Development Bank, the Asian Development Bank, the Bank of England, the Financial Services Authority, and the European Union, among others. Many of the figures I draw on about the state of the world economy in 2010 come from these sources.

A number of books listed below are important for their own analyses of the causes of the crisis. Perhaps I have given more prominence

than others to the more basic issues of globalization—the global sourcing of goods and its consequences and the unsupervised global flows of
capital—and so I have started my account with the forces I first saw at
work in the Asian crisis.

Others have looked at the whole period of what is called "the Washington Consensus." There is a great deal of work now available on the
history of monetary policies pursued in America and elsewhere in the
last two decades.

Some books focus in on what has been called the savings glut, and
others on the imbalances caused by the growth of substantial trade surpluses and deficits. More than one study—for example Rajan, Stiglitz,
and Krugman—has focused on rising inequality in America in the last
twenty-five years and its consequences.

The roots of the crisis within the financial system have been examined
by a number of brilliant authors. Some have joined official reports from
governments' central banks, regulatory agencies, and parliamentary and
congressional committees in highlighting the shortage of capital, the use
of off-balance sheet vehicles, and the extraordinary speed and potential
destructiveness of the growth of certain derivatives. Some have focused
on the experience of hedge funds, especially after LTCM, the impact of
the bonus culture and the failures of corporate governance, and the use
of offshore financial centers. When looking specifically at weaknesses in
supervision, many have emphasized the procyclicality of too many regulatory instruments, and the failure to grasp the complexity and interconnectedness of the new instruments. Although I do not say much about
this, accountants, auditors, and credit rating agencies have rightly come
under the microscope. Very good studies have appeared on the experience—and in most cases, the failings—of individual companies at the
center of the financial storm.

There is also a new body of writing about the lessons "economics"
is learning. First a series of books and articles reminded us of both the
uses of Keynesian economics and the study of behavioral economics.
Now, as people reflect even more deeply, there is a wider questioning
of what the future nature of capitalism will be and what is the right
relationship in a global economy between governments and markets.
The study of political economy is back on the agenda, and there can be

little doubt that the teaching of economics will change radically. But we should look to the future as well as reflect on the past. I hope there will also be a new interest in what I will call "global growth economics"—in charting how coordinated approaches by individual countries and continents can yield mutual benefits and rescue parts of the world from low growth, high unemployment, and extreme poverty.

Ahamed, Liaquat. *Lords of Finance: The Bankers Who Broke the World*. New York: Penguin Press, 2009.

Akerlof, George A., and Robert J. Shiller. *Animal Spirits: How Human Psychology Drives the Economy, and Why It Matters for Global Capitalism*. Princeton, NJ: Princeton University Press, 2009.

Anderson, Chris. *The Long Tail: Why the Future of Business Is Selling Less of More*. New York: Hyperion, 2006.

Authers, John. *The Fearful Rise of Markets: Global Bubbles, Synchronized Meltdowns, and How to Prevent Them in the Future*. London: FT Press, 2010.

Bardhan, Pranab. *Awakening Giants, Feet of Clay: Assessing the Economic Rise of China and India*. Princeton, NJ: Princeton University Press, 2010.

Beech, Matt. *The Political Philosophy of New Labour* (International Library of Political Studies). UK: Tauris Academic Studies, 2005.

Belich, James. *Replenishing the Earth: The Settler Revolution and the Rise of the Angloworld, 1783–1939*. New York: Oxford University Press, 2009.

Bhagwati, Jagdish. *In Defense of Globalization*. New York: Oxford University Press, 2004.

Bremmer, Ian. *The End of the Free Market: Who Wins the War Between States and Corporations?* New York: Portfolio, 2010.

Cable, Vince. *The Storm: The World Economic Crisis and What It Means*. UK: Atlantic Books, 2009.

Caldwell, Christopher. *Reflections on the Revolution in Europe: Immigration, Islam, and the West*. New York: Doubleday, 2009.

Clarke, Peter. *Keynes: The Rise, Fall, and Return of the 20th Century's Most Influential Economist*. London: Bloomsbury Publishing, 2009.

Cohen, Adam. *Nothing to Fear: FDR's Inner Circle and the Hundred Days That Created Modern America*. New York: Penguin Press, 2009.

Cohen, Ronald. *The Second Bounce of the Ball: Turning Risk into Opportunity*. London: Weidenfeld & Nicolson, 2007.

Commers, M.S. Ronald, Wim Vandekerckhove, and An Verlinden, eds. *Ethics in an Era of Globalization* (Ethics and Global Politics). Burlington, VT: Ashgate Publishing Company, 2008.

Corthorn, Paul, and Jonathan Davis, eds. *The British Labour Party and the Wider*

World: Domestic Politics, Internationalism and Foreign Policy (International Library of Political Studies). UK: Tauris Academic Studies, 2008.

Das, Gurcharan. *India Unbound: The Social and Economic Revolution from Independence to the Global Information Age.* New York: Random House, 2001.

Davies, Gavyn. FT Blog. London, 2010.

Davies, Howard. *Banking on the Future: The Fall and Rise of Central Banking.* Princeton, NJ: Princeton University Press, 2010.

———, and David Green. *Global Financial Regulation: The Essential Guide.* Malden, MA: Polity Press, 2008.

Dumas, Charles. *Globalisation Fractures: How Major Nations' Interests Are Now in Conflict.* London: Profile Books, 2010.

Earls, Mark. *Herd: How to Change Mass Behaviour by Harnessing Our True Nature.* West Sussex, UK: John Wiley & Sons, 2009.

Easterbrook, Gregg. *Sonic Boom: Globalization at Mach Speed.* New York: Random House, 2009.

Eichengreen, Barry. *Globalizing Capital: A History of the International Monetary System.* Princeton, NJ: Princeton University Press, 2008.

Felice, William F. *The Global New Deal: Economic and Social Human Rights in World Politics.* Lanham, MD: Rowman & Littlefield, 2010.

Ferguson, Niall. *The Ascent of Money: A Financial History of the World.* New York: Penguin Press, 2008.

Findlay, Robert, and Kevin H. O'Rourke. *Power and Plenty: Trade, War, and the World Economy in the Second Millennium.* Princeton, NJ: Princeton University Press, 2007.

Folkerts-Landau, David, and Carl-Johan Lindgren. *Toward a Framework for Financial Stability* (World Economic and Financial Surveys). Washington, DC: International Monetary Fund, 1998.

Fraser, Ian. *Examining HBOS.* http://www.ianfraser.org/examining-hbos/. June 9, 2009.

Friedman, Thomas L. *Hot, Flat, and Crowded: Why We Need a Green Revolution—and How It Can Renew America.* New York: Farrar, Straus and Giroux, 2008.

———. *The World Is Flat: A Brief History of the Twenty-first Century.* New York: Farrar, Straus, and Giroux, 2005.

Furman, Jason, and Jason E. Bordoff, eds. *Path to Prosperity: Hamilton Project Ideas on Income Security, Education, and Taxes.* Washington, DC: Brookings Institution Press, 2008.

Galbraith, John Kenneth. *The Great Crash 1929.* Boston: Houghton Mifflin, 1955.

———. *A Short History of Financial Euphoria.* New York: Penguin Books, 1990.

Gamble, Andrew. *The Spectre at the Feast: Capitalist Crisis and the Politics of Recession*. New York: Palgrave Macmillan, 2009.

Gasparino, Charles. *The Sellout: How Three Decades of Wall Street Greed and Government Mismanagement Destroyed the Global Financial System*. New York: HarperBusiness, 2009.

Gelinas, Nicole. *After the Fall: Saving Capitalism from Wall Street and Washington*. New York: Encounter Books, 2009.

Goldin, Claudia, and Lawrence F. Katz. *The Race Between Education and Technology*. Cambridge, MA: Belknap Press, 2008.

Green, Stephen. *Good Value: Reflections on Money, Morality and an Uncertain World*. London: Penguin Books, 2009.

Greenspan, Alan. *The Age of Turbulence: Adventures in a New World*. New York: Penguin Press, 2007.

Halpern, David. *The Hidden Wealth of Nations*. Cambridge, UK: Polity, 2009.

Harrison, Maureen, and Steve Gilbert, eds. *Barack Obama: Speeches 2002–2006*. Carlsbad, CA: Excellent Books, 2007.

Hutton, Will. *Them and Us: Politics, Greed, and Inequality—Why We Need a Fair Society*. London: Little, Brown, 2010.

Institute of New Economic Thinking, Inaugural Conference: The Economic Crisis and the Crisis in Economics, King's College, Cambridge, England. Proceedings of Conference, April 8–11, 2010. http://ineteconomics.org/initiatives/conferences/kings-college/proceedings.

James, Harold. *The End of Globalization: Lessons from the Great Depression*. Cambridge, MA: Harvard University Press, 2001.

Johnson, Simon. *13 Bankers: The Wall Street Takeover and the Next Financial Meltdown*. New York: Pantheon, 2010.

Kaletsky, Anatole. *Capitalism 4.0: The Birth of a New Economy in the Aftermath of Crisis*. New York: PublicAffairs, 2010.

Kay, John. *The Truth About Markets: Their Genius, Their Limits, Their Follies*. UK: Penguin, Allen Lane, 2003.

Keegan, William. *The Prudence of Mr. Gordon Brown*. London: John Wiley & Sons, 2003.

Kepel, Giles. *Beyond Terror and Martyrdom: The Future of the Middle East*. Cambridge, MA: Belknap Press, 2008.

Kristof, Nicholas D., and Sheryl WuDunn. *Half the Sky: Turning Oppression into Opportunity for Women Worldwide*. New York: Vintage Books, 2010.

Krugman, Paul. *The Conscience of a Liberal*. New York: W. W. Norton, 2007.

———. *The Return of Depression Economics and the Crisis of 2008*. New York: W. W. Norton, 2008.

Kung, Hans. *Global Ethic for Global Politics and Economics*. New York: Oxford University Press, 1997.

———. *Global Responsibility: In Search of a New World Ethic.* Eugene, OR: Wipf & Stock Publishers, 2004.

Layard, Richard. *Happiness: Lessons from a New Science.* New York: Penguin Press, 2005.

Levitt, Steven D., and Stephen J. Dubner. *SuperFreakonomics: Global Cooling, Patriotic Prostitutes and Why Suicide Bombers Should Buy Life Insurance.* New York: William Morrow, 2009.

Lewis, Michael. *The Big Short: Inside the Doomsday Machine.* New York: W. W. Norton, 2010.

Lietaer, B.A. The *Future of Money: Creating New Wealth, Work and a Wiser World.* Century, 2001.

Lowenstein, Roger. *The End of Wall Street.* New York: Penguin Press, 2010.

Lukacs, John. *Five Days in London: May 1940.* New Haven, CT: Yale Nota Bene, 2001.

Mahbubani, Kishore. *The New Asian Hemisphere: The Irresistible Shift of Global Power to the East.* New York, NY: PublicAffairs, 2009.

McLean, Iain. *Adam Smith Radical and Egalitarian: An Interpretation for the 21st Century.* Edinburgh: Edinburgh University Press, 2006.

Moran, Theodore H. *International Political Risk Management: Exploring New Frontiers* (Working Papers Series on Contemporary Challenges for Investors, Lenders, and Insurers). World Bank Publications, 2001.

Nilekani, Nandan. *Imagining India: The Idea of a Renewed Nation.* New York: Penguin Press, 2009.

Nirmalya, Kumar. *India's Global Powerhouses: How They Are Taking on the World.* Cambridge, MA: Harvard Business School Press, 2009.

Phelps, Edmund S. *Rewarding Work: How to Restore Participation and Self-Support to Free Enterprise.* Cambridge, MA: Harvard University Press, 1997.

Pogge, Thomas, ed., and Keith Horton, ed. *Global Ethics: Seminal Essays: II* (Paragon Issues in Philosophy). St. Paul, MN: Paragon House Publishers, 2008.

Porritt, Jonathan. *Capitalism As If the World Matters.* Sterling, VA: Earthscan, 2007.

Posner, Richard A. *A Failure of Capitalism: The Crisis of '08 and the Descent into Depression.* Cambridge, MA: Harvard University Press, 2009.

Prasch, Robert E. *How Markets Work: Supply, Demand, and the "Real World."* Edward Elgar Publishing, 2008.

Prins, Nomi. *It Takes a Pillage: Behind the Bailouts, Bonuses, and Backroom Deals from Washington to Wall Street.* New York: Wiley, 2009.

Rajan, Raghuram G. *Fault Lines: How Hidden Fractures Still Threaten the World Economy.* Princeton, NJ: Princeton University Press, 2010.

Redleaf, Andrew, and Richard Vigilante. *Panic: The Betrayal of Capitalism by Wall Street and Washington.* Minneapolis: Richard Vigilante Books, 2010.

Reinhart, Carmen M., and Kenneth Rogoff. *This Time Is Different: Eight Centuries of Financial Folly.* Princeton, NJ: Princeton University Press, 2009.

Report of the Commission of Exports of the Presidents of the General Assembly.

Reynolds, David. *America, Empire of Liberty: A New History of the United States.* New York: Basic Books, 2009.

Robinson, Ken, and Lou Aronica. *The Element: How Finding Your Passion Changes Everything.* New York: Viking, 2009.

Rodrik, Dani. *One Economics, Many Recipes: Globalization, Institutions, and Economic Growth.* Princeton, NJ: Princeton University Press, 2007.

Romm, Joseph. *Hell and High Water: Global Warming—the Solution and the Politics—and What We Should Do.* New York: HarperCollins, 2007.

Roubini, Nouriel, and Stephen Mimm. *Crisis Economics.* New York: Penguin Press, 2010.

Runciman, W. G. *Great Books, Bad Arguments: Republic, Leviathan, and The Communist Manifesto.* Princeton, NJ: Princeton University Press, 2010.

Rubin, Robert E. *In an Uncertain World: Tough Choices from Wall Street to Washington.* New York: Random House, 2003.

Sachs, Jeffrey. *The End of Poverty: Economic Possibilities for Our Time.* New York: Penguin Press, 2005.

Sacks, Jonathan. *Future Tense: A Vision for Jews and Judaism in the Global Culture.* London: Hodder & Stoughton, 2009.

Salmon, Patrick, Keith Hamilton, and Stephen Robert Twigge, eds. *German Unification 1989–90: Documents on British Policy Overseas.* New York: Routledge, 2010.

Sandel, Michael J. *Justice: What's the Right Thing to Do?* New York: Farrar, Straus, and Giroux, 2009.

Sarotte, Mary Elise. *1989: The Struggle to Create Post–Cold War Europe.* Princeton, N.J.: Princeton University Press, 2009.

Saul, John Ralston. *The Collapse of Globalism: And the Reinvention of the World.* New York: Overlook Hardcover, 2005.

Sen, Amartya. *The Idea of Justice.* Cambridge, MA: Belknap Press of Harvard University Press, 2009.

Shiller, Robert J. *Irrational Exuberance.* Princeton, NJ: Princeton University Press, 2000.

Shirky, Clay. *Cognitive Surplus: Creativity and Generosity in a Connected Age.* New York: Penguin Press, 2010.

———. *Here Comes Everybody: The Power of Organizing Without Organizations.* New York: Penguin Press, 2008.

Skidelsky, Robert. *Keynes: The Return of the Master.* New York: PublicAffairs, 2009.

Smith, Adam, Ryan Patrick Hanley, ed., and Amartya Sen. *The Theory of Moral Sentiments.* New York: Penguin Classics, 2010.

Smith, Yves. *ECONNED: How Unenlightened Self-Interest Undermined Democracy and Corrupted Capitalism.* New York: Palgrave Macmillan, 2010.

Solnit, Rebecca. *A Paradise Built in Hell: The Extraordinary Communities That Arise in Disaster.* New York: Viking, 2009.

Sorkin, Andrew Ross. *Too Big to Fail: The Inside Story of How Wall Street and Washington Fought to Save the Financial System—and Themselves.* New York: Viking, 2009.

Soros, George. *Open Society: Reforming Global Capitalism.* New York: PublicAffairs, 2000.

Sperling, Gene. *The Pro-Growth Progressive: An Economic Strategy for Shared Prosperity.* New York: Simon & Schuster, 2005.

Stiglitz, Joseph. *Freefall: Free Markets and the Sinking of the Global Economy.* New York: Penguin Press, 2010.

———. *Making Globalization Work.* New York: W. W. Norton, 2006.

Taleb, Nassim Nicholas. *The Black Swan: The Impact of the Highly Improbable.* New York: Random House, 2007.

Taylor-Gooby, Peter. *New Risks, New Welfare: The Transformation of the European Welfare State.* New York: Oxford University Press, 2005.

Tett, Gillian. *Fool's Gold: How Unrestrained Greed Corrupted a Dream, Shattered Global Markets and Unleashed a Catastrophe.* New York: Free Press, 2009.

Tough, Paul. *Whatever It Takes: Geoffrey Canada's Quest to Change Harlem and America*

Tvede, Lars. *Business Cycles: History, Theory, and Investment Reality.* New York: Wiley, 2006.

Wallis, Jim. *Rediscovering Values on Wall Street, Main Street, and Your Street: A Moral Compass for the New Economy.* New York: Howard Books, 2010.

Whelon, Fenton. *Lessons Learned: How Good Policies Produce Better Schools.* Fenton Whelan, 2009.

Wolfensohn, James D. *A Global Life: My Journey Among Rich and Poor, from Sydney to Wall Street to the World Bank.* New York: PublicAffairs, 2010.

———. *Voice for the World's Poor: Selected Speeches and Writings of World Bank President James D. Wolfensohn, 1995–2005.* Washington: World Bank Publications, 2005.

Wolf, Martin. *Fixing Global Finance.* Baltimore, MD: Johns Hopkins University Press, 2008.

———. *Why Globalization Works.* New Haven, CT: Yale University Press, 2004.

Zakaria, Fareed. *The Post-American World.* New York: W. W. Norton, 2008.

INDEX

INDEX

ABOUT THE AUTHOR

Gordon Brown served as British Prime Minister and leader of the Labour Party from 2007 to 2010. He served as Chancellor of the Exchequer from 1997 to 2007, making him the longest-serving Chancellor in modern history. Brown's time as Chancellor was marked by major reform of Britain's monetary and fiscal policy and sustained investment in health, education, and overseas aid. As Prime Minister, his tenure coincided with the recent financial crisis, and he was one of the first to initiate calls for global financial action; his administration also simultaneously introduced a range of rescue measures within the country. Brown has a Ph.D. in history from the University of Edinburgh, and he spent his early career working as a lecturer. He has been a Member of Parliament since 1983. He is married to Sarah Brown, a charity campaigner, and the couple has two young sons.